The Encyclopedia Of Taekwon-Do Patterns
*The Complete Patterns Resource For Ch'ang Hon,
ITF & GTF Students Of Taekwon-Do*
Volume 2

*CheckPoint
Press*

The Encyclopedia Of Taekwon-Do Patterns

The Complete Patterns Resource For Ch'ang Hon, ITF & GTF Students Of Taekwon-Do

Volume 2

By Stuart Anslow

Warning

This book contains dangerous techniques which can result in serious injury or death. Neither the author nor publishers can accept any responsibility for any prosecution or proceedings brought or instituted against any person or body as a result of the use or misuse of information or techniques described or detailed within this book or any injury, loss or damage caused thereby. Some of the techniques and training methods described in this book require high levels of skill, control and fitness and should only be practiced by those in good health and under the supervision of a qualified instructor.

The Encyclopaedia Of Taekwon-Do Patterns

The Complete Patterns Resource For Ch'ang Hon, ITF & GTF Students Of Taekwon-Do

Volume 2

By Stuart Anslow
2nd Edition

Photographs by Kate Barry, Colin Avis & Stuart Anslow
Cover and Chapter Graphics by Jonathan Choi & Liam Cullen
Cover & Interior Layout by Stuart Anslow
Proof Read & Edited by Lyndsey Reynolds
Secondary Proof Reading by John Dowding

Copyright © 2010 Stuart Paul Anslow

All rights reserved

No parts of this publication may be reproduced, stored in a retrieval system, or transmitted in any form or by any means, electronic, mechanical, photocopying, recording or otherwise without the prior permission of the copyright owner.

British Library Cataloguing In Publication Data
A Record of this Publication is available
from the British Library

ISBN 978-1-906628-16-1

First Published 2010 by
CheckPoint Press, Dooagh, Achill Island, Co.Mayo, Republic of Ireland,
Tel: 00353 9843779   www.checkpointpress.com

For
'A TKD Student'
Loyal, but Open Minded

Acknowledgements

I would like to express my gratitude to the following students and instructors of our wonderful art who have helped turn this collection of books into a reality.

First of all I would like to thank many of my own students who were involved in this project, some in multiple roles; Kate Barry and Colin Avis who both assisted me in taking the thousands of photographs, as well as being in them. Lyndsey Reynolds who proof read every page and posed for the Silla Knife Pattern chapter; Vikram Gautam, Parvez Sultan, Sushil Punj, Marek Handzel, Richard Baker and Jonathan Choi who all posed for various chapters as well, with Jonathan editing many of the various poses that accompany the start of each chapter, along with Liam Cullen (a friend rather than one of my own students) who also edited the graphics for the book covers, which is work that I could not do myself, as my initial attempts were poor to say the least.

I extend my gratitude and sincere thanks to my friends and fellow instructors Gordon Slater and Elliot Walker who posed for some of the chapters in these books, as well as John Dowding who performed a secondary proof read for me. Mr Slater also authored a great forward for this book series.

A big thank you to Master George Vitale, a true Taekwon-Do historian and researcher, for his most in-depth historical piece on the 'True' and 'Complete' history of Taekwon-Do, commissioned especially for these books (which can be found in appendix v, in Volume 1), as well as his help with research into the patterns, which along with Dani Steinhoff's research (thank you Dani) I was able to combine with my own to publish what I believe is the most definitive history of those Taekwon-Do pioneers that were involved in the actual creation of the individual patterns. I am very grateful to Gerald Robbins, creator of the Taekwondo Hall of fame website (www.taekwondohalloffame.com) for allowing me to use photographs from the site so that I could include as many recent photographs of these legendary pioneers as possible.

I would also like to express my appreciation to my friends; Yi, Yun Wook for assisting me in the correct hangul translations for each pattern, as well as the book title hangul and various bits of terminology. I am grateful to Master Paul McPhail (ITFNZ) for allowing me to use his work on the various motions employed by the ITF as well as a study on the sine wave and my friend Piotr Bernat for his help regarding the Global Taekwon-Do Federation (GTF) patterns featured in these books.

I extend my thanks to Master Keith Yates for clarifying the patterns of Grandmaster Jhoon-Rhee, Kevin McClear for clarifying the correct order of the patterns practiced by students of Grandmaster Hee, Il Cho as members of the Action International Martial Arts Association (AIMAA) and Daniel Gaul (Chun Kuhn Do) for clarifying the Kihap points used by Grandmaster Kim, Bok Man.

I also wish to thank a number of people who have contributed indirectly to this book, by either clarifying certain points for me, clarifying terminology or contributing in other ways. These people are Master Parm Rai (ITF), Master Ha Xuan (GTF), Master Earl Weiss (ITF), Stephen Gell (GTF), Art van der Lee (Oh Do Kwan), Patrick Steele (ITF), John A. Johnson (ITF), Philip Hawkins, Joseph Marrero, Chris Spiller (ITF) and Paul Mitchell (TAGB) - I thank you all as your input has shaped these books in some fashion.

Of course, I couldn't conclude these acknowledgements without thanking my instructors, David Bryan and John Pepper who set me on the right path and taught me most of the patterns I now practice and teach myself. And of course all those who helped pioneer the patterns founded by General Choi, Hong Hi, as well as Grandmaster Park, Jung Tae and Grandmaster Kim, Bok Man for the patterns they further devised, developed and instituted.

Foreword By Master George Vitale, 8th Degree

It is my pleasure to write this foreword for Mr. Stuart Anslow's latest gem, a book series on Taekwon-Do patterns. Mr. Anslow, a talented and dedicated martial artist and black belt instructor has made a name for himself in the martial art world as a steadfast defender of Taekwon-Do's ability to provide sound self defence skills to its students. The basis for his claim, which I steadfastly agree with, is to return to the roots of Taekwon-Do, when it was developed in the Republic of Korea's Army as an effective military means for self defence. This was during a period when strong defence skills were necessary to survive on the rough streets of Korea and during the protracted periods of war time that Korea was engaged in. The effectiveness of this new Korean martial art, a compilation of the fighting systems available at the time (1950s and 60s) has been well documented on the field of battle as well as reported in the periodicals of the day.

The soldiers who originally developed this Korean martial art were led by a legendary Major-General and Ambassador Choi Hong Hi, one of the founding members of the ROK Army. Gen. Choi over his lifetime (1918-2002) devised 25 patterns, called Tuls in Korean. These martial art 'forms', as many call them, are comprised as Gen. Choi would say, of "various fundamental movements, most of which represent either attack or defence techniques, set to a fixed and logical sequence". According to Gen. Choi training with these patterns will improve flexibility of your movements, build your muscles, assist with body shifting, help with one's breathing, develop fluid motions and allow for rhythmic movements that are aesthetically pleasing. Finally he felt that patterns provide a "critical barometer in evaluating an individual's technique".

Training with the patterns has become an important part of Taekwon-Do's syllabus for both promotion and competition. Additionally to not only helping to develop technical proficiency, diligent study and practice of these patterns is needed to help the student grow their mental or spiritual discipline. Adherence to the strict instruction of one's master instructor or the established criteria of competition allows the student numerous opportunities to enhance character traits necessary to build discipline. Knowledge of the meanings of the patterns and the great Korean patriots and significant events in Korean history that they are named after, also affords each student with fine examples to mentor and strive towards, which assists in developing their individual character further.

General Choi not only developed the original Taekwon-Do patterns, but he had the foresight to name them after these figures and events so details of Korea's history and culture would not only be spread around the world, but would be safeguarded against eradication, in case Korea ever suffered under the brutality of an occupying force again, as they were disseminated globally through his Taekwon-Do. These patterns became an important part in making his Taekwon-Do a distinctly Korean martial art. They, like other martial art forms, Katas, Poomsae or Hyungs, help to define their art. The Chang Hon patterns are like Gen. Choi's signature. Signatures are unique and much like another patriot, John Hancock, who signed America's Declaration of Independence in a large, bold way, allowing him to stand out during their late 18th century struggle for freedom. This is his fingerprint, his legacy, what he left behind as a gift for mankind for all of eternity. The 24 patterns he left us with reflect 24 hours, one day, or all of his life that he lived in the 20th century and into the next millennium.

These books cover not only the 24 patterns left to us by General Choi, but also Ko-Dang as well. This Tul, at times referred to as the lost pattern is contained within this work. The only other books to do this to my knowledge is the Patterns Handbook published by the United States Taekwon-Do Federation, which contains text instructions only and Hee Il Cho's Volume 3. The 39 moves of this pattern however are captured in this work with both photos and diagrams, in addition to the all important written instructions. Of course the older books written by General Choi contained just four of them in 1959 and only 20 in 1965. His other later books published through the International Taekwon-Do Federation (ITF) contained just 24, either with Ko-Dang or Juche, with none of them containing the detail that is presented here.

There have been other books on the Chang Hon patterns like the series of 5 books by Jhoon Rhee that only covered 9 color belt Hyungs up to red belt level. Hee Il Choi's series of 3 books still contain only the first 20 patterns developed by Gen. Choi and his soldiers. Never before have all 25 been covered in such detail. Additionally the 3 fundamental exercises required for promotion and advancement 4 direction punch, 4 direction block for 10th gup white belt beginners and 4 direction thrust for 2nd kup red belts are included as well.

These books also contain the Silla Knife pattern created by Grandmaster Kim Bok Man. Grandmaster Kim was a Sgt-Major under the command of Gen. Choi in the ROK Army. He was a member of the historic Taekwon-Do demonstration team that first took Taekwon-Do abroad when they toured Vietnam and Taiwan in 1959. Sgt-Major

Kim also went to Malaysia in 1963 where he helped General Choi finalize 16 of the Chang Hon Tuls. He was responsible for helping Taekwon-Do spread through out South East Asia. This pioneer was also a founding member of the ITF in 1966 and now teaches his art of Chun Kuhn Do.

Finally Mr. Anslow's series of books feature the patterns devised by the late Grandmaster Park Jung Tae, often referred to as the People's Master and used by the Global Taekwon-Do Federation (GTF). It is believed that no other book contains these patterns. So this work is a great resource for GTF students, who also do the ITF patterns as well. Grandmaster Park was a key right hand man to General Choi throughout the 1980s, as the former ITF Secretary General and Chairman of the ITF Instruction Committee. He was instrumental in creating Juche, Taekwon-Do's final pattern and the most Korean of all of the original Tuls.

Stuart has included Kihap points as emphasized by various groups or instructors. His true history section helps to sort out the confused and muddied story of Taekwon-Do's development. He takes the time to credit the original pioneers for some of their many contributions, so his books are most inclusive, as should be and as few, if any are. The studies written by Master Paul McPhail, one of the ITF's most technically savvy researchers, will help students understand the ways of motion, that are often confusing and hard to understand.

As an instructor Stuart Anslow teaches and focuses on Chang Hon Taekwon-Do. He does not get bogged down by organizational constraints or the politics that often can be in play. Therefore his work transcends these boundaries. In the words of a Pioneer Grandmaster Rhee Ki Ha, instrumental in assisting with the development and the spread of Taekwon-Do worldwide and the first person promoted to IX Dan (9th Degree) by the principle founder, Gen. Choi, we are ITF, "International Taekwon-Do Family". These works, along with his previous work are major steps forward in uniting this original Taekwon-Do family. Unity within the Tae Kwon Do community is long overdue. When one studies this recent project and his past contributions, it becomes increasingly clear that we have so much more in common than that which separates us. We are after all one Art and in addition we share aspects with all Martial Arts. Unity among "ITF stylists" should come first, followed by all Tae Kwon Do groups. Then it will be easier to see how we are all "just martial artists". These books, like Mr. Anslow's previous works on the hidden applications of the patterns is a must have for any serious martial artist.

Foreword By Gordon Slater, 6th Degree

Patterns, Kata's, Forms, Drills, whatever you want to call them are a basis…a foundation of many of the martial arts in the present and the past.

So what are the benefits of performing and perfecting of patterns? Some will say; *"It is a method of putting individual techniques into a logical sequence, it is building muscle content to perform techniques, improving ones stances and applications. It is a attacking and defence system."*

I explain to my own students; *"Patterns are like learning a foreign language, each technique is an individual word within that language, but to speak the language you have to put the words into sentences, Patterns are forming those sentences to enable you to speak the language, perform the art."*

Like all traditional martial arts, Patterns have been handed down from founder to student, who eventually becomes a Master, Master to instructors, instructors to senior students and so on. Also like all martial arts in our modern world, splits occur within organisations. How big would the founding body that first came to these shores (the U.K.) be today if it were not for all the splits and the birth of new organisations?

Today many martial arts schools are becoming independent, or merely affiliated to other larger groups to allow some recognition. And then there is evolution, some groups have changed techniques within the patterns or modified them. Some have stayed with tradition. I am sure Masters could debate the pros and cons of change and tradition until the end of time.

"If it is not broken why fix it?" Vs "If one doesn't change, one gets left behind."

What I am trying to point out here, is the evident dilution of the patterns gene pool. Different groups many have a slight difference (or big difference depending how they view it) in the performance of different patterns. What this book had tried to encompass is most people's views. It is unbiased, it does not judge the rights and wrongs of each difference in start position, finish position, speed of technique, where to Kihap, sine wave, hip twist etc.

What it does do is try and show all Taekwon-Do styles a logical way of performing each technique. These books demonstrate, in printed form, extensive photographic sequences of all the Ch'ang Hon patterns. Use it as a guide, use it as a bible, use it how you wish. Right or wrong opinions collected together give you a better understanding of anything i.e. Politics, the best system of an attacking football team, how to get from A to B the quickest route etc. View this book with an open mind, please do not be blinkered.

Mr. Anslow has spent many an hour sourcing information and different opinions to enable him to produce these volumes. He has sought out Masters and students alike to get their views, and ask the questions of 'why and how?' in order to define the small differences and make them as accurate and applicable to all as possible. With all this knowledge, he has then burnt much midnight oil in putting it all together, something many of us want to do, but never quite get around to. Therefore I have nothing but praise for Mr. Anslow in his tireless work to produce these volumes. A job very well done. Congratulations!

Finally, with regards to rank. My views are; *"A belt does not say how good you are, only what grade you are."*.

"Don't dismiss an opinion because of rank, 40 years experience doesn't always mean they have the greater knowledge."

If you judge a person on indepth knowledge opposed to time served, then from my opinion Mr. Anslow is of Master status!

Thank you Mr. Anslow for allowing us to share your knowledge!

About The Author

Stuart Anslow received his black belt in the art of Taekwon-Do in 1994 and is now a 5th degree.

He is Chief Instructor of the renowned Rayners Lane Taekwon-do Academy, which was established in 1999 and is based in Middlesex, UK.

During his martial arts career, Stuart has won many accolades in the sporting arena, including national and world titles. His Academy is one of the most successful in the country winning numerous gold medals at every martial arts championship his students enter, a testament to his abilities as an instructor.

In 2000, Stuart won a gold and silver medal at Grandmaster Hee Il Cho's 1st AIMAA Open World Championships in Dublin, Ireland and in 2004 he returned with 14 of his students to the 2nd AIMAA Open World Championships where they brought home 26 medals between them, 7 of them becoming World Champions in their own right, 2 became double world gold medallists, all from a single school of Taekwon-do.

In 2002, Stuart founded the International Alliance of Martial Arts Schools (IAOMAS) which drew martial artists from around the world together, growing from a few schools to over 400 in under a year. This non-profit organization is an online student and instructor support group that gives travelling students the ability to train at over hundreds of affiliated schools worldwide and is truly unique in the way it operates.

Stuart has been a regular writer for the UK martial arts press, having written many articles for *'Taekwon-do and Korean Martial Arts'*, *'Combat'*, *'Martial Arts Illustrated'* and *'Fighters'* magazines, as well as taking part in interviews for some of them. His numerous articles (which can now be found on the Academy web site) cover the many related subjects of martial arts from training to motivation, but his main love is Taekwon-do.

As well as his Academy, Stuart is the Chief martial arts instructor for two local schools (one private, one comprehensive), one of which was the first school in the country to teach martial arts as part of its national curriculum.

In 2002, Stuart received an award from the Hikaru Ryu Dojo, a martial arts academy in Australia, presented by their Chief Instructor and fellow IAOMAS member Colin Wee when he visited Stuart's Academy in the UK. In recognizing Stuart's contribution, Colin stated (referring to IAOMAS) that "*nothing to date has been so foresighted and effective as Stuart's work in establishing this worldwide online martial arts community.*"

In October 2003, Stuart was inducted into the world renowned Combat Magazines '*Hall Of Fame 2003*' for his work within the field of martial arts on a worldwide level. Combat magazine is the UK and Europe's biggest martial arts publication.

In 2004 he was selected as the Assistant Coach for the Harrow Borough Karate team, to compete at the prestigious London Youth Games held at Crystal Palace and has held this position ever since. During the same year Stuart also received various Honorary awards for his work in the International field of martial arts. From the USA he received a '*Yap Suk Dai Ji Discipleship*' award for his innovative work within IAOMAS and '*T'ang Shou*` society award for promoting martial arts on a worldwide scale.

In 2006 he was presented with a '*Certificate Of Appreciation*' from the members of IAOMAS Canada which read '*In recognition of your un-dying contribution to the evolution of martial arts and your inspirational and innovative formation of the International Alliance Of Martial Art Schools*`. Though just a humble instructor or student as he refers to himself, he continues to inspire others.

Also in 2006 he released his first book relating to Taekwon-do; '*Ch'ang Hon Taekwon-do Hae Sul: Real Applications To The ITF Patterns*' which explored the applications of patterns techniques contained within the Ch'ang Hon patterns, away from what was considered the '*norm*' for applications in favour of more realistic (and ultimately more beneficial) techniques. The book was extremely well received and became an instant success, seen as a 'must have' by both instructors and students worldwide.

In 2009, his love for Taekwon-do and disappointment with the coverage in the various Taekwon-do magazines led him to publish his own online magazine '*Totally Tae Kwon Do*'; a free, downloadable magazine for all students of the art. Supported by his friends, Tae Kwon Do instructors and students around the world it too became a worldwide success.

Stuart is well known in the UK and internationally and apart from being a full time instructor of Taekwon-do, teaching at local schools and running Self Protection courses for groups associated with his local Council, he is the father of four beautiful children, one with Downs Syndrome, whom he supports and cherishes to the best of his ability, despite his hectic work schedule.

Though a full time instructor, his reputation is gained not only by his own career but also by his uncompromising approach to teaching and the standards within his Academy and that of his students. The students quality are testament of his *'no short cuts'* approach to how martial arts in general and Taekwon-Do in particular, should be taught. His classes flourish with quality students despite much local competition from schools with a more *relaxed* approach to teaching and gradings. Many of his senior students feature in the photographs within this book.

Chloe, Callum, Logan and Jorja Anslow

Table Of Contents

Acknowledgements vii
Foreword By George Vitale, VIII ix
Foreword By Gordon Slater, VI xiii
About The Author xv

Introduction 1
A Brief History Of Taekwon-Do 5
The True History Of The Ch'ang Hon Patterns 9

Differences Between Organisations 13
    - Chambering Positions When Executing Blocking Techniques 13
    - Chambering Positions When Executing Striking Techniques 14
    - Knifehands 15
    - Ways Of Moving Between Stances 16
    - Stepping Between Stances 17
    - Spot Turning / Centre-Line Turns 18
    - Hip Twist, Sine-Wave And Knee-Springs 19

How To Use This Book 21
Standards For Pattern Performance 24

Po-Eun Tul 25
    - Tips For Po-Eun Tul 45

Ge-Baek Tul 47
    - Tips For Ge-Baek Tul 65

Jee-Goo Hyung (GTF Pattern) 67
    - Tips For Jee-Goo Hyung 82

Eui-Am Tul 83
    - Tips For Eui-Am Tul 100

Choong-Jang Tul 101
    - Tips For Chong-Jang Tul 121

Juche Tul 123
    - Tips For Juche Tul 148

Ko-Dang Tul 151
- Tips For Ko-Dang Tul 167

Jook-Am Hyung (GTF Pattern) 169
- Tips For Jook-Am Hyung 218

Sam-Il Tul 221
- Tips For Sam-Il Tul 236

Yoo-Sin Tul 237
- Tips For Yoo-Sin Tul 266

Appendices 269
- Appendix i: *Pattern Speeds* 270
- Appendix ii: *Pattern Orders Of Taekwon-Do Organisations* 273
- Appendix iii: *Kihaps In Patterns* 276
- Appendix iv: *Sine Wave Study* 281
- Appendix v: *Performers Biographies* 284

Introduction

Originally it was my wish to produce a single book covering all the patterns in the Ch'ang Hon system, but sadly it was not to be as the cost would have been too prohibitive, so it was divided into three volumes.

So this series of books has come together to be a comprehensive reference for all students of Taekwon-do that follow the Ch'ang Hon system originally devised by General Choi, Hong Hi, including those that parted ways during Taekwon-do's history to date. This means they are suitable as a reference guide not just for those in the ITF (International Taekwon-Do Federation), but for those in organisations that are no longer connected to the ITF, such as the USTF, GTF, UITF, GTI, TAGB, AIMAA, BUTF, PUMA or indeed any Organisation, Federation, Association, Club, School, Academy or group that follows the patterns listed in this book; *The Ch'ang Hon Patterns*, *Blue Cottage Forms*, *ITF Patterns* or *Chon-Ji Forms* as they are also known. These books also include the Global Taekwon-Do Federation's Hyung's (the preferred term of Grandmaster Park, Jung Tae) and Silla knife pattern; patterns which were created or devised by pioneering instructors along the same lineage stemming from General Choi and are thus now part of the Taekwon-Do worlds collection of patterns.

Taekwon-Do's history stretches from before 1955 (when it was actually named) to the present and a consequence of this is that there are various styles of the art which were the pinnacle of the Ch'ang Hon system at certain points in time. For example, a student who's instructor started teaching in the 1970's and continues to teach the way he was taught will learn and perform slightly different from a student who's instructor started in the 1990's or one that is very current with any ITF changes. When writing these books I wanted to take this into account, so rather than simply show things the way I teach or learned them I enlisted help from some instructors that have come from different lines to me and thus perform their patterns slightly differently and as such, the various time periods are represented as well. As the books are designed to be an encyclopedia for all students of Taekwon-Do rather than students from a particular organisation I felt it was a good idea to have the various stages/differences represented. Throughout the book, the students and instructors that pose for the various photographs have performed, trained and/or taught patterns within the UKTA, ITF, GTI, TAGB and BUTF and as well as independently, thus representing a large portion of students throughout the world who perform them in a similar manner.

The Taekwon-do world has many organisations, each having minor differences with how they do things. For example, one organisations L-Stance may be slightly different in width than another's or some will execute a Forefist Punch using 'hip twist', while others will use 'sine wave' etc. and so the differences in *basics* can be numerous. However, all organisations that can trace their roots back to General Choi have one constant and that is the patterns themselves; as although an L-Stance may be of a slightly different width, or the way they move between techniques may be different, in the main, with a few minor exceptions (which I have tried to note in these volumes), the actual techniques each organisations students execute within each of the 25 Ch'ang Hon patterns remain pretty much the same. It is with this in mind that I wrote these books. It differs from other books of this type as it doesn't tell you how you *must* perform the basics (though it gives examples) or how long or wide your stances *must* be or whether to use sine-wave or hip twist, it simply tells you what each move is, what stance it is in and just as importantly, how to get from one technique to another.

Over the years there have been many good books published on the Taekwon-do patterns, many of which I own. Indeed General Choi himself has written both the 15 volume encyclopedia, as well as a condensed version. However, the former is expensive and hard to get and the latter only details the patterns in text form, with few pictures, neither of which contain the pattern *'Ko-Dang'* which many Taekwon-do students are required to learn and practice. Consequently, those books that do contain *'Ko-Dang'* do not contain the pattern *'Juche'* which again, many students need to learn and practice. In some organisations *'Juche'* replaced *'Ko-Dang'*, while others never instituted *'Juche'* to begin with. To complicate matters more, years later, some organisations once again replaced *'Juche'* back with the original *'Ko-Dang'*, with one organisation renaming *'Juche'* to *'Ch'ang Hon'* (ICTF) and another renaming it to *'Ko-Dang'* (ITF under Grandmaster Choi, Jung Hwa) despite keeping all the moves the same. These books include both *'Ko-Dang'* and *'Juche'* to cover this gap.

Furthermore, some of the earlier released books while good, only contained the first 20 patterns but over the years, General Choi developed a total of 25 Ch'ang Hon patterns and this book includes them all. These books also include the 3 Saju exercises he developed which rarely appear in other books. Only *Saju Jirugi'* and occasionally *'Saju Makgi'* have been documented in other books, but these books also include *'Saju Tulgi'*.

Some pioneering instructors who once helped developed the original patterns went on to institute or develop their own. In order to make this book collection a true *Encyclopedia Of Taekwon-Do Patterns* I have included these as well. Apart from the historical merit these patterns have, it is important for those students in the GTF (Global Taekwon-Do Federation) as they have to learn 30 patterns in total and as yet, I haven't seen any books that show them at all, so I hope I have done them justice. These are the six *'Jee-Goo Hyung'* developed by Grandmaster Park, Jung Tae. Though some simply call them the *new GTF patterns* others refer to them as *Jee-Goo hyung* because *Jee-Goo* means *Global*.

I have also included the *'Silla Knife Pattern'*, instituted by legendary Taekwon-Do instructor Grandmaster Kim, Bok Man because it is one of the most requested patterns I have come across on various Taekwon-Do internet forums, possibly because some schools wish to add a weapons form but want one that is Korean based with the added benefit that it comes from such a pioneering instructor. Grandmaster Kim, Bok Man instituted many additional forms for his own students, both empty handed and weapon based forms but the *Silla Knife Pattern* is the only one which is mentioned. That said, I would have liked to include more, but space did not permit it so I have represented this great master with the Silla Knife Pattern.

Aside from having a complete collection of patterns in a single set of books, a small bug-bear of mine is that previous patterns books often show individual pictures of each move within each pattern (of the ones they cover), from the point of view of an examiner watching you. This is fine (and is the way I have also laid out these books) until the student is travelling back to his or her start position and facing away from the examiner, where by many books simply show a photo of the pattern performers back and you cannot even see the technique at all - this has been corrected in these volumes as most techniques have a full size, forward facing shot.

One of the biggest problems I have seen with virtually all *'step by step'* pattern books is that while decent, they are not really a true *'step by step'* guide. They simply show each technique at its final stage, then the next and the next etc. but they never actually show you how to get from one to another, how to execute the actual technique fully, the chamber positions and how your feet move with the various spins, pivots and slides. This for many students is very confusing. In these books I have tried to correct this by showing the movements from one technique to another by way of multiple pictures of the performer moving between techniques and nearly every technique is covered in this way.

Coupled with the *'step by step'* photographs, each movement is described in text form, along with directional arrows and detailed foot diagrams, showing both previous and current foot positions to make it even easier for the first time performer of a pattern to grasp them. On occasion, when one *count* is actually two movements (for example move #12 of Hwa-Rang tul is both a Side Piercing Kick and a Knifehand Strike), these have further been split into 'A' and 'B' shots in order to show the performance of the whole movement.

These volumes also list many of the minor differences in various organisations, such as the various motions used by the ITF, Kihap points for those that utilise them, the actual order of patterns organisations require and a sine wave study.

As part of this book I wanted to have a section on the history of the patterns and pay homage to those that helped in their creation. Most know that General Choi, Hong Hi always had the final say on the patterns contained within his system, but many others helped devise them (to various degrees) and they have never been given full credit, so part of this book finally acknowledges their contribution to the patterns of Taekwon-do. I also wanted to include a 'History of Taekwon-Do' section, but as these books relate to just the patterns I included a 'Brief History' at the beginning of each volume, but also a more complete history section as an appendix in volume 1, which is possibly the most concise and researched, not to mention true history ever to appear in a Taekwon-Do book that isn't a history book per se.

Finally, I have not listed specific applications within these volumes because; firstly I know that when a student passes a grading and needs to learn a new pattern, the actual applications are very much secondary to learning the *pure* techniques of the pattern themselves. This is what I refer to as *'stage 1'* of patterns training, with *'stage 2'* being learning them in-depth, with as much detail as possible, which this book also covers. *'Stage 3 and 4'* are learning, applying and training realistic applications which are covered in the book *'Ch'ang Hon Taekwon-do Hae Sul: Real Applications To The ITF Patterns'*. Secondly, the sheer amount of information within these books on the patterns alone means there was little space for discussing applications anyway. As these are covered in my other book it seemed ultimately pointless trying to squeeze applications into these volumes. In any event, the ITF (as well as other organisations) already have various applications to the movements contained within their own patterns. Those who have already read *'Ch'ang Hon Taekwon-do Hae Sul'* will know my personal views regarding this particular issue, so I wouldn't feel comfortable listing standard applications as portrayed in certain other books. Finally of course, this series of books are for learning and performing solo patterns.

This second volume features all the Dan grade patterns in the Ch'ang Hon system of Taekwon-Do from *Po-Eun* (1st Dan) to *Yoo-Sin* (3rd Dan), used by both the *International Taekwon-Do Federation* (ITF) and other *Ch'ang Hon* based organisations, as well as the *Global Taekwon-Do Federation* (GTF) patterns required at the same Dan grade levels. It also features all both *Ko-Dang* and *Juche* so no matter which one your organisation requires it can be referenced here. I hope you find them a useful reference tool.

A Brief History Of Ch'ang Hon Taekwon-Do

Contrary to popular belief, Taekwon-Do is not a 2,000 year old Korean martial art and its connection to the ancient Korean art of Taek-Kyon is tenuous at best. It is in fact derived, for the most part, from Shotokan Karate. It also has other martial arts (such as Judo, Hapkido, Boxing, Wrestling and even Chinese Martial Arts influences) fused into what is now know as 'The Art of Hand and Foot' aka Taekwon-Do.

In 1945 Korea was liberated from the Japanese and Korea officially formed its armed forces (its modern military). Although Japanese martial arts remained being taught in Korea (by Korean instructors) in the various Kwan's (gyms), General Choi, Hong Hi wanted to break away from the arts of Japan, to have a martial art to train his soldiers in that had Korean values and at the same time instil national pride following the devastating effects of his country being occupied by Japan. He had learned Karate in Japan during the occupation of his country and had been teaching it to the soldiers under his command since 1946.

General Choi, Hong Hi

In 1954 during the Korean war, President Syngman Rhee saw a demonstration by the military Korean martial arts masters under General Choi's leadership and was so impressed he ordered that it be taught to all military personnel. This blessing from the president propelled Korean martial arts forward like a rocket. General Choi is known to have been teaching martial arts to his 29th Infantry Division on Cheju Island already and in 1954 he founded the Oh Do Kwan (Gym of My Way), along with Lieutenant Nam, Tae Hi, which was seen as the catalyst for the formation of Tae Kwon Do, as while General Choi taught the soldiers Karate he was, at the same time, formulating Taekwon-Do

President Syngman Rhee

Colonel Nam, Tae Hi

A unification effort was made to unite the various Kwans that were teaching in Korea, in order to make them a unified single Korean martial art and despite opposition, the art was officially named on the 11th of April 1955, known as the birth date of Taekwon-Do, a name put forward by General Choi. Despite this, for many years only General Choi's soldiers in the Oh Do Kwan and their civilian counter parts in the Chung Do Kwan used the term 'Tae Kwon Do'.

Photograph from the meeting when they named Taekwon-do with many martial arts masters present. General Choi can be seen at the head of the table. circa 1955

Naming this emerging art was simply the beginning, in fact even when officially named not one of the patterns were fully formulated, though in 1955 the first Ch'ang Hon pattern (Hwa-Rang) was finished. Over time Tae Kwon Do moved further away from its Karate roots by devising more new patterns, named after Korean historical figures or events; emphasising the rising and dropping into techniques (which was later termed sine-wave) as opposed to the Karate way of keeping the head the same height throughout; and of course introducing many more kicking techniques. Eventually, Taekwon-Do broke the chains of its roots and became distinct in its own right.

Even though Taekwon-Do has evolved into a martial art for all, including a large sport based side, it should be remembered that it was formulated as an art of self-defence, by soldiers, for soldiers and its effectiveness was no more evident than when it was actually used on the battle fields of Vietnam, where it was so feared by the Viet Cong that soldiers were told to avoid engaging in combat, even when Korean soldiers were unarmed, due to their knowledge of Taekwon-do![1]

Taekwon-Do is one of only a few martial arts that have a proven, battlefield tested, track record. Following the battle of Tra Binh Dong,[2] Times magazine ran an article that stated *"It was knife to knife and hand-to-hand—and in that sort of fighting the Koreans, with their deadly tae kwon do (a form of karate), are unbeatable. When the action stopped shortly after dawn, 104 enemy bodies lay within the wire, many of them eviscerated or brained"*[3].

> (On the night of St. Valentine's Day, a North Vietnamese regiment of 1,500 men struck at the 254 man Korean Company.)
> It was knife to knife and hand-to-hand and in that sort of fighting the Koreans, with their deadly (a form of Tae kwon Do), are unbeatable. When the action stopped shortly after dawn, 104 enemy bodies lay within the wire, many of them eviscerated or brained. All told, 253 Reds were killed in the clash, while the Koreans lost only 15 dead and 30 wounded.
> —Time— 24 Feb 1967

'A Savage Week'. Time Magazine, 24 February 1967

1959 was an influential year for Taekwon-Do as well as the start of the Vietnam war. The Korean Taekwon-Do Association (KTA) was formed, an armed forces demonstration team toured Taiwan and South Vietnam and General Choi published his first book on the art of Taekwon-Do and in 1962 the first Taekwon-Do tournament was held.

1962 was also the year that General Choi was forced to retire from the military due to his lack of support for President Park, Jung Hee who took power following a bloodless coup in 1961. Instead, General Choi was made an Ambassador and shipped off to Malaysia where he continued to teach and formulate Taekwon-Do, which included formulating 15 more Ch'ang Hon patterns.

General Choi finally returned to Korea in 1964 only to find that, due to politics, the Korean Taekwon-Do Association (KTA) had ceased to exist and had been replaced with the Korean Tae Soo Do Association (KTA) which was formed in 1962. However, in 1965 General Choi was elected as President of the KTA and managed to return the name to the Korean Taekwon-Do Association. He also published his second book on Taekwon-Do and lead a demonstration team around South East Asia and Europe. This demonstration tour was called the 'Kuk Ki Taekwon-Do Good-will Mission'!

On the 22nd March, 1966 General Choi formed the International Taekwon-Do Federation in Seoul, South Korea, with Master Kim, Jong Chan designing both the ITF badge (logo) and the ITF flag.

---

[1] 'Captured Viet Cong orders now stipulate that contact with the Koreans is to be avoided at all costs unless a Viet Cong victory is 100% certain. Never defy Korean soldiers without discrimination, even when are not armed, for they all well trained with Taekwondo.' - An excerpt from an enemy directive seized. - July 22, 1966

[2] A full transcript of the battle of Tra Binh Dong, including how Taekwon-Do was used in it to great effect, can be found in the book *'Ch'ang Hon Taekwon-do Hae Sul'* by the same author.

[3] 'A Savage Week', Time Magazine, 24 February 1967

As General Choi became more and more opposed (and vocal) to President Park's regime he eventually self-exiled himself to Canada in 1972, where he also relocated the ITF headquarters, as well as publishing his third book on Taekwon-Do (known as the Bible of Taekwon-Do). This was the first book to contain all of the 24 patterns of Taekwon-Do.

Taekwon-Do's history is full of politics and it was due to this that the International Taekwon-Do Federation (ITF) headquarters relocated to Canada instead of staying in Korea. It was due to politics that General Choi exiled himself to Canada in 1972 and it was politics that lead to the formation of the World Taekwondo Federation (WTF) in 1973. Sadly, politics has plagued Taekwon-Do all through it short life and continues to do so to this day, even after General Choi passed on the 15th June, 2002.

To read a more in-depth history of Taekwon-Do, please read *'The True And More Complete History Of Taekwon-Do'*, written especially for this book by Taekwon-Do researcher and historian Master George Vitale - it can be found as appendix v, in Volume 1.

Further to this, if you enjoy learning about the history of Taekwon-Do then I wholeheartedly recommend the following books:

A Killing Art: The Untold History Of Tae Kwon Do
by Alex Gillis

The Korean Martial Art Of Tae Kwon Do & Early History
by Grandmaster Choi, Chang Keun

The Taegeuk Cipher
by Simon John O'Neill

Finally, though I have learned a lot by studying these patterns to ensure they are as correct as possible, I have come to realize just what a momentous task General Choi executed by putting together the original *'Encyclopedia of Taekwon-Do'* as, even with the digital age this was a difficult task, so I can only imagine what it was like in 1983 and just how difficult a task it was with just a 35mm camera and a type writer, even with some of the most gifted and hard-working students (aka the pioneers), the Taekwon-Do world will ever see.

The True History Of The Ch'ang Hon Patterns

The patterns of Ch'ang Hon Taekwon-Do are the signature of the systems creator General Choi Hong Hi. When Taekwon-Do was officially named on 11th April, 1955 not one of the final 24 patterns of Ch'ang Hon Taekwon-do had been finalized, as at this time Taekwon-do still used the Kata from its father art of Shotokan Karate, though this was due to change.

(2 Star) General Choi, Hong Hi

Of course all pattern development was overseen by General Choi himself. He had major technical input into them as well as the final word on them, he was like the director, but other Masters acted out the movements and added their input which helped immensely in their formulation, but they have never received proper credit for it, until now.

Colonel Nam, Tae Hi

A popular misconception is that the patterns were created in order, from *Chon-Ji* onwards, but actually the first official pattern ever devised was *Hwa-Rang*, which was created with the help of Colonel Nam, Tae Hi and Sergeant Han, Cha Kyo in 1955. *Choong-Moo* was the second pattern created in 1955, again with the help of Colonel Nam, Tae Hi, with the third pattern created for the Ch'ang Hon Taekwon-do system being *Ul-Ji* which again, was created with the help of Sergeant Han, Cha Kyo in 1957. Sometime prior to 1958/59 pattern *Sam-Il* was created by General Choi (with the help of the soldiers of the Oh Do Kwan) and it was included in his first book on Taekwon-Do, published in 1959.

It wasn't until 1961 that the next pattern would be finalised. This would be pattern *Ge-Baek* and it was created with the help of Master C.K.Choi, another soldier.

Sergeant Han, Cha Kyo

When General Choi was sent to Malaysia in 1962 fifteen more patterns were created, bringing the total to twenty. It was between 1962 and 1964, with the assistance of his soldiers Master Woo, Jae Lim and Master Kim, Bok Man (who attained the highest non-commissioned officer rank of Sgt. Major) that patterns *Chon-Ji, Dan-Gun, Do-San, Won-Hyo, Yul-Gok, Joong-Gun, Toi-Gye, Kwang-Gae, Po-Eun, Ko-Dang, Choong-Jang, Choi-Yong, Yoo-Sin, Se-Jong* and *Tong-Il* were created, although the actual order is unclear.

Master C.K. Choi

Sometime around 1968 patterns *Eui-Am, Moon-Moo, Yon-Gae* and *So-San* were formulated with the assistance of Master Cho, Sang Min, bringing the final number of patterns to '24', General Choi's ideal number. Master J.C. Kim, Master Park, Jong Soo and Master Lee, Byung Moo among others, may also have helped formulate these patterns.

Master Woo, Jae Lim

Following a trip to North Korea in the early 1980's to secure support for the ITF, pattern *Ko-Dang* was removed and replaced with a new pattern called *Juche*. The reasons for this are discussed all over the internet, as are the merits or demerits of it all. However, whatever ones point of view is, the simple fact remains that it was changed by the founder himself and thus around 1981 pattern *Juche* was created and became an official ITF pattern between 1983 to 1985. It is believed that Master Park, Jung Tae played a major role (if not the major role) in the development of pattern *Juche*, along with assistance form Master Choi, Jung Hwa (General Choi's son), Michael McCormack (General Choi's son-in-law) and Master Lim, Won Sup.

Just prior to this trip, Master Kim, Bok Man, who helped with the formulation of at least 15 patterns in Malaysia between 1962 and 1964 released a book which shows he introduced 4 new patterns for his students called the Silla patterns. These consisted of two empty hand patterns, one knife pattern and a pole pattern. Many believe that Master Kim, Bok Man was opposed to Taekwon-do being a totally empty handed system and wished to have weapons included in its curriculum. The Silla patterns are said to come from the time of the Hwa-rang warriors who existed during the Silla Dynasty in Korea, hence their name.

Master Kim, Bok Man

In 1990 Master Park, Jung Tae parted company with General Choi and the ITF. Up until this point he had been the ITF Secretary-General as well as Chairman of the ITF Instruction Committee, and the man responsible for teaching virtually all Taekwon-do techniques and how they were executed and performed. In 1990 Master Park, Jung Tae formed the Global Taekwon-do Federation (GTF) and further developed six new patterns, often referred to as the *Jee-Goo hyung*. Students within this federation now perform 30 patterns in total including all the original Ch'ang Hon patterns (with *Ko-dang* rather than *Juche*), along with the six new patterns created by Master Park.

Master Cho, Sang Min

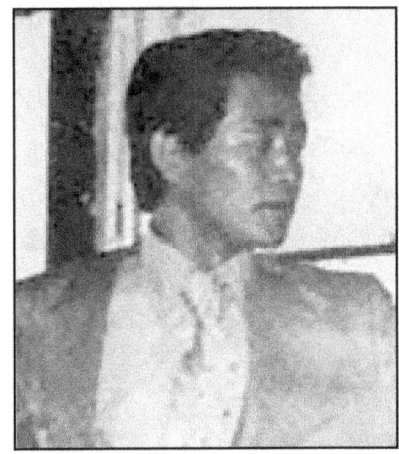
Master J.C. Kim

As a consequence of Master Park, Jung Tae leaving the ITF the sine-wave motion changed once again. The previous up/down motion was changed to a newer down/up/down motion and later refined to a relax/up/down motion by some organisations, however it is still referred to as *'sine wave'* forcing practioners of the original or older version to rename what they do as *'Natural Motion'*.

In 2005 the International Ch'ang Hon Taekwon-Do Federation (ICTF) renamed pattern *'Juche'* as *'Ch'ang Hon'* after General Choi's penname and in 2009, the ITF under Grandmaster Choi, Jung Hwa renamed pattern *'Juche'* as *'Ko-Dang'*, however the movements in both cases remain the same as the original pattern *Juche*.

It should be noted that I have referred to those who helped in the formulation of the Ch'ang Hon patterns by the term Master, when some are now actually Grandmasters. This is not a sign of disrespect for them, but rather a sign of respect for those whose status I do not know.

Though often referred to as the ITF patterns, their correct name is the *Ch'ang Hon* patterns. *Ch'ang Hon* was the pseudonym of General Choi and means *'Blue Cottage'*, so sometimes they are referred to as the *Blue Cottage* patterns or even the *Chon-Ji* patterns, after the first pattern in the set.

Master Park, Jong Soo

Originally they were referred to by their Korean name of *Hyung*, which means *form*, but General Choi later changed this terminology to *tul*, which means *pattern*, as he felt it was a better description of them and was a uniquely Korean term. Master Park, Jung Tae preferred to use the term *hyung*, so when describing his patterns I follow suit, as I have also done with Master Kim, Bok Man's *Silla pattern*, as that was the terminology he chose to use.

Finally, it is interesting to note that originally, all the patterns were named after famous Korean historical figures or groups, except the first and last ones. The first

Master Lee, Byung Moo

pattern, '*Chon-Ji*' represents the creation of the world, therefore the creation of Korea as well as the beginning for Taekwon-do students. The last pattern, '*Tong-Ill*' represents the reunification of North and South Korea which was General Choi's lifelong dream; the beginning and the end so to speak. With the change of '*Ko-Dang*' to '*Juche*' however, this changes the equation slightly, but I feel the names of the first and last patterns in the set were highly significant to General Choi and his Korean heritage and ideals.

Master Park, Jung Tae

In an interview conducted in 1999 General Choi was asked how long it took to research his patterns, to which he replied "*I began my research in March 1946 into what was to be named Taekwon-do on April 11, 1955. My research ended in 1983. The patterns represent my study of the Art in this period.*"

Sadly Master Han, Cha Kyo passed in 1996, Master Park, Jung Tae passed away on the 11th April, 2002; 47 years to the day that Taekwon-Do was officially named and General Choi passed away on 15th June 2002. Each has left an enduring mark in Taekwon-do's history and between them they have left their legacy of Taekwon-Do with us.

Differences Between Organisations

Different Taekwon-Do organisations often require their students to perform basic movements in a way that is particular to that organisation. This is mostly due to the time period that the Taekwon-Do organisation base their patterns on i.e. When they separated paths from the ITF or another group, and though there can be minor differences in the way certain techniques are executed, such as aligning a forefist punch with the shoulder, rather than the centre of the body, in the main, these differences are minute and will easily be honed by your own instructor to organisational requirements.

With that said, there are two main areas that do vary from association to association; these are the way blocks are chambered and the way a student moves from one stance to the next and its these differences we detail here. It should be noted that none of them are unequivocally the right way and consequently, none are incorrect either, it is all down to organisational preference.

Chambering Positions When Executing Blocking Techniques

Across the organisations of Taekwon-Do there are 3 main ways that blocks (and some strikes) are chambered. For the examples below we will use the chambering position of a *Left Low Outer Forearm Block*:

A. Wrist to Wrist - A student would align the back of his left wrist, above (or on top) of his left wrist, to the side of his body and execute the block from this position.

B. Forearm to Forearm - A student would align the his left outer forearm above the lower portion of his right outer forearm (sometimes referred to as inside the forearm), to the side of his body and execute the block from this position.

C. Far Back - A student would bring his blocking arm (in this case the left arm) as far back as is possible, bringing it around the body as far as he can reach. For low block this would mean above the shoulder, to the side and execute the block from this position.

Chambering Positions When Executing Striking Techniques

Punch and Backfist Chambering Positions

Most organisation execute closed fist striking techniques from similar positions, with minor variations.

Punches are usually executed from the hip, whereas back fists and knifehand strikes are executed from similar positions as blocks; from the side of the body.

Palm and Knifehand Chambering Positions

Palm techniques are usually executed from the chest, however some organisations execute them from the hips.

Fingertip thrusts are also mostly executed from chest height, however some organisations execute them from the hips.

Straight Fingertip Thrust, Flat Fingertip Thrust and Upset Fingertip Thrust Chambering Positions

In some Taekwon-Do organisations they still use the older chambering motion for a Straight Fingertip Thrust, where the thrusting hand starts from the hip, comes up slightly and shoots forwards (similar to pulling and pointing a pistol from a cowboy style holster).

Older Straight Fingertip Thrust Chamber Position

Knifehands

One quite big difference that needs to be noted relates to knifehands and how they are chambered and travel to their point of impact. Many organisations form the knifehand position from the offset; opened and formed at the chamber position and allow it to travel relaxed but formed to its point of impact. However, some organisations, specifically ITF ones, require the student to chamber a knifehand as a closed fist which travels towards it target relaxed but still closed, only opening into the knifehand at the last possible moment. This applies to both knifehand blocks and knifehand strikes.

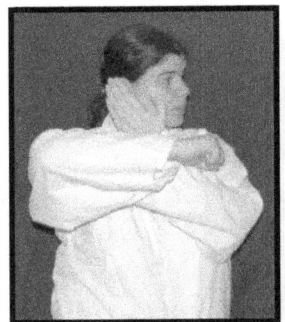  

Above And Below Show The Two Different Methods Of Executing A Knifehand Strike

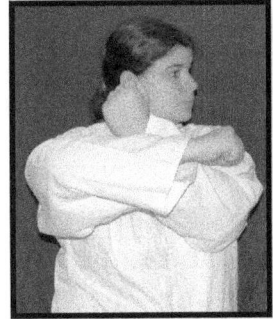  

Ways Of Moving Between Stances

As with chambering blocks there are various ways of moving from one stance to the next that the various Taekwon-Do organisations require. These are usually related to a specific time period in Taekwon-Do's development and are down to organisational preference. There are 3 main ways of moving:

A. Horizontal Wave - This method sees the student travelling from one stance to the next keeping their head at the same height, with little or no vertical movement. The knees are bent to compensate for the rising of the body as the student moves from one stance to the next. This method is usually utilized by organisations that separated from the ITF in its early years.

B. Natural Motion - This methods sees the students travelling in a natural way from one stance to the next. It allows the natural raising of the body as the student moves forwards before dropping into the technique. This method usually incorporates hip twist as well (see above) and was originally called 'sine-wave' but was changed by some pioneers as a way to distinguish it from the newer version of sine-wave detailed next. This method is usually utilized by organisations that separated from the ITF in the mid 80's or early 90's.

C. Sine-Wave - This method sees the student dropping slightly (or relaxing as some term it) just prior to the start of the movement, then rising as they move forwards before finally dropping into the technique. This method is usually utilized by organisations that remain part of the ITF following the departure of Master Park Jung Tae in the early 90's.

Stepping Between Stances

Like the vertical motions (or lack of) employed when stepping forwards or backwards between stances, the motion the feet travel in also varies and can be separated into 3 distinct methods. In these examples we use the transfer from a left walking stance, stepping forwards into a right walking stance.

A. In & Out - This method sees the students right foot travel in so it is next to the left foot, before moving outwards again into the stance.

B. Skating - This method, commonly referred to as *skating* sees the students right foot travel in a small arc as it moves forwards. At a maximum it comes only half a shoulder width in, but usually it is much less than that.

C. Parallel - This method see the student move forwards without moving his foot in at all, as if walking along a set of train tracks.

Spot-Turning / Centre-Line Turns

There are many ways of turning that General Choi employed in the patterns which are referenced in the relevant chapters, however the most common one found is *'Spot-Turning'* (Gujari Dolgi) or as many know it; a *'Centre-Line Turn'* as seen between moves #2 and #3 in Do-San tul and many other places.

Different organisations perform them differently, with some stepping straight across the centre-line and simply turning around (left diagram on page 19), with others moving the front foot 'in' and 'back' before turning and then moving the (now) front foot forwards again (right diagram on page 19). For the sake of uniformity, in these books they are named *'Centre-Line Turns'*.

Methods of Spot Turning/Centre Line Turns

Hip Twist, Sine Wave And Knee-Springs

The two ways that many organisations utilize when striking or blocking are hip twist or sine-wave, with a third way being a combination of the two. These are separate from the *Ways Of Moving Between Stances* as they refer to ways blocks or strikes are executed with or without the forward momentum of moving the whole body. These methods are used when both moving or stationary, with the addition of 'Knee-Spring' that some organisations used for executing techniques stationary, as explained below:

A. Hip Twist - This involves holding the hip back as a student moves or executes a technique before finally flicking it forwards at the last moment to add power into the strike or block. This method is often utilized in conjunction with the horizontal wave (detailed previously). When stationary (as in the pictures above) a student simply withdraws the hip back, then shoots it forwards again as they strike or block.

B. Sine-Wave - A student would drop into a stance to execute a technique and rely solely on the sine-wave relax/up/down motion to add power into the technique without additional hip twist. When stationary (as in the pictures on the previous page) the student simply relaxes, rises and drops again while executing the strike or block. This method is almost specifically used by current ITF students.

C. Combination - The final method is a combination of both the previous methods and utilizes dropping into stance's as well as hip twist to add power. The student would rise naturally as they move or use a knee-spring if stationary (see below), holding the hip back slightly, before flicking it into place as the student drops and executes the technique. This method is most often used in conjunction with the *Natural Motion* way of moving.

Knee-Spring

A knee-spring is utilized by some organisations when executing stationary techniques. It sees the student raising their rear heel and relaxing their rear knee; a slight rising of the body is often seen, as is some hip twist but both are minimal compared to using sine-wave or hip twist alone. As the technique is executed, the rear heel thrusts back to the floor and the rear knee locks straight creating forward power for the block or strike.

How To Use This Book

The main pages of this book are laid out in a specific way in order to transmit as much information as possible to the student. Students have various combinations in the way they like to learn; some can relate straight away to pictures, others like pictures combined with text etc.

Each of the main chapters start with an introduction page, displaying the name of the pattern itself, its standard definition, its diagram and the number of movements it contains.

The pages of each patterns chapter (as well as the saju's) displays two or three large numbered pictures of the movement in each patterns sequence. This is combined with various arrows (which are detailed overleaf), which show direction of movement, transition of stances and head (facing) direction amongst other things.

The majority of all the main pictures are shown forward or side facing so techniques can be seen clearly, but where a movement is facing away, a smaller picture appears inset in the main picture to show the correct facing direction it should be executed in. All patterns are shot as if being watched by an examiner.

Underneath the main picture is the terminology of the movement in both Korean and English, and underneath this is a foot diagram showing the previous foot positions as *greyed out* and the new foot positions as black footprints. Below this the movements are described in text form, for example:

Nopunde Bakat Palmok Yop Makgi
High Outer Forearm Side Block

32. Pivot your left foot 90 degrees anti-clockwise into a *Left Walking Stance*, whilst executing a *High Outer Forearm Side Block* with your left arm.

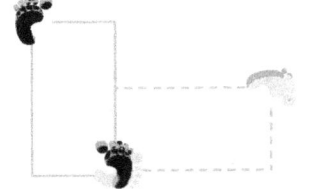

Finally, at the bottom of each page are a number of small pictures showing how to move from the previous technique to the next, for all the techniques listed on that page. These include the movements in the correct facing direction, as well as chambers and various parts of the transitions from one move to the next.

Previous

Moves 31, 32 & 33

The arrows that accompany the main pictures represent the following:

A *large solid arrow* shows the *direction of movement* from one stance to the next in the form of a step (either forwards, backwards or other direction) or a kick.

A *large dashed arrow* shows the *facing direction* following a movement where there is more than just a simple step involved. A *dashed arrow* is used to show that the footwork is more detailed and thus needs to be looked at within the written descriptions. An example of this would be the 2nd movement of Saju Jirugi that has you turning 90 degrees to block, but the foot of the rear leg travels backwards, in the opposite direction to where you are facing. Other examples would be changing from one stance to another without a step forwards, spot-turning/centre-line turns, a step backwards, a spin or a foot shift such as the 2nd and 3rd movements of Won-Hyo tul, where you only shift your front foot forwards from an L-Stance to form a fixed stance.

If there are *no arrows*, then there is no change of stance and no forwards or backwards movement and it is simply an execution of another technique. For example, the Low Block and Rising Block combination in Dan-Gun tul.

Two arrows together show direction of movement while facing another direction, for example, the Back Fist Strike in Toi-Gye tul. The *larger arrow* represents the direction of movement (which may or may not be dashed as detailed above), while the *shorter dashed arrow* represents the way you face upon completion or during execution of the technique.

Finally, a *short dashed arrow* on its own indicates the facing direction of a movement if it changes from the previous movement but doesn't have a step involved. For example, the Low Reverse Knifehand Blocks in Ge-Baek tul, where the stance remains the same, but the facing changes to the opposite side.

Stances and foot positions are represented by footprints upon a rectangle:

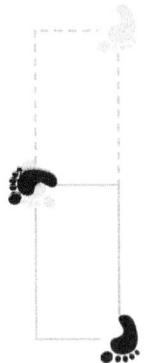

The *rectangle* represents the average length and width of a basic Walking Stance, with other stances as slight variations on them. They are incorporated to show how the feet are repositioned in relation to the previous stance of a technique/move. They are used in conjunction with foot prints to show foot placement, with a dashed rectangle with *light foot prints* representing the previous foot positions of the last stance used and *dark foot prints* representing the current foot positions of the new stance or position. The example to the left shows how the student steps from a Right Walking Stance into a Right L-Stance.

On some pages a *boxed piece of text* holds information for students who follow specific systems and holds information pertinent to them, that may be of use as a general note as well. They give information relating to certain sets of movements, for example if combinations are performed in various motions such as Connecting, Continuous, Fast Motion etc.

| ITF Note: ..... |

Finally, at the back of each book are tables relating to pattern orders used by many of the big associations (as they do vary), Kihap points that some organisations use, as well as an in-depth description of various motions and a sine wave study for those that utilise it.

Standards For The Performance Of Patterns

No matter which organisation you practice under, there are a number of standards or rules that are applicable to the way patterns are executed as a solo exercise and include the Saju exercises. These are as follows:

1. **All patterns start and finish on the same spot.**
2. **Each pattern should be performed in a rhythmic motion without stiffness.**
3. **Each technique should be fully formed before moving onto the next.**
4. **Techniques should be performed with realism.**
5. **Correct breathing should be performed throughout each pattern.**
6. **Correct posture and muscle tension should be utilized in all techniques.**
7. **Each pattern should be perfected before moving onto the next.**

Finally, all students of Taekwon-do should remember that *patterns are a series of defensive and offensive movements, set in a logical order against one or more imaginary opponents* and as such, are a core element of Taekwon-Do and its related self defence.

Though there are many benefits to practicing patterns, such as health, flexibility and balance etc., learning them to simply pass a grading or win a medal at a competition is the least important factor of patterns, as without understanding and appreciating them fully, they become little more than a dance routine - and there is so much more to them!

Po-Eun
Chong Mong-Chu

Po-Eun has 36 movements. Po-Eun is the pseudonym of a loyal subject Chong Mong-Chu (1400) who was a famous poet and whose poem *"I would not serve a second master though I might be crucified a hundred times"* is known to every Korean. He was also a pioneer in the field of physics. The diagram represents his unerring loyalty to the king and country towards the end of the Koryo Dynasty.

Narani Sogi Hanulson
*Parallel Stance
with Heaven Hand*

**Kaunde Palmok
Daebi Makgi**
Middle Forearm Guarding Block

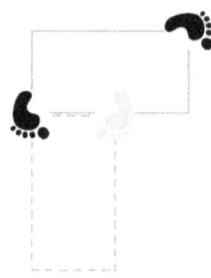

1. From *Parallel Stance with Heaven Hand*, step to your Left and form a *Right L-Stance*, executing a *Middle Forearm Guarding Block*.

From the ready posture to move 1

Waebal Sogi
One Leg Stance
(raising both fists)

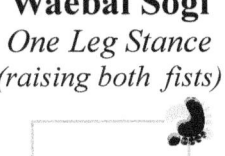

Outward Pressing Kick
Bakuro Noollo Chagi

2. Relax slightly then bring your Right foot to your Left knee into a *Left One Leg Stance*. As you do this throw your hands upwards behind you (formed into fists) simulating the motion of upward punches. Turn your head in the opposite direction as you complete the movement.

3. Maintain your position of hands/arms and execute an *Outward Pressing Kick* with your Right leg.

Previous

Moves 2 & 3

Kaunde Sonkal Yop Taeragi
Middle Knifehand Side Strike

Kyockja Jirugi
Angle Punch

---

4. Following the kick, land in a Sitting Stance and execute a *Middle Knifehand Side* Strike with your Right hand.

5. Maintain your stance and execute an *Angle Punch* with your Left fist.

Previous — *Moves 4 & 5*

**Forefist Pressing Block /
Middle Side Inner Forearm
Front Block**
*Ap Joomok Noollo Makgi /
Kaunde Yop An Palmok Ap Makgi*

**Forefist Pressing Block /
Middle Side Inner Forearm
Front Block**
*Ap Joomok Noollo Makgi /
Kaunde Yop An Palmok Ap Makgi*

6. Maintain your stance and simultaneously execute a *Left Forefist Pressing Block* and *Right Middle Side Inner Forearm Front Block*.

7. Maintain your stance and simultaneously execute a *Right Forefist Pressing Block* and *Left Middle Side Inner Forearm Front Block*.

Kaunde An Palmok Hechyo Makgi
Middle Inner Forearm Wedging Block

Dwit Palkup Tulgi
Back Elbow Thrust

8. Maintain your stance and execute a *Middle Inner Forearm Wedging Block*.

9. Maintain your stance and execute a *Back Elbow Thrust* with your Right elbow, placing your Left palm on top of your closed fist while executing the technique.

Kaunde Ap Joomok Jirugi
Middle Forefist punch

Dwit Palkup Tulgi
Back Elbow Thrust

10. Maintain your stance and execute a *Right Middle Forefist Punch* slipping the palm of your Left hand on top of your elbow joint.

11. Maintain your stance and execute a *Back Elbow Thrust* with your Left elbow, placing your Right palm on top of your closed fist while executing the technique.

Previous — *Moves 10 & 11*

Soopyong Jirugi
Horizontal Punch

Najunde Palmok Ap Makgi
Low Forearm Front Block

> **ITF Note:** Movements 6 to 12 are performed in *'Continuous Motion'*

12. Maintain your stance and execute a *Horizontal Punch* to your Right side.

13. Travelling to your Right, move your Left leg to form a *Right X-Stance* and execute a *Low Forearm Front Block* with your Right arm. Place the finger belly of your Left hand on your Right under-forearm (i.e. in front).

Previous — *Moves 12 & 13*

Digutja Japgi
U-Shape Grasp

Sang Soopyong Yop Palkup Tulgi
Twin Horizontal Side Elbow Thrust
(slow motion)

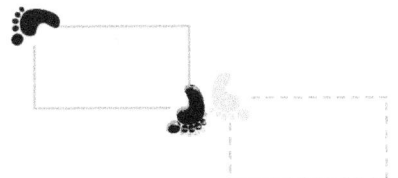

14. Continue in the same direction by moving your Right foot to form a *Left L-Stance* and execute a *U-Shape Grasp*.

15. Bring your Left foot to your Right to form a *Closed Stance* and execute a *Twin Horizontal Side Elbow Thrust*, turning your head to face left. This is performed in slow motion.

Note: The direct translation of *'Moa' (for move #15 etc.)* is actually *'Close'*, but most use the terminology *'Closed'*, so I have stayed with the most common term used throughout this book.

Previous — *Moves 14 & 15*

Dung Joomok Yop Dwit Taeragi
Back Fist Side Back Strike

Najunde Palmok Ap Makgi
Low Forearm Front Block

16. Step your Left foot back in the opposite direction (to your left) and form a *Sitting Stance* while simultaneously executing a *Back Fist Side Strike* with your Right fist. Bringing your Left arm downwards to a Low Block position. Look forwards.

17. Step to your left with your Right foot in front, to form an *Left X-Stance* and execute a *Low Forearm Front Block* with your Left arm, placing the finger belly of your Right hand on the side of your fist.

Previous — *Moves 16 & 17*

Najunde Sonkal Dung Daebi Makgi
Low Reverse Knifehand Guarding Block

Kaunde Palmok Daebi Makgi
Middle Forearm Guarding Block

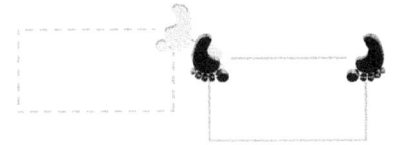
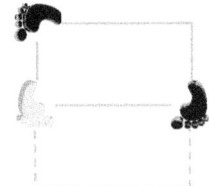

18. Step your left foot out to form a *Sitting Stance* and execute a *Low Reverse Knifehand Guarding Block*. Perform in a circular motion.

19. Shift your Right foot to form a *Left L-Stance*, turn to face the opposite direction and execute a *Middle Forearm Guarding Block*.

Waebal Sogi
One Leg Stance
(raising both fists)

Outward Pressing Kick
Bakuro Noollo Chagi

20. Relax slightly then bring your Left foot to your Right knee into a *Right One Leg Stance*. As you do this throw your hands upwards behind you (formed into fists) simulating the motion of upward punches. Turn your head in the opposite direction as you complete the movement.

21. Maintain the position of your hands/arms and execute an *Outward Pressing Kick* with your Left leg.

Previous   *Moves 20 & 21*

Kaunde Sonkal Yop Taeragi
Middle Knifehand Side Strike

Kyockja Jirugi
Angle Punch

21. Following the kick land in a Sitting Stance and execute a *Middle Knifehand Side* Strike with your Left hand.

22. Maintain your stance and execute an *Angle Punch* with your Right fist.

**Forefist Pressing Block /
Middle Side Inner Forearm
Front Block**
*Ap Joomok Noollo Makgi /
Kaunde Yop An Palmok Ap Makgi*

**Forefist Pressing Block /
Middle Side Inner Forearm
Front Block**
*Ap Joomok Noollo Makgi /
Kaunde Yop An Palmok Ap Makgi*

24. Maintain your stance and simultaneously execute a *Right Forefist Pressing Block* and *Left Middle Side Inner Forearm Front Block.*

25. Maintain your stance and simultaneously execute a *Left Forefist Pressing Block* and *Right Middle Side Inner Forearm Front Block.*

Previous — *Moves 24 & 25*

Kaunde An Palmok Hechyo Makgi
Middle Inner Forearm Wedging Block

Dwit Palkup Tulgi
Back Elbow Thrust

26. Maintain your stance and execute a *Middle Inner Forearm Wedging Block*.

27. Maintain your stance and execute a *Back Elbow Thrust* with your Left elbow, placing your Right palm on top of your closed fist while executing the technique.

Previous — *Moves 26 & 27*

Kaunde Ap Joomok Jirugi
Middle Forefist punch

Dwit Palkup Tulgi
Back Elbow Thrust

28. Maintain your stance and execute a *Left Middle Forefist Punch* slipping the palm of your Right hand on top of your elbow joint.

29. Maintain your stance and execute a *Back Elbow Thrust* with your Right elbow, placing your Left palm on top of your closed fist while executing the technique.

Previous — *Moves 28 & 29*

Soopyong Jirugi
Horizontal Punch

Najunde Palmok Ap Makgi
Low Forearm Front Block

> **ITF Note:** Movements 24 to 30 are performed in *'Continuous Motion'*

30. Maintain stance and execute a *Horizontal Punch* to your Left side.

31. Travelling to your Left, move your Right leg to form a *Left X-Stance* and execute a *Low Forearm Front Block* with your Left arm. Place the finger belly of your Right hand on your Left under-forearm (i.e. in front).

Previous — *Moves 30 & 31*

Digutja Japgi
U-Shape Grasp

Sang Soopyong Yop Palkup Tulgi
Twin Horizontal Side Elbow Thrust
(slow motion)

32. Continue in the same direction by moving your Right foot to form a *Right L-Stance* and execute a *U-Shape Grasp*.

33. Bring your Right foot to your left to form a *Closed Stance* and execute a *Twin Horizontal Side Elbow Thrust*, turning your head to face right. This is performed in slow motion.

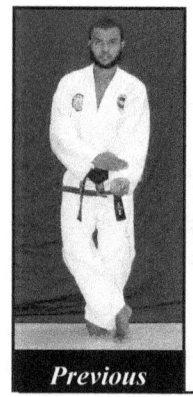

Dung Joomok Yop Dwit Taeragi
Back Fist Side Back Strike

Najunde Palmok Ap Makgi
Low Forearm Front Block

34. Move your Right foot back in the opposite direction (to your Right) to form a *Sitting Stance* while simultaneously executing a *Back Fist Side Strike* with your Left fist, bringing your Right arm downwards to a *Low Block* position. Look forwards.

35. Step to your Right with your Left foot in front to form an *Right X-Stance* and execute a *Low Forearm Front Block* with your Right arm, placing the finger belly of your Left hand to the side of your fist.

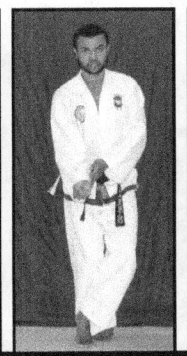

Moves 34, 35 & 36 (shown from right to left) — *Previous*

Najunde Sonkal Dung Daebi Makgi
Low Reverse Knifehand Guarding Block

Narani Sogi Hanulson
*Parallel Stance
with Heaven Hand*

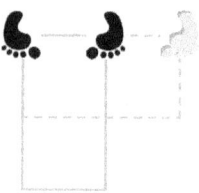

36. Move your Right foot out to form a *Sitting Stance* and execute a *Low Reverse Knifehand Guarding* Block. Perform in a circular motion.

Return. Bring your Left foot back to the Ready Posture.

Move 36 & return to Ready Stance

Tips For Po-Eun Tul

1. When moving from moves #1 to #2 or moves #19 to #20 (from the Forearm Guarding Blocks), don't forget to turn the hand covering your solar plexus so it is palm facing the ground, in order to fully twist both hands into the next technique.

2. Keep the Knifehand Strike chambered as you turn and strike out at the last second, as opposed to rotating and bringing the Knifehand Strike in a wide arc around the body.

3. Beginners at this pattern often find it hard to remember which arm punches downwards first on moves #6 and #24, following the Angle Punch! Just remember, the same arm that performs the Angle Punch is the arm that executes the first Downward punch in the combinations that follow.

4. Following the Wedging Blocks (Move #8 and move #26) many find it hard to remember which arm performs the first Back Elbow Thrust. To remember, thrust first with the elbow that is on the side of the direction you are travelling in already.

5. Before performing the Horizontal Punch (moves #12 and #30) raise both hands to chest height first.

6. On the Low Forearm Blocks in X-Stance the order of the blocking arm is Right then Left (on the first half of the patterns), then Left and Right (on the second half of the pattern), whilst the placement of the finger belly is always front first, followed by side (when travelling back again).

7. Although moves #18 and #36 should be performed in a circular motion, the Reverse Knifehands cut down in a straight diagonal line at the apex of the circular motion. See small chapter pictures for more details on how these are executed.

Ge-Baek
Great Korean General

Ge-Baek has 44 movements. Ge-Baek is named after Ge-Baek, a great General in the Baek Je Dynasty (660 AD). The diagram represents his severe and strict military discipline.

Narani Junbi Sogi
Parallel Ready Stance

Kyocha Sonkal Kaunde Makgi
X-Knifehand Middle Block

Najunde Bituro Chagi
Low Twisting Kick

1. From *Parallel Ready Stance*, step back with your Right foot to form a *Right L-Stance* and execute a *X-Knifehand Middle Block*.

2. Keeping your hands in the same position, execute a *Low Twisting Kick* with your Right leg.

> **ITF Note:** For ITF Students this is a *X-Knifehand Checking Block (*Kyocha Sonkal Momchau Makgi) and comes straight out from chest height.

From the ready posture to moves 1 & 2

Kaunde Baro Ap Joomok Jirugi
Middle Obverse Forefist Punch

Bandae Ap Joomok Jirugi
Middle Reverse Forefist Punch

Bakat Palmok Chookyo Makgi
Outer Forearm Rising Block

ITF Note: Movements 3 & 4 are performed in *'Fast Motion'*

3. Following the kick, land in a *Right Walking Stance* and execute a *Middle Obverse Forefist Punch*.

4. Maintain your *Walking Stance* and execute a *Middle Reverse Forefist Punch*.

5. Step backwards to form a *Left Walking Stance* and execute a *Left Outer Forearm Rising Block*.

Previous — Moves 3, 4, 5 & 6

Najunde Bakat Palmok Makgi
Low Outer Forearm Block

Doo Bandalson Nopunde Makgi
Double Arc-Hand High Block

Goburyo Junbi Sogi 'A'
Bending Ready Stance 'A'

ITF Note: Movements 5 & 6 are performed in *'Continuous Motion'*

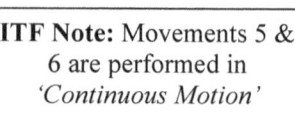

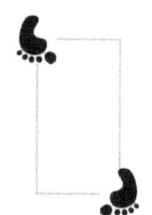

6. Maintain your *Walking Stance*, execute a *Low Outer Forearm Block* with Left arm.

7. Maintain your *Walking Stance*, execute a *Double Arc-Hand High Block*.

8. Raise your Left leg and form a *Bending Ready Stance 'A'*.

Previous — *Moves 7, 8, 9, 10 & 11*

Sonbadak Duro Makgi
Palm Scooping Block

Kaunde Ap Joomok Jirugi
Middle Forefist Punch

Dung Joomok Ap Taeragi
Backfist Front Strike

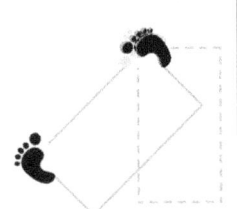

ITF Note: Movements 9 & 10 are performed in *'Connecting Motion'*

9. Lower your Left leg into a *Sitting Stance* at an angle of 45 degrees and execute a *Palm Scooping Block* with your Left palm.

10. Remain in a *Sitting Stance* and execute a *Left Middle Forefist Punch* to your centre.

11. Remain in a *Sitting Stance*, extend your Left fist underneath your Right arm (relaxing it slightly), then draw it back and execute a *Backfist Front Strike* to your centre with your Left fist.

Performing Double Arc-Hand High Block

| **Kaunde Sonkal Daebi Makgi**
Middle Knifehand Guarding Block) | **Najunde Ap Cha Busigi**
Low Front Snap Kick | **Baro Opun Sonkut Tulgi**
Obverse Flat Fingertip Thrust |

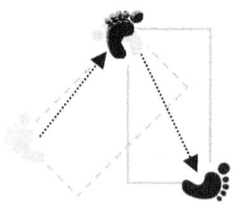

12. Move your Right foot back and across roughly inline with your Left foot (approx. 1 shoulder width), then move your Left foot forward to form a *Right L-Stance* and execute a *Middle Knifehand Guarding Block*.

13. Execute a *Low Front Snap Kick* with your Left leg without moving forwards, keeping your hands in the *Knifehand Guarding Block* position.

14. Following the Front Snap Kick, land in a *Left Low Stance* and execute an *Obverse High Flat Fingertip Thrust* with your Left hand.

Previous — Moves 12, 13, 14, 15, 16 & 17 - The stepping motions from Sitting Stance to L-Stance (11 to 12)

 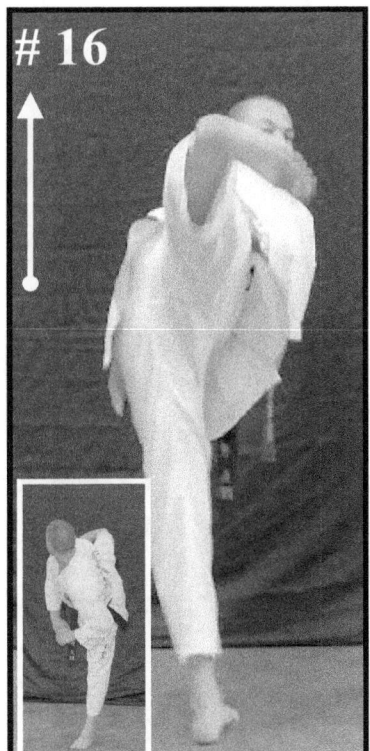 

Bandae Opun Sonkut Tulgi
Reverse Flat Fingertip Thrust

Kaunde Yop Cha Jirugi
Middle Side Piercing Kick

Kaunde Palmok Daebi Makgi
Middle Forearm Guarding Block

15. Remain in your *Low Stance* and execute a *Reverse High Flat Fingertip Thrust* with your Left hand.

16. From the previous movement, grab your Left hand and simultaneously execute a *Middle Side Piercing Kick*, whilst pulling back with your hands.

17. Following the Side Piercing Kick, land in a *Right L-Stance* and execute a *Middle Forearm Guarding Block* facing the opposite direction of the kick you have just performed.

Reverse view of the combination (Moves 15 to 17)

Kaunde Palmok Daebi Makgi
Middle Forearm Guarding Block

Kaunde Sonkal Daebi Makgi
Middle Knifehand Guarding Block

Gutja Makgi
9-Shape Block

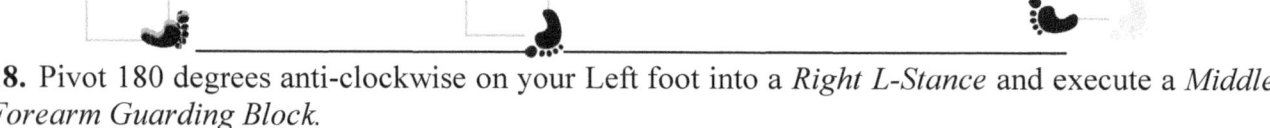

18. Pivot 180 degrees anti-clockwise on your Left foot into a *Right L-Stance* and execute a *Middle Forearm Guarding Block*.

19. Pivot 180 degrees anti-clockwise on your Right foot into a *Right L-Stance* and execute a *Middle Knifehand Guarding Block*.

20. Move your Left foot into a *Sitting Stance* (clockwise) and execute a Right *9-Shape Block*. The arm travelling downwards goes inside.

Previous — *Moves 18, 19 & 20* — *Performing 9-Shape Block*

Sonkal Najunde Makgi
Knifehand Low Block

Kaunde Dollyo Chagi
Middle Turning Kick

ITF Note: Movements 22 & 23 are performed in *'Fast Motion'*

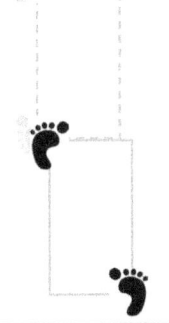

21. Pivot 270 degrees anti-clockwise on your Left foot into a *Walking Stance* and execute a *Knifehand Low Block* with your Left hand.

22. Execute a *Middle Turning Kick* using your Right leg. This kick is usually performed at a 30 degree angle.

     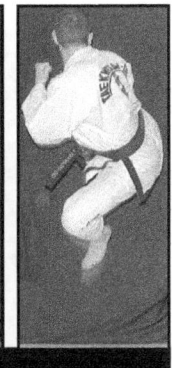

Previous — *Moves 21, 22 & 23*

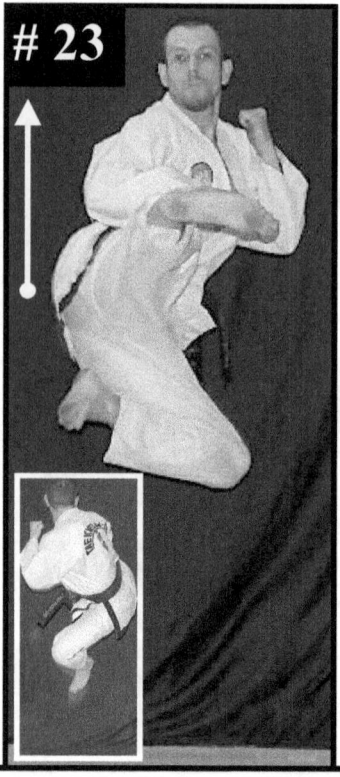

Twimyo Yop Cha Jirugi
Flying Side Piercing Kick

Nopunde Sang Sewo Jirugi
High Twin Vertical Fist Punch

Doo Bandalson Nopunde Makgi
Double Arc-Hand High Block

ITF Note: Movements 22 & 23 are performed in *'Fast Motion'*

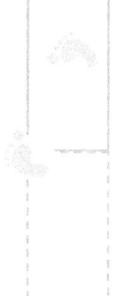

23. Upon completing the Turning Kick, execute a *Flying Right Side Piercing Kick*, using a twin foot take off. The kick should travel at least 1 stance length.

24. Following the Flying Side Kick, land in a *Right Walking Stance* and execute a *High Twin Vertical Fist Punch*.

25. Maintain your current stance and execute a *Double Arc-Hand High Block*.

Dwijibo Jirugi
Upset Punch

Ap Palkup Taeragi
Front Elbow Strike

Kyocha Sogi, Nopunde Doo Palmok Makgi
X-Stance, High Double Forearm Block

 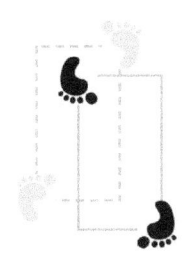 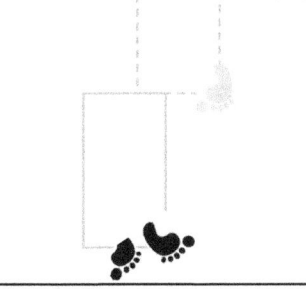

26. Maintain your current stance and execute a *Left Upset Punch*.

27. Perform a centre-line turn to form a *Left Walking Stance* and execute a *Front Elbow Strike*. Strike into your Left palm with your Right elbow.

28. Jump forward into a right *X-Stance* and execute a *High Double Forearm Block*.

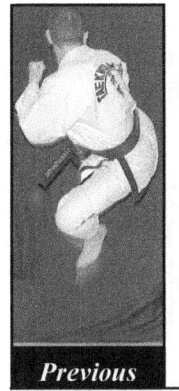      

Previous — Moves 24, 25, 26, 27, 28 & 29

Sonbadak Duro Makgi
Palm Scooping Block

Kaunde Ap Joomok Jirugi
Middle Forefist Punch

**Dung Joomok
Ap Taeragi**
Backfist Front Strike

ITF Note: Movements 29 & 30 are performed in *'Connecting Motion'*

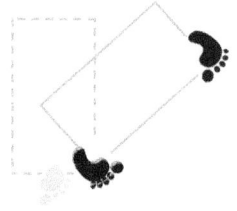  

29. Move your Left foot into a *Sitting Stance* at 45 degrees and execute a *Right Palm Scooping Block*.

30. Maintain your *Sitting Stance* and execute a *Middle Punch* with Left fist.

31. Maintain your *Sitting Stance* and extend your Right fist, underneath your Left arm (relaxing it slightly), then draw it back and execute a *Backfist Front Strike* to your centre with your Left fist.

Previous | *All the motions involved in the combination*

Nopunde Sonkal Dung Taeragi
High Reverse Knifehand Strike

Kaunde Dollyo Chagi,
with side step
Middle Turning Kick

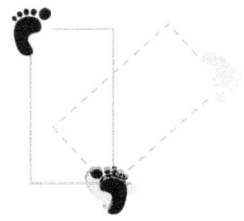

32. Pivot anti-clockwise on your Right foot to form a *Left Walking Stance* whilst executing a *High Reverse Knifehand Strike*

33. Move your Left foot sideways (to your Left) approx. 1 shoulder width and execute a *Middle Turning Kick* with your Right leg, directly inline with the previous position of the Left foot in move #32.

Previous — *Moves 30, 31, 32 & 33*

Nopunde Sang Sewo Jirugi
High Twin Vertical Fist Punch

Joongi Joomok Kaunde Dwijibo Jirugi
Middle Knuckle Fist Upset Punch

Gutja Makgi
9-Shape Block

34. Following the kick, land and perform a centre-line turn (anti-clockwise) to form a *Left Walking Stance*, whilst executing a *High Punch with Twin Vertical Fist*.

35. Without moving forwards, switch from a Left Walking Stance to a Right L-Stance by shifting your front foot and execute a *Middle Knuckle Fist Upset Punch* with your Right fist, grabbing and pulling your Left fist to your Right shoulder.

36. Moving your Right foot, pivot 180 degrees clockwise into a *Sitting Stance* and execute a *Left 9-Shape Block*

     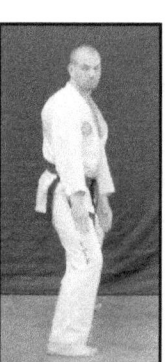

Previous — *Moves 34, 35, 36, 37 & 38*

Sonkal Dung Najunde Daebi Makgi
Low Reverse Knifehand Guarding Block

Sonkal Najunde Daebi Makgi
Low Knifehand Guarding Block

ITF Note: Movements 37 & 38 are performed in *'Continuous Motion'*

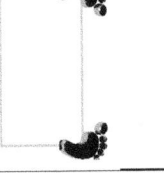

37. Maintain your *Sitting Stance* whilst executing a *Low Reverse Knifehand Guarding Block* to your Left-hand side - Perform in a circular motion and end looking in that direction. *Note: Some groups teach this to be performed by without the circular motion, as per the next move.*

38. While maintaining your Sitting Stance, Raise your arms straight up and execute a *Low Knifehand Guarding Block* in a straight diagonal line to your Right side.

Low Section Reverse Knifehand Guarding Block - Clockwise Circular motion

San Makgi
W Block

San Makgi
W Block

39. Pivot 180 degrees clockwise on your Right foot and *stamp* your Left foot into a *Sitting Stance* whilst executing a *W Block*.

40. Pivot 180 degrees clockwise on your Right foot and *stamp* your Left foot into *Sitting Stance* and execute a *W Block*.

Previous — Moves 39, 40, 41 & 42

Palmok Chookyo Makgi
Forearm Rising Block

Bandae Ap Joomok Jirugi
Reverse Forefist Punch

Palmok Chookyo Makgi
Forearm Rising Block

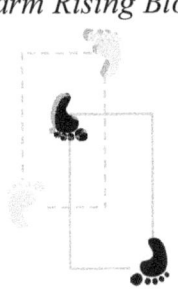

41. Step forwards with your Right foot and form a *Right Walking Stance*, whilst executing a *Forearm Rising Block* with your Right outer forearm.

42. Maintain your *Walking Stance* and execute a *Reverse Forefist Punch* with your Left fist.

43. Perform a centre line turn, ending up in a *Left Walking Stance* and execute a *Forearm Rising Block*, with your Left outer forearm.

Previous — *Performing the W Blocks*

Kaunde Bandae Ap Joomok Jirugi
Middle Reverse Forefist Punch

Narani Junbi Sogi
Parallel Ready Stance

44. Maintain your *Walking Stance* and execute a *Reverse Forefist Punch* with your Right fist.

Return. Upon completion of the pattern, bring your Right leg forwards to *Parallel Ready Stance*.

Previous — *Moves 42, 43, 44* — *Return*

Tips For Ge-Baek Tul

1. Move #2, the Low Twisting Kick works on an 'S' type motion, meaning the knee of the kicking leg comes in and then outwards. General Choi liked this kick to be held out for a split second (i.e. posed).

2. For moves #7 & #25, start the Double Arc-Hand High Block with the palms facing the opposite way to where they finish, with your hands not too close together, as this allows for the correct motion of the blocks.

3. The transition from move #11 to #12 sees you moving your Right foot back, but inline with your Left foot before stepping your left foot forwards to form the Right L-Stance.

4. When performing the Flying Side Piercing Kick (move#23) you will find it easier if, following the previous Turning Kick, you lower your Right foot in line with your Left foot so your hips are at the correct angle for the twin foot jump prior to executing the Flying Side Piercing kick.

5. Do not rush through moves #24, #25 and #26.

6. Do not rush the last movements of the pattern following the W Blocks.

All the motions involved in the combination of moves 9, 10 & 11

Jee-Goo
The Globe

Jee-Goo means *'The Globe'* or *'Global'*. Jee-Goo has 30 movements which consist of the numbers 24, 4 and 2. The number 24 represents the 24 hours of the day. The number 4 represents the 4 directions of North, South, East and West and covers all nations and people. The number 2 is demonstrated by student performing twice in each direction in order to underline the will to attain world peace and harmony. The ready posture of Parallel Ready Stance with the forearms crossed symbolizes the crossing out of the years of strife in Taekwon-Do.

Narani Sogi, Kyocha Paldung
Parallel Stance with Forearms Crossed

Najunde Bakat Palmok Makgi
Low Outer Forearm Block

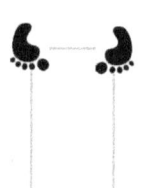 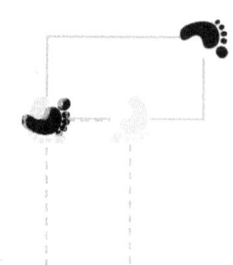

1. From the Ready Posture; *Parallel Stance with Forearms Crossed*, step to your Left into a *Left Walking Stance* and execute a *Low Outer Forearm Block* with your Left arm.

From the Ready Posture to move 1

Nopunde Ap Cha Busigi
High Front Snap Kick

Kaunde Ap Joomok Jirugi
Middle Forefist Punch

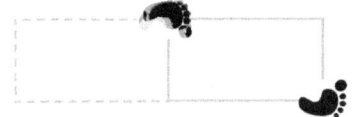

2. Execute a *High Front Snap Kick* with your Right leg.

3. Following the kick, place your Right foot down to form a *Right Walking Stance* while executing a *Middle Forefist Punch* with your Right fist.

Previous

Moves 2 & 3

Najunde Bakat Palmok Makgi
Low Outer Forearm Block

Nopunde Ap Cha Busigi
High Front Snap Kick

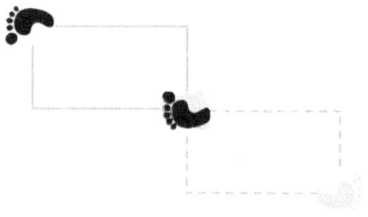

4. Pivot 180 degrees clockwise, moving your Right foot to form a Right Walking Stance while executing a *Low Outer Forearm Block* with your Right arm.

5. Execute a *High Front Snap Kick* with your Left leg.

Previous — *Moves 4 & 5*

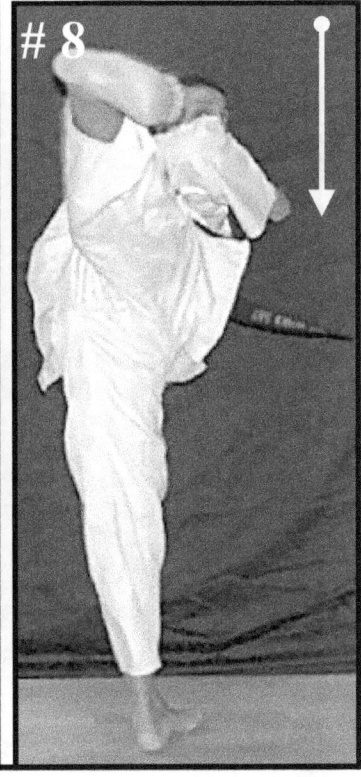

Kaunde Ap Joomok Jirugi
Middle Forefist Punch

Dollimyo Makgi
Circular Block

Nopunde Yop Cha Jirugi
High Side Piercing Kick

> **GTF Note:** Move 7 was originally performed as *a Low Outer Forearm Block* with the left arm.

6. Following the kick, place your Left foot down to form a *Left Walking Stance* while executing a *Middle Forefist Punch* with your Left fist.

7. Move your Left foot 90 degrees anti-clockwise to form a *Left Walking Stance* while executing an *Inner Forearm Circular Block* with your Right arm.

8. Execute a *High Side Piercing Kick* with your Right Leg.

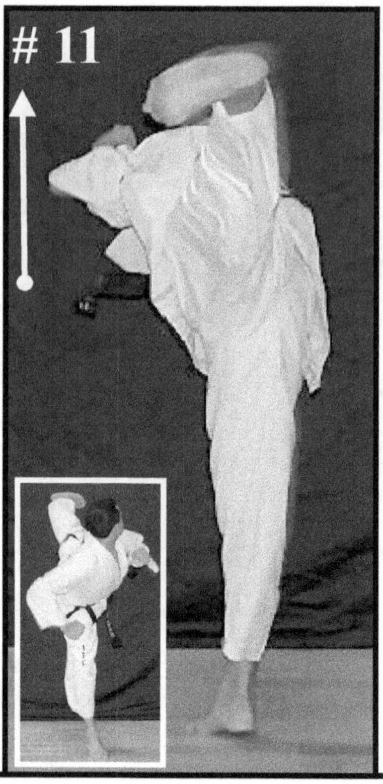

| **Kaunde An Palmok Makgi** *Middle Inner Forearm Block* | **Dollimyo Makgi** *Circular Block* | **Nopunde Yop Cha Jirugi** *High Side Piercing Kick* |

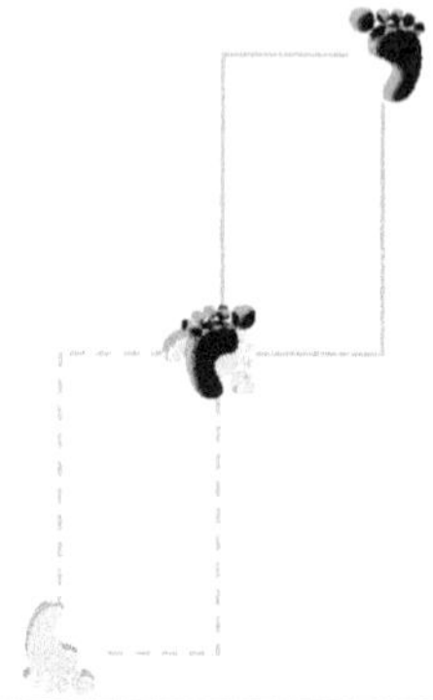

9. Following the kick, lower your Right foot in front to form a *Left L-Stance* while executing a *Middle Inner Forearm Block* with your Right arm.

10. Moving your Right foot, pivot 180 degrees clockwise to form a Right Walking Stance while executing an *Inner Forearm Circular Block* with your Left arm.

11. Execute a *High Side Piercing Kick* with your Left Leg.

Kaunde An Palmok Makgi
Middle Inner Forearm Block

Nopunde Bakat Palmok Yop Makgi
High Outer Forearm Side Block

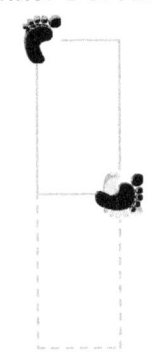 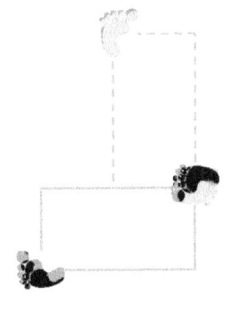

12. Following the kick, lower your Left foot in front to form a *Right L-Stance* while executing a *Middle Inner Forearm Block* with your Left arm.

13. Moving your Left foot, pivot 90 degrees anti-clockwise into a *Left Walking Stance* executing a *High Outer Forearm Side Block* with your Left arm.

Previous — *Moves 12 & 13*

Nopunde Dollyo Chagi
High Turning Kick

Nopunde Doo Palmok Makgi
High Double Forearm Block

14. Execute a *High Turning Kick* with your Right Leg.

15. Following the kick, lower your Right foot in front to form a *Right Walking* while executing a *High Double Forearm Block*.

Previous — *Moves 14 & 15*

Nopunde Bakat Palmok Yop Makgi
High Outer Forearm Side Block

Nopunde Dollyo Chagi
High Turning Kick

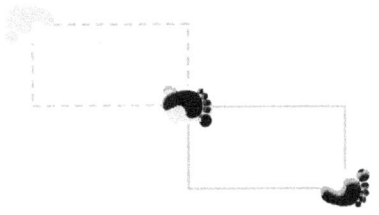

16. Moving your Right foot, pivot 180 degrees clockwise into a *Right Walking Stance* executing a *High Outer Forearm Side Block* with your Left arm.

17. Execute a *High Turning Kick* with your Left Leg.

Previous   *Moves 16 & 17*

Nopunde Doo Palmok Makgi
High Double Forearm Block

Sang Palmok Makgi
Twin Forearm Block

18. Following the kick, lower your Left foot in front to form a *Left Walking* while executing a *High Double Forearm Block*.

19. Moving your Left foot, pivot 90 degrees anti-clockwise to form a *Right L-Stance* while executing a *Twin Forearm Block*.

Previous

Moves 18 & 19

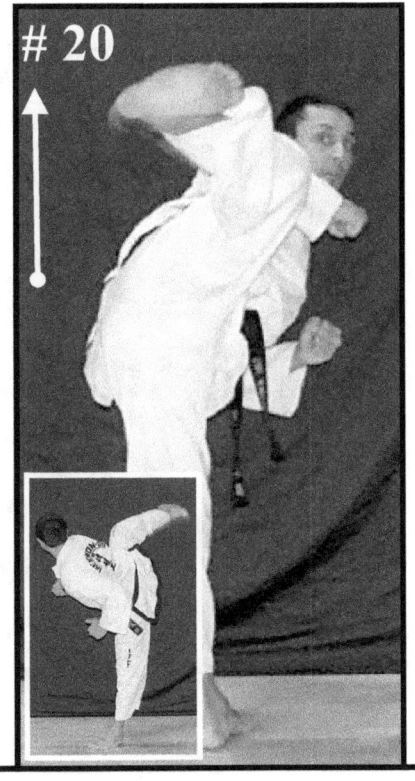

Nopunde Bandae Dollyo Goro Chagi
High Reverse Hooking Kick

Sonkal Yop Taeragi
Knifehand Side Strike

Sang Palmok Makgi
Twin Forearm Block

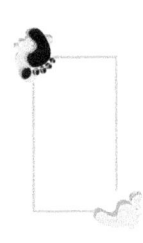

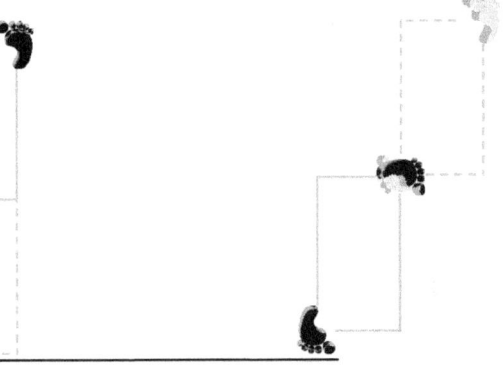

20. Execute a *High Reverse Hooking Kick* with your Right leg, spinning 180 degrees clockwise.

21. Following the kick, lower your Right foot to form a *Left L-Stance* while executing a *Knifehand Side Strike* with your Right hand.

22. Moving your Right foot, pivot 180 degrees clockwise into a *Left L-Stance* while executing a *Twin Forearm Block*.

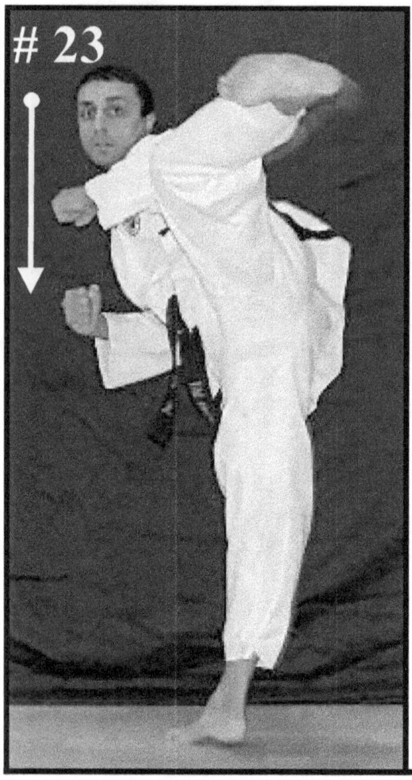

| # 23 | # 24 | # 25 |

Nopunde Bandae Dollyo Goro Chagi
High Reverse Hooking Kick

Sonkal Yop Taeragi
Knifehand Side Strike

Nopunde Ap Joomok Jirugi
High Forefist Punch

23. Execute a *High Reverse Hooking Kick* with your Left leg, spinning 180 degrees anti-clockwise.

24. Following the kick, lower your Left foot to form a *Right L-Stance* while executing a *Knifehand Side Strike* with your Left hand.

25. Step forwards into a *Right Walking Stance* while executing a *High Forefist Punch* with your Right fist.

Previous — Moves 23, 24 & 25

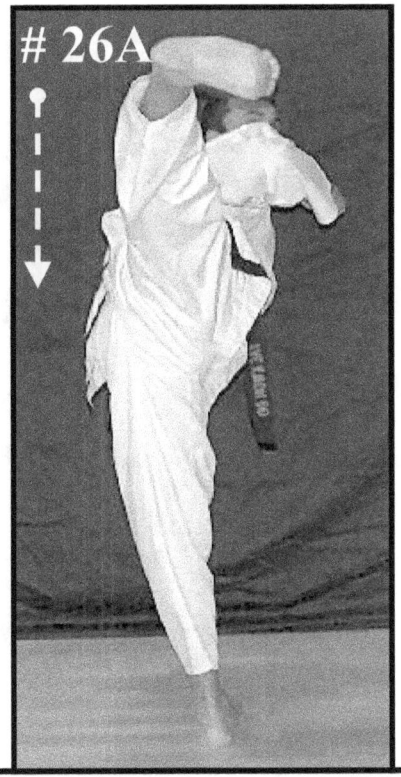

**Nopunde Bakuro
Sewo Cha Momchugi**
*High Outward Vertical
Checking Kick*

Nopunde Yop Cha Jirugi
High Side Piercing Kick

**Kaunde Bandae
Ap Joomok Jirugi**
*Middle Reverse
ForeFist Punch*

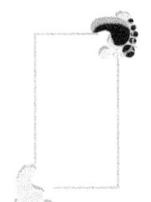

Note: Movements 26a & 26b are performed in *'Consecutive Motion'*

26a. Taking your weight on your Left foot, execute a *High Outward Vertical Checking Kick* with your Right (front) leg.

26b. Without placing your Right foot down, immediately execute a *High Side Piercing Kick* with your Right leg.

27. Following the kick, lower your Right foot behind to form a *Left Walking Stance* while executing a *Middle Reverse Forefist Punch* with your Right fist.

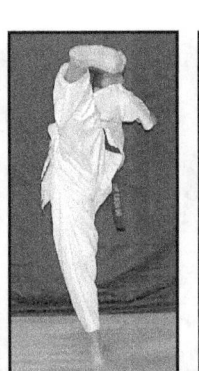

Previous — *Moves 26a, 26b & 27*

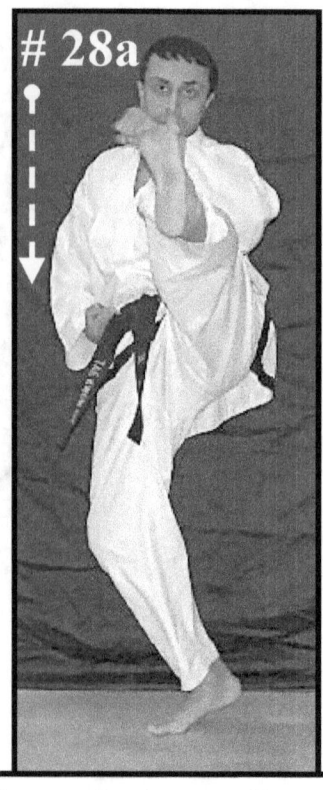

Nopunde Anuro Sewo Cha Momchugi
High Inward Vertical Checking Kick

Nopunde Yop Cha Jirugi
High Side Piercing Kick

Kaunde Palmok Daebi Makgi
Middle Forearm Guarding Block

Note: Movements 28a & 28b are performed in *'Consecutive Motion'*

28a. Taking your weight on your Right foot, execute a High Inward Vertical Checking Kick with your Left (front) leg.

28b. Without placing your Left foot down, immediately execute a *High Side Piercing Kick* with your Left leg.

29. Following the kick, lower your Left foot behind to form a *Left L-Stance* while executing a *Middle Forearm Guarding Block*.

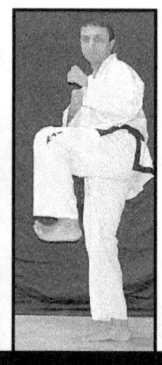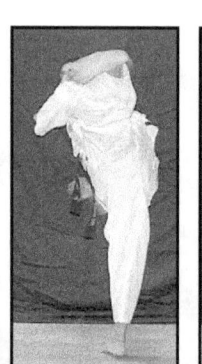

Previous — *Moves 28a, 28b & 29*

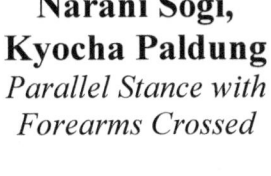

**Kaunde Bandae
Ap Joomok Jirugi**
*Middle Reverse
Forefist Punch*

**Narani Sogi,
Kyocha Paldung**
*Parallel Stance with
Forearms Crossed*

29. Maintaining your stance, execute a *Middle Reverse Forefist Punch* with your Left fist.

Return. Bring your Left foot forwards to the Ready Posture (*Parallel Stance with Forearms Crossed*)

Previous — *Move 30 & Return To Ready Posture*

Tips For Jee-Goo Hyung

1. Be sure to return to the chamber position following the High Turning Kicks (moves #14 and #17) rather than simply dropping your leg as it makes it difficult to land in a correct width Walking Stance, but just as importantly it gives you better time to chamber the next movement (Double Forearm Block) properly.

2. Be careful not to over-spin on moves #20 and #23 (High Reverse Hooking Kick) as it makes landing in the following L-Stance difficult and unwieldy.

3. You really need to flick your Right leg outwards with a bit of force on the High Outward Vertical Checking Kick (move #26a), as it comes off the front leg.

4. Don't forget that following Checking Kick/Side piercing Kick combinations the kicking leg lands behind.

Eui-Am
Son Byong Hi

Eui-Am is the pseudonym of Son Byong Hi, leader of the Korean independence movement (formed 1st March, 1919). Eui-Am has 45 movements which refer to his age when he changed the name of Dong Hak (Oriental culture) to Chondo Kyo (Heavenly way religion) in 1905. The diagram represents his Indomitable Spirit, displayed while dedicating himself to the prosperity of his nation.

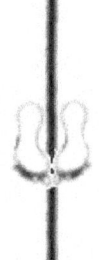

Moa Junbi Sogi 'D'
Closed Ready Stance 'D'

Sonkal Najunde Anuro Makgi
Knifehand Low Inward Block

Nopunde Bakat Palmok Yop Makgi
High Outer Forearm Side Block

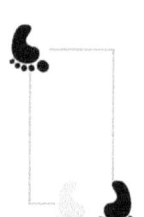

1. From *Closed Ready Stance 'D'*, move your right foot backwards to form *a Left Walking Stance* while executing a *Knifehand Low Inward Block* with your Right hand, pulling your Left fist to the front of your Right shoulder.

2. Move your Left leg backwards to form a *Right Walking Stance* while executing a *High Outer Forearm Side Block* with your Left arm.

Running from right to left - From the ready posture to moves 1 & 2

  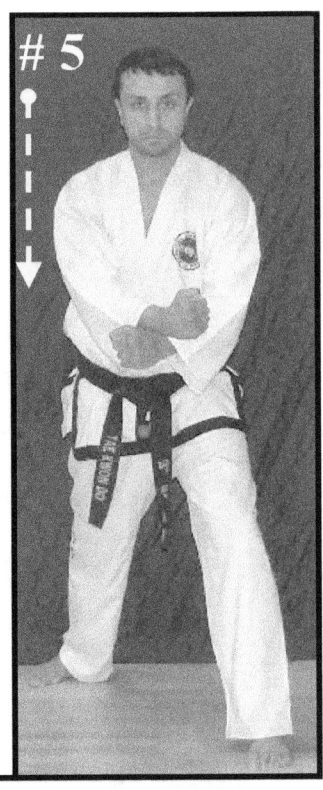

Kaunde Ap Joomok Jirugi
Middle Forefist Punch

Najunde Bituro Chagi
Low Twisting Kick

Kyocha Joomok Naeryo Makgi
X-Fist Downward Block

3. Maintain your stance and execute a *Middle Forefist Punch* with your Right fist.

4. Execute a *Low Twisting Kick* with your Left leg, keeping your hands in their previous position.

5. Following the kick, step down to form a *Left Walking Stance* while executing an *X-Fist Downward Block*.

     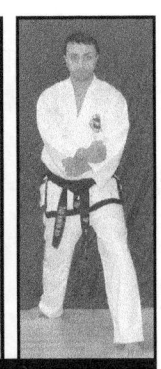

Previous — *Moves 3, 4 & 5*

Sonkal Chookyo Makgi
Knifehand Rising Block

Dung Joomok Nopunde Yop Taeragi
Back Fist High Side Strike

Kaunde Ap Joomok Jirugi
Middle Forefist Punch

ITF Note: Movements 5 & 6 are performed in *'Continuous Motion'*

6. Maintain your stance and immediately execute a *Knifehand Rising Block* with your Right hand.

7. Jump forwards to form a *Right X-Stance* while executing a *Back Fist High Side Strike* with your Right fist, bringing the finger belly of your Left hand to the side of your fist.

8. Pivot 180 degrees on your Right foot, moving your Left foot to form a *Right L-Stance* while executing a *Middle Punch* with your Left fist.

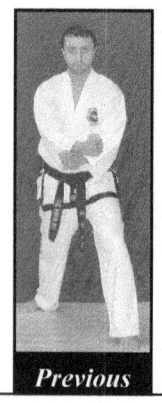     

Previous — Moves 6, 7 & 8

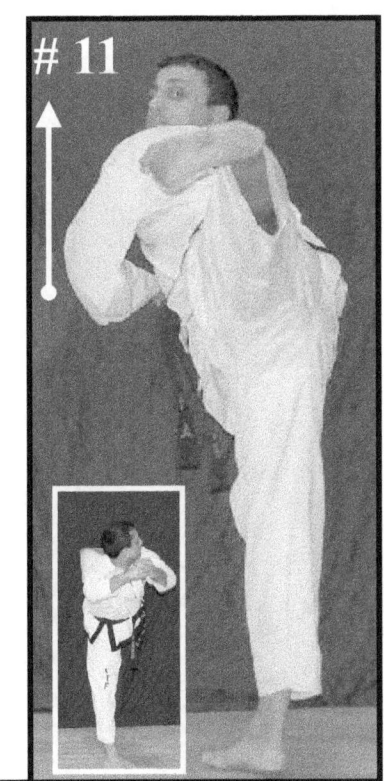

Kaunde Bandae Dollyo Chagi
Middle Reverse Turning Kick

Sonkal Yop Taeragi
Knifehand Side Strike

Kaunde Yop Cha Jirugi
Middle Side Piercing Kick

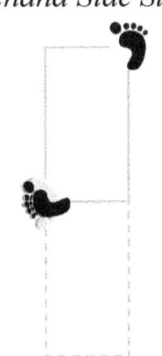

9. Execute a *Middle Reverse Turning Kick* with your Right leg at a 30 degree angle.

10. Following the kick, stamp your Right foot to form a *Sitting Stance* while executing a *Knifehand Side Strike* with your Right hand.

11. Grab hold of your Knifehand and execute a *Middle Side Piercing Kick* with your Left leg, pulling your hands back as you execute the kick.

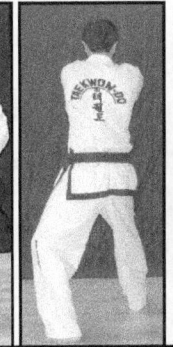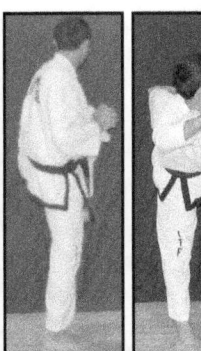

Previous — *Moves 9, 10 & 11*

Nopunde Bandal Jirugi	**Kaunde Dollyo Jirugi**	**Sonkal Najunde Anuro Makgi**
High Crescent Punch	*Middle Turning Punch (slow motion)*	*Knifehand Low Inward Block*

12. Following the kick, lower your Left foot to form a *Left Walking Stance* while executing a *High Crescent Punch* with your Right fist.

13. Move your Right foot forwards to form a *Parallel Stance* while executing a *Middle Turning Punch* with your Left fist. Perform move in slow motion.

14. Move your Left foot backwards to form a Right Walking Stance while executing a *Knifehand Low Inward Block* with your Left hand, pulling your Right fist to the front of your Left shoulder.

Previous — *Moves 12, 13 & 14*

  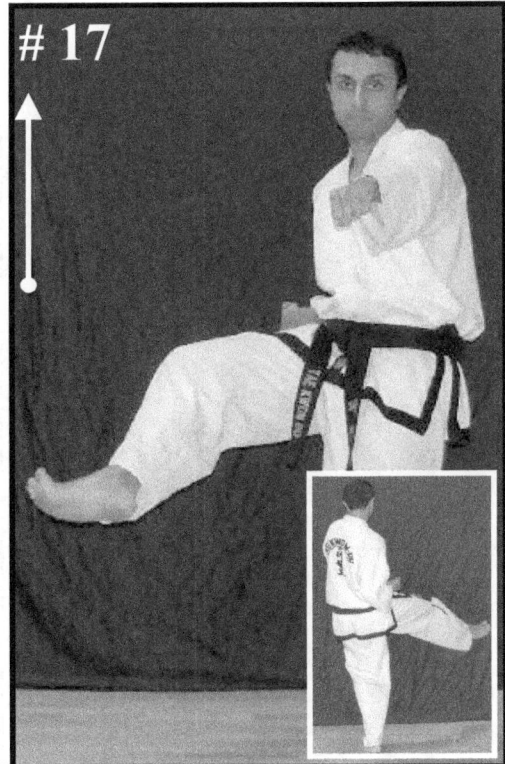

Nopunde Bakat Palmok Yop Makgi
High Outer Forearm Side Block

Kaunde Ap Joomok Jirugi
Middle Forefist Punch

Najunde Bituro Chagi
Low Twisting Kick

 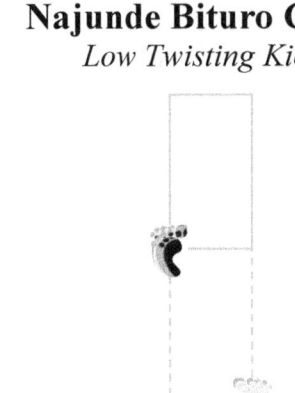

15. Move your Right leg backwards to form a *Left Walking Stance* while executing a *High Outer Forearm Side Block* with your Right arm.

16. Maintain your stance and execute a *Middle Forefist Punch* with your Left fist.

17. Execute a *Low Twisting Kick* with your Right leg, keeping your hands in their previous position.

Previous — *Moves 15, 16 & 17*

Kyocha Joomok Naeryo Makgi
X-Fist Downward Block

Sonkal Chookyo Makgi
Knifehand Rising Block

Dung Joomok Nopunde Yop Taeragi
Back Fist High Side Strike

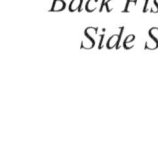

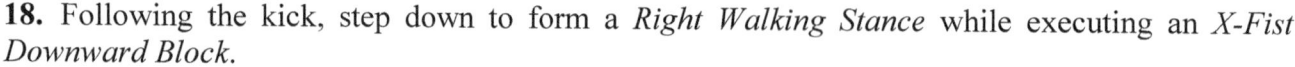

18. Following the kick, step down to form a *Right Walking Stance* while executing an *X-Fist Downward Block*.

19. Maintain your stance and immediately execute a *Knifehand Rising Block* with your Left hand.

20. Jump forwards to form a *Left X-Stance* while executing a *Back Fist High Side Strike* with your Left fist, bringing the finger belly of your Right hand to the side of your fist.

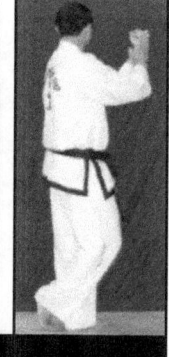

Previous — *Moves 18, 19 & 20*

 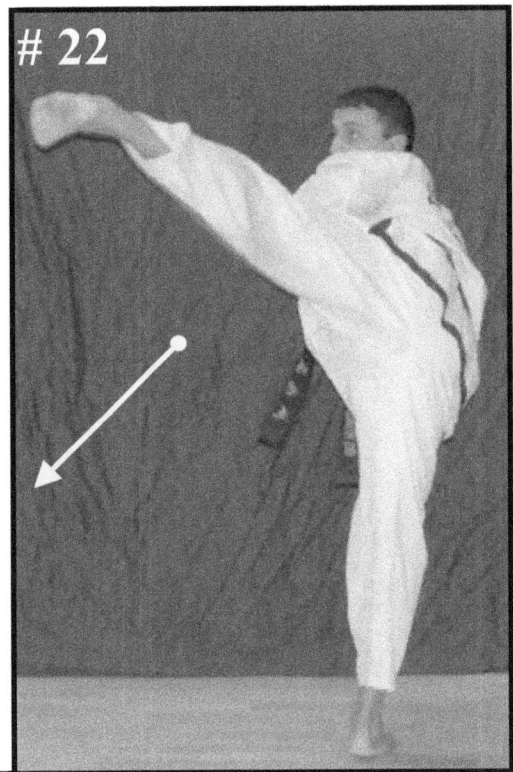 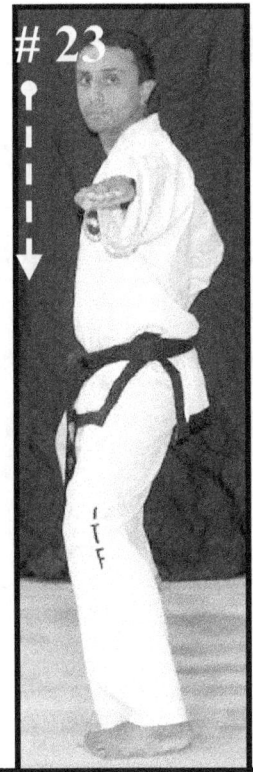

**Kaunde Ap
Joomok Jirugi**
Middle Forefist Punch

**Kaunde Bandae
Dollyo Chagi**
Middle Reverse Turning Kick

Sonkal Yop Taeragi
Knifehand Side Strike

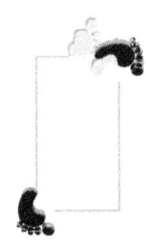  

21. Pivot 180 degrees on your Left foot, moving your Right foot to form a *Left L-Stance* while executing a *Middle Punch* with your Right fist.

22. Execute a *Middle Reverse Turning Kick* with your Left leg at a 30 degree angle.

23. Following the kick, stamp your Left foot to form a *Sitting Stance* while executing a *Knifehand Side Strike* with your Left hand.

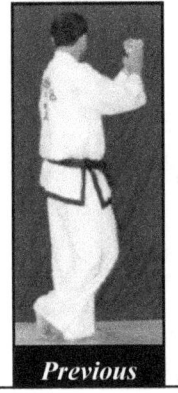  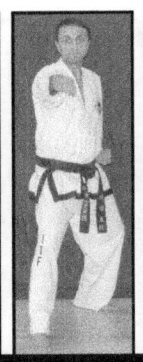    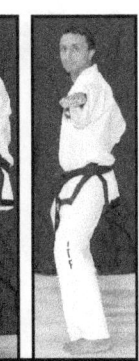

Previous | *Moves 21, 22 & 23*

Kaunde Yop Cha Jirugi
Middle Side Piercing Kick

Nopunde Bandal Jirugi
High Crescent Punch

Kaunde Dollyo Jirugi
Middle Turning Punch
(slow motion)

24. Grab hold of your Knifehand and execute a *Middle Side Piercing Kick* with your Right leg, pulling your hands back as you execute the kick.

25. Following the kick, lower your Right foot to form a *Right Walking Stance* while executing a *High Crescent Punch* with your Left fist.

26. Move your Left foot forwards to form a *Parallel Stance* while executing a *Middle Turning Punch* with your Right fist. Perform move in slow motion.

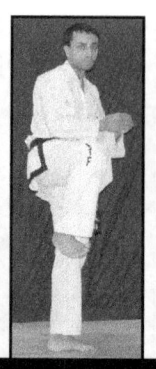

Previous — Moves 24, 25 & 26

Kaunde Sonkal Hechyo Makgi
Middle Knifehand Wedging Block

Sonkal Dung Dollimyo Makgi
Reverse Knifehand Circular Block

Sang Sonbadak Naeryo Makgi
Twin Palm Downward Block

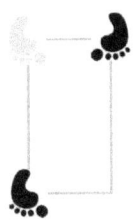  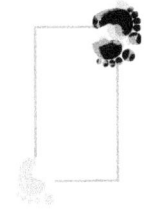

27. Step forwards with your Right leg to form a *Right Walking Stance*, executing a *Middle Knifehand Wedging Block*.

28. Maintain your stance and execute a *Reverse Knifehand Circular Block* with your Left hand.

29. Keep facing the same direction and withdraw your Right leg backwards to form a *Left Rear Foot Stance* while executing a *Twin Palm Downward Block*.

Previous — *Moves 27, 28 & 29*

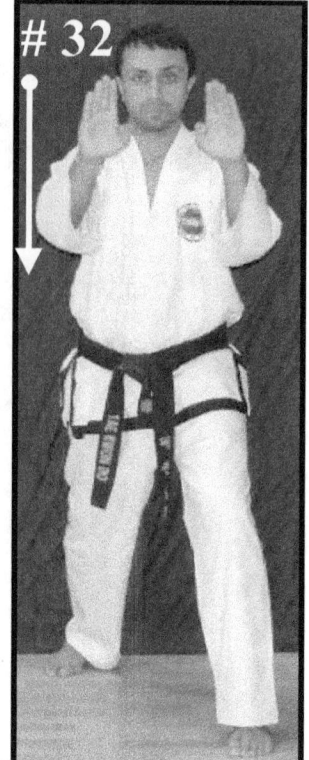

Kaunde Ap Joomok Jirugi
Middle Forefist Punch

Sonkal Dung Najunde Anuro Makgi
Reverse Knifehand Low Inward Block

Kaunde Sonkal Hechyo Makgi
Middle Knifehand Wedging Block

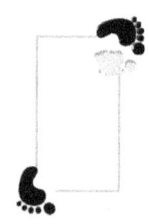
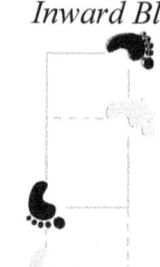

30. Move your Right foot forwards again to form a *Left L-Stance* while executing a *Middle Forefist Punch* with your Left fist.

31. Shift both feet backwards while maintaining your *Left L-Stance*, simultaneously executing a *Reverse Knifehand Low Inward Block* with your Right hand while bringing your Left fist to the front of your Right shoulder.

32. Step forwards with your Left leg forwards to form a *Left Walking Stance*, executing a *Middle Knifehand Wedging Block*.

Previous — *Moves 30, 31 & 32*

Sonkal Dung Dollimyo Makgi
Reverse Knifehand Circular Block

Sang Sonbadak Naeryo Makgi
Twin Palm Downward Block

Kaunde Ap Joomok Jirugi
Middle Forefist Punch

33. Maintain your stance and execute a *Reverse Knifehand Circular Block* with your Left hand.

34. Keep facing the same direction and withdraw your Left leg backwards to form a *Right Rear Foot Stance* while executing a *Twin Palm Downward Block*.

35. Step your Left foot forwards again to form a *Right L-Stance* while executing a *Middle Forefist Punch* with your Right fist.

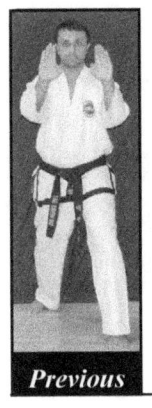      

Previous — *Moves 33, 34 & 35*

Sonkal Dung Najunde Anuro Makgi
Reverse Knifehand Low Inward Block

Nopunde Bandae Dollyo Chagi
High Reverse Turning Kick

Kaunde Palmok Daebi Makgi
Middle Forearm Guarding Block

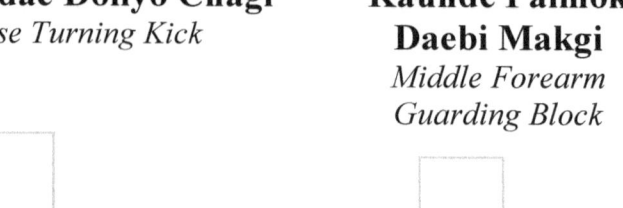
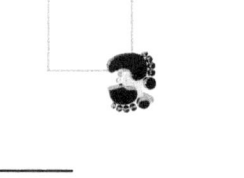

36. Shift both feet backwards while maintaining your *Right L-Stance*, simultaneously executing a *Reverse Knifehand Low Inward Block* with your Left hand while bringing your Right fist to the front of your Left shoulder.

37. Execute a *High Reverse Turning Kick* with your Right leg at a 30 degree angle.

38. Following the kick, lower your Right foot to form a *Left Rear Foot* Stance while executing a *Middle Forearm Guarding Block*.

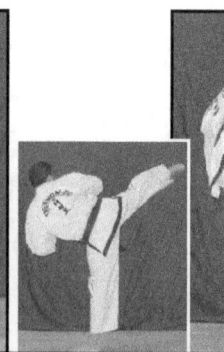

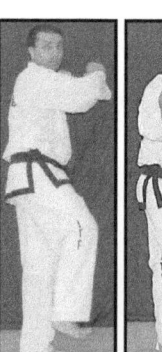

Previous — *Moves 36, 37 & 38*

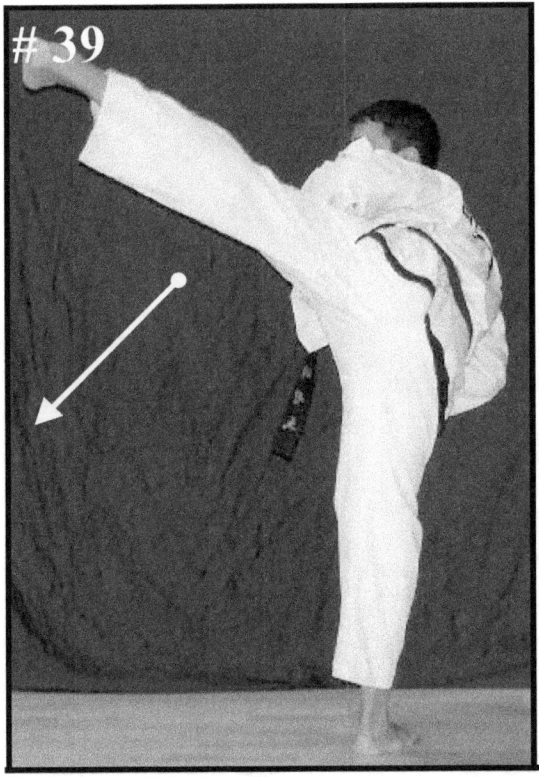

Nopunde Bandae Dollyo Chagi
High Reverse Turning Kick

Kaunde Palmok Daebi Makgi
Middle Forearm Guarding Block

Najunde Sonkal Makgi
Low Knifehand Block

39. Execute a *High Reverse Turning Kick* with your Left leg at a 30 degree angle.

40. Following the kick, lower your Left foot to form a *Right Rear Foot* Stance while executing a *Middle Forearm Guarding Block*.

41. Move your Left foot backwards, just past your Right foot, then move your Right foot backwards to form a *Right L-Stance* while executing a *Low Knifehand Block* with your Left hand. This is known as *'Backwards Double Stepping'* (Ibo Omgyo Didimyo Duruogi)

Previous — *Moves 39, 40 & 41*

Kaunde Bandae Ap Joomok Jirugi
Middle Reverse Forefist Punch

Najunde Sonkal Makgi
Low Knifehand Block

Kaunde Bandae Ap Joomok Jirugi
Middle Reverse Forefist Punch

42. Move your rear foot (Right) outwards to the side to form a *Left Walking Stance* while executing a *Middle Reverse Forefist Punch* with your Right fist.

43. Move your Right foot backwards to form a *Left L-Stance* while executing a *Low Knifehand Block* with your Right hand.

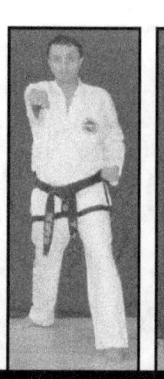

Previous — Moves 42, 43 & 44

Nopunde Ap Joomok Jirugi
High Forefist Punch

Moa Junbi Sogi 'D'
Closed Ready Stance 'D'

 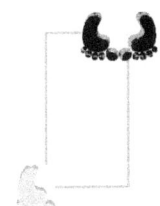

44. Move your rear foot (Left) outwards to the side to form a *Right Walking Stance* while executing a *Middle Reverse Forefist Punch* with your Left fist.

45. Maintain your stance and execute a *High Forefist Punch* with your Right fist.

Return. Bring your Right foot back to the Ready Posture *(Closed Ready Stance 'D')*.

Previous — *Moves 51 & 52 and Return to Ready Posture*

Tips For Eui-Am Tul

1. Sometimes students get confused about which way round there arms should be following the Low Twisting Kick, so that the X-Fist Downward Block is executed correctly to allow for the following Knifehand Rising Block, which needs the hand on top. Just remember, the leg that performs the Twisting Kick is the same as the arm that goes 'underneath' on the X-Fist Downward Block, so opposite hand is free to execute the proceeding Knifehand Rising Block (which is a reverse block).

2. Ensure your execute moves #9 and #22 (Middle Reverse Turning Kick) at a 30 degree angle (i.e. not straight in front) as this is the correct position (though some say 45 degrees) and it allows you to correct prep the chamber and 'step down' for the next movement and stance.

3. Moves #13 and #25 (Middle Turning Punch) are often performed the same as Angle Punch's but an Angle Punch is executed at shoulder level and in-line with the Left or Right shoulder, whereas a Turning Punch is executed to the centre of the body at solar plexus level.

4. Many students tend to dip too much on the Middle Knifehand Wedging Block due to the next move being a Knifehand Circular Block. However, this technique should be executed with no more 'dip' than you do with the Wedging Block's in Do-San tul.

5. Moves #31 and #36 (the slide back into Reverse Knifehand Low Inward Block) are difficult to perform at first because you are shifting in an L-Stance. To execute them, try tilting your body slightly forward while preparing the chamber movement, then throw your body backwards as you slide the L-Stance back and execute the block.

6. Ensure your execute moves #37 and #39 (High Reverse Turning Kick) at a 30 degree angle (i.e. not straight in front) as this is the correct position (though some say 45 degrees) and it allows you to correctly step down into the Rear Foot Stance.

7. The first two Reverse Turning Kicks are 'Middle', whilst the last two are 'High'.

Choong-Jang
General Kim Duk Ryang

Choong-Jang has 52 movements. Choong-Jang is the pseudonym given to General Kim Duk Ryang who lived during the Lee Dynasty in the 14th century. This pattern ends with a left-hand attack to symbolize the tragedy of his death at 27 in prison before he was able to reach full maturity.

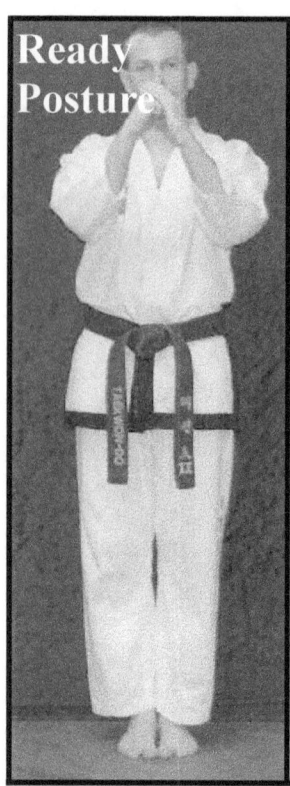  

Moa Junbi Sogi 'A'
Closed Ready Stance 'A'

High Side Front Block & Low Outer Forearm Block.
An Palmok Nopunde Yop Ap Makgi & Najunde Bakat Palmok Makgi
- Alternate sides -

---

1. From *Closed Ready Stance 'A'*, move your Right foot to form *a Sitting Stance* and execute a *High Side Front Block* with your Right arm whilst simultaneously executing a *Low Block* with your Left arm.

2. Maintain your stance and execute a *High Side Front Block* with your Left arm whilst simultaneously executing a *Low Block* with your Right arm.

Running from right to left - From the ready posture to moves 1 & 2

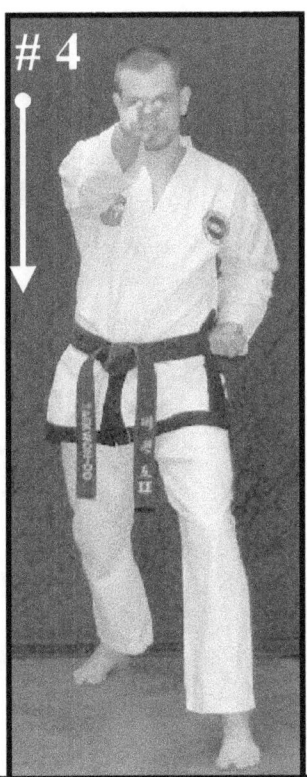

Kyockja Jirugi
Angle Punch
(slow motion)

Nopunde Doo Songarak Tulgi
High Double Finger Thrust

Nopunde Doo Songarak Tulgi
High Double Finger Thrust

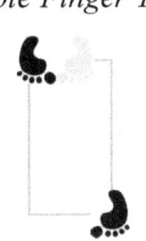

3. Move your Right foot to your Left to form a *Closed Stance* and execute an *Angle Punch* with your Left arm. This is performed in slow motion.

4. Move forwards with your Left foot into a *Walking Stance* and execute a *High Double Finger Thrust* with your Right hand.

5. Move forwards with your Right foot into a *Walking Stance* and execute a *High Double Finger Thrust* with your Left hand.

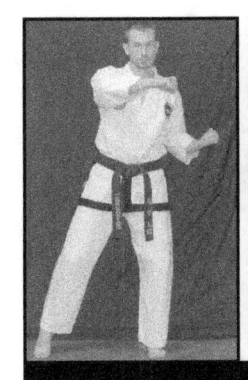

Previous — *Moves 3, 4 & 5*

Dung Joomok Ap Taeragi	**Chookyo Makgi**	**Kaunde Ap Joomok Jirugi**
Backfist Front Strike	*Rising Block*	*Middle Forefist Punch*

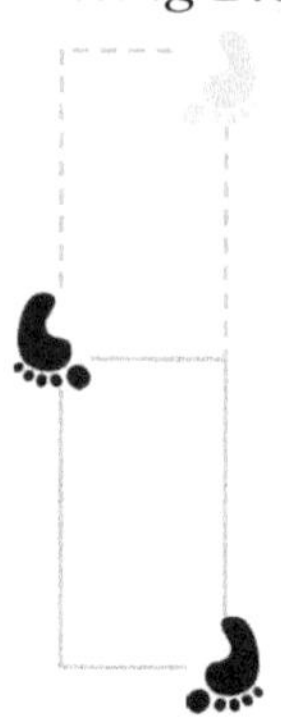

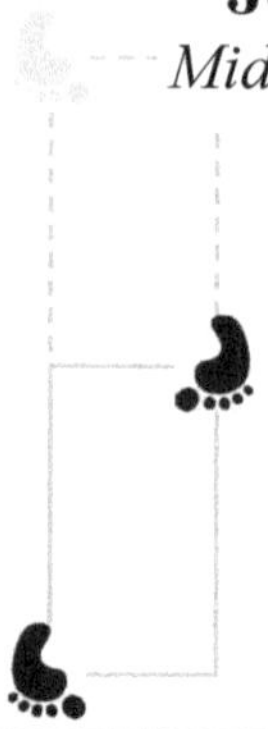

6. Maintain your *Walking Stance* and execute a *Backfist Front Strike* with your Right arm, bringing your left arm underneath your Right arm, with a closed fist.

7. Move forwards into a *Left Walking Stance* and execute a *Rising Block* with your Left arm.

8. Move forwards into a *Right Walking Stance* and execute a *Right Middle Forefist Punch*.

Previous   *Moves 6, 7 & 8*

Kaunde Palmok Daebi Makgi
Middle Forearm Guarding Block

Najunde Ap Cha Busigi
Low Front Snap Kick

Nopunde Opun Sonkut Tulgi
High Flat Fingertip Thrust

Note: The movement between # 8 & #9 are termed *'Backwards Step Slide Turning'* - Dwiro Omgyo Didigo Mikulmyo Dolgi

9. Spin backwards 180 degrees anti-clockwise to form a *Right L-Stance* while executing a *Middle Forearm Guarding Block*.

10. Maintain your hand position and execute a *Low Front Snap Kick* with your Right leg.

11. Land in a *Right Low Stance* and execute a *High Flat Fingertip Thrust* with your Right hand.

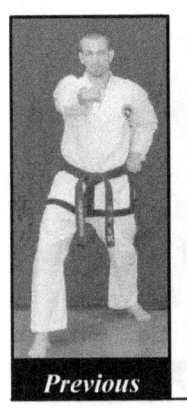   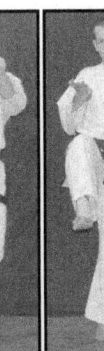    

Previous | *Moves 9, 10 & 11* | *The spin from moves 8 to 9*

Nopunde Dollyo Chagi
High Turning Kick

Nopunde Jirugi
High Punch

Yop Palmok Tulgi
Side Elbow Thrust

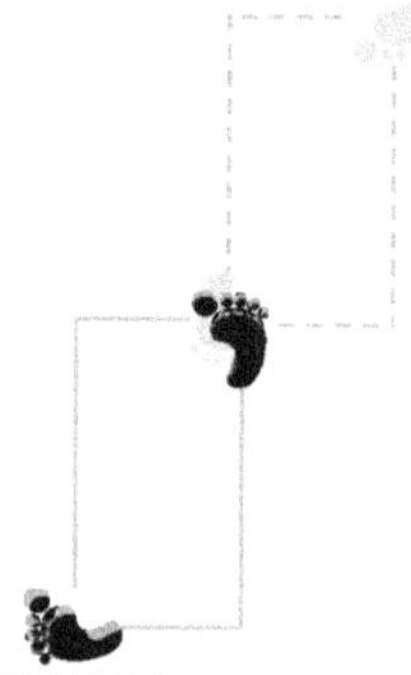

12. Drop down sideways onto your Left knee, supporting yourself with both hands and execute a *High Turning Kick* with your Right leg.

13. Lower kick into a kneeling position (Right knee forwards) and execute a *High Punch* with your Right fist, placing your left hand in line with your foot - arched as if covering an opponents foot.

14. Rise up and spin 180 degrees anti-clockwise, sliding into a *Left L-Stance* and execute a *Side Elbow Thrust* with your Left elbow.

Moves 12, 13 & 14

Palmok Daebi Makgi
Forearm Guarding Block

Sonbadak Duro Makgi
Palm Scooping Block

Kaunde Sonkal Taeragi
Middle Knifehand Strike

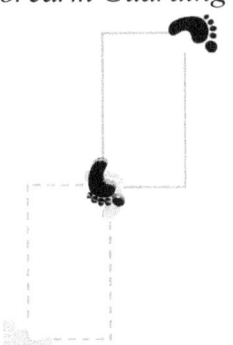 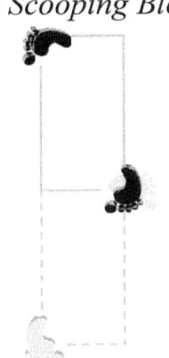 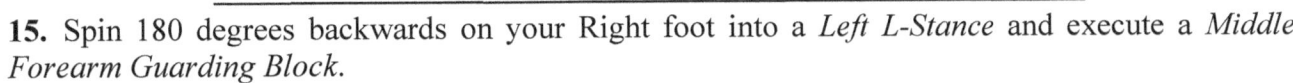

15. Spin 180 degrees backwards on your Right foot into a *Left L-Stance* and execute a *Middle Forearm Guarding Block*.

16. Move backwards into a *Right L-Stance* and execute a *Palm Scooping Block* with your Left hand.

17. Move backwards into a *Left L-Stance* and execute a *Middle Knifehand Strike* with your Right hand.

Previous — *Moves 15, 16 & 17*

Kyocha Joomok Noollo Makgi
X-Fist Pressing Block

Najunde Moorup Chagi
Low Knee Kick

Sonkal Daebi Makgi
Knifehand Guarding Block

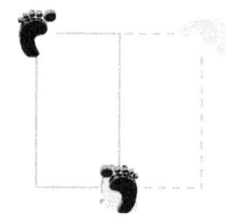
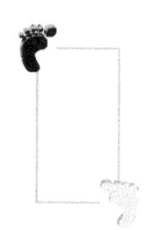
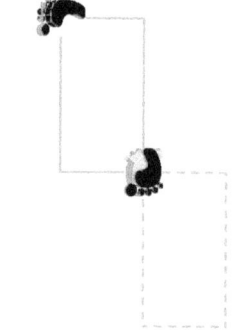

18. Perform a centre-line turn into a *Left Walking Stance* and execute an *X-Fist Pressing Block*.

19. Pull your arms to your right (as if grabbing your opponents leg) while simultaneously executing a *Low Knee Kick* (this is often termed Low front Snap Kick with knee) with your Right knee

20. Lower your Right foot as you pivot 180 degrees anti-clockwise on your Left foot to form a *Right L-Stance* while executing a *Middle Knifehand Guarding Block*.

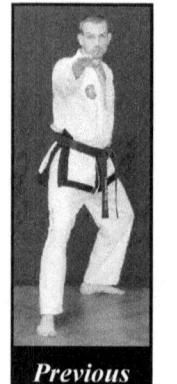

Previous — *Moves 18, 19 & 20* — *Reverse view of moves 18 & 19*

 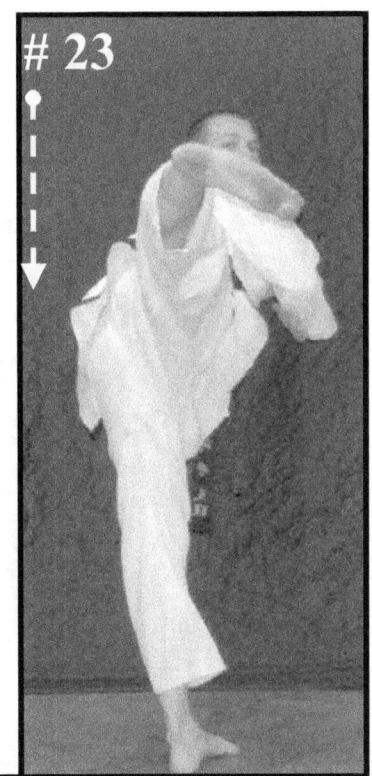

Yop Palmok Tulgi
Side Elbow Thrust

Sonkal Najunde Makgi
Knifehand Low Block

Kaunde Yop Cha Jirugi
Middle Side Piercing Kick

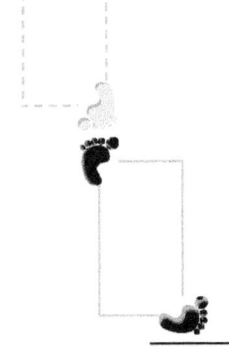 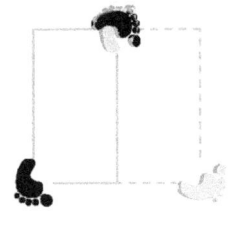 

21. Pivot 180 degrees anti-clockwise and slide into a *Right L-Stance* executing a *Side Elbow Thrust* with your Right elbow.

22. Without moving forwards, turn to face the direction of your elbow strike and move your Right foot sideways to form a *Left L-Stance* and execute a *Middle Knifehand Guarding Block*.

23. Without stepping forwards, take your weight onto your Left leg and execute a *Middle Side Piercing Kick* off your front leg pulling your hands backwards. When you land you will be facing the opposite way round.

Previous — *Moves 21, 22 & 23*

Sang Sonbadak Noollo Makgi
Twin Palm Pressing Block

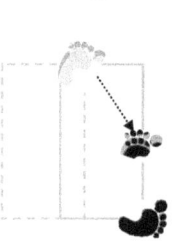

Nopunde Ap Makgi
High Front Block

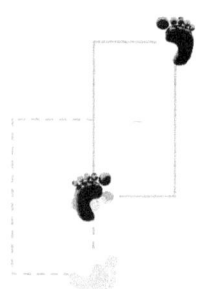

Nopunde Dung Joomok Yop Taeragi
High Back Fist Side Strike

24. Following the Side Piercing Kick, land by bringing your Right foot to your Left, pivoting 180 degrees anti-clockwise, into a *Right Rear Foot Stance* and execute a *Twin Palm Pressing Block*.

25a. Move forwards into a Right Walking Stance and execute an Outer Forearm High Front Block with your Right arm.

25b. Maintain your stance and execute a *High Back Fist Side Strike* with the same arm (Right). This is performed immediately upon completion of the previous block, with no gap between moves.
Note: 25A and 25B were counted as a single move by General Choi.

Previous | Moves 24 & 25 (A & B) plus side views of the Twin Palm Pressing Block

Nopunde Opun Sonkut Tulgi
High Flat Fingertip Thrust

Najunde Ap Cha Busigi
Low Front Snap kick

Both Fists To Right Hip
(slow motion)

26. Pivot 180 degrees anti-clockwise on your Right foot and move your Left foot across into a *Right L-Stance* and execute a *High Flat Fingertip Thrust* with your Left hand.

27. Place your Right palm over your Left hand while simultaneously executing a *Low Front Snap Kick* with your Right leg.

28. Lower your Right foot down in front of you and pivot 180 degrees anti-clockwise, on you Left foot. Slide your Right foot backwards slowly to form a *Left Walking Stance* bringing both fists to your Right hip. Keep your Left fist (in Side Fist Position) on the Right fist. Perform whole movement in slow motion.

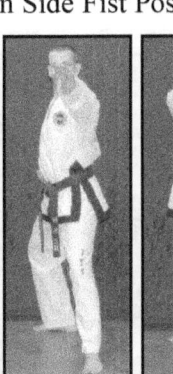
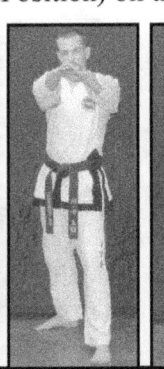

Previous — *Moves 26, 27 & 28* — *# 28 Side View*

Sondung Naeryo Taeragi
Backhand Downward Strike

Ap Joomok Jirugi
Forefist Punch

Sondung Naeryo Taeragi
Backhand Downward Strike

29. Without moving forwards, execute a stamp with your Left foot, forming a *Right L-Stance* while executing a *Backhand Downward Strike* with your Left Back hand.

30. Maintain your stance and execute a *Right Middle Punch* to your Left palm.

31. Move forwards executing a stamp with your Right foot and form a *Left L-Stance* while executing a *Backhand Downward Strike* with your Right Back hand.

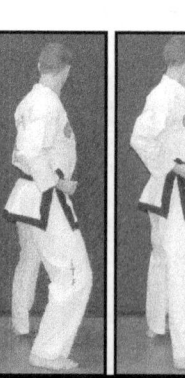

Previous — *Moves 29, 30 & 31* — *# 29 & 30 (Side View)*

Kaunde Ap Joomok Jirugi
Middle Forefist Punch

Kaunde Sonkal Yop Taeragi
Middle Knifehand Side Strike

Dung Joomok Nopunde Yop Ap Taeragi
Back Fist High Side Front Strike

32. Maintain your stance and execute a *Left Middle Punch* to your Right palm.

33. Pivot 180 degrees clockwise on your Right foot, stamping your Left foot as you form a *Right L-Stance* and execute a Middle *Knifehand Side Strike* with your Left hand.

34. Without moving forwards, move your Left foot to form a *Left Walking Stance* and execute a *Back Fist High Side Front Strike* with your Right arm, striking your Left palm with your forearm.

Previous | Moves 32, 33 & 34

Kaunde Sonkal Yop Taeragi
Middle Knifehand Side

Dung Joomok Nopunde Yop Ap Taeragi
Back Fist High Side Front Strike

Sonkal Dung Najunde Daebi Makgi
Reverse Knifehand Low Guarding Block

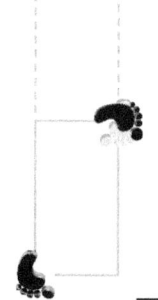  

35. Move forwards into a Left L-Stance, stamping your Right foot as you execute a Middle *Knifehand Side Strike* with your Right hand.

36. Without moving forwards, move your Right foot to form a *Right Walking Stance* and execute a *Back Fist High Side Front Strike* with your Left arm, striking your Right palm with your forearm.

37. Pivot around 180 degrees anti-clockwise on your Right foot to form a *Right L-Stance* and execute a *Reverse Knifehand Low Guarding Block*.

Previous — *Moves 35, 36 & 37*

Choong-Jang
General Kew-Duk Kyung

Gutja Makgi
9-Shape Block

Sonkal Dung Najunde Daebi Makgi
Reverse Knifehand Low Guarding Block

Gutja Makgi
9-Shape Block

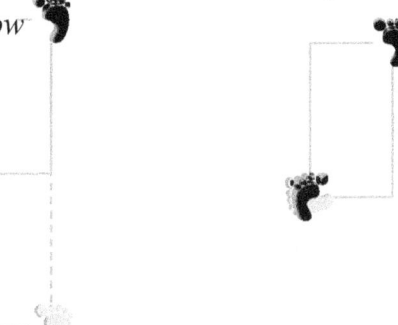

38. Without moving forwards, step your Left foot to form a *Left Walking Stance* and execute a *Right 9-Shape Block*.

39. Move your Right foot wards to form a *Left L-Stance* and execute a *Reverse Knifehand Low Guarding Block*.

40. Without moving forwards, move your Right foot to form a *Right Walking Stance* and execute a *Left 9-Shape Block*.

Previous — *Moves 38, 39 & 40*

Sang Sonkal Soopyong Taeragi
Twin Knifehand Horizontal Strike

Bandalson Nopunde Bandae Taeragi
Arc-Hand High Reverse Strike

41. Move backwards into a *Left Walking Stance* while executing a *Twin Knifehand Horizontal Strike*.

42. Maintain your *Walking Stance* and execute an *Arc-Hand High Reverse Strike* with your Right hand.

Previous — *Moves 41, 42, 43, 44 & 45*

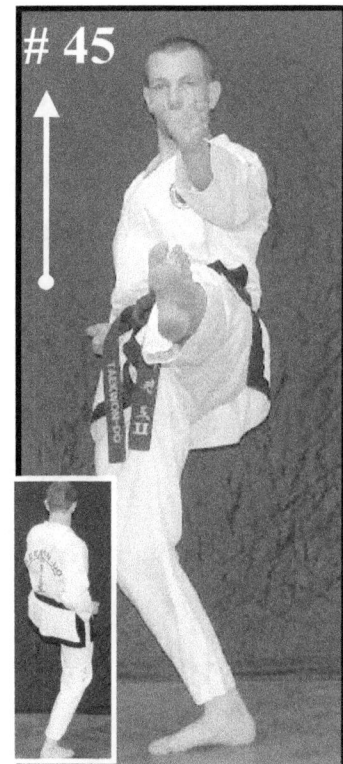

Kaunde Ap Cha Busigi	**Bandalson Nopunde Bandae Taeragi**	**Kaunde Ap Cha Busigi**
Middle Front Snap Kick	*Arc-Hand High Reverse Strike*	*Middle Front Snap Kick*

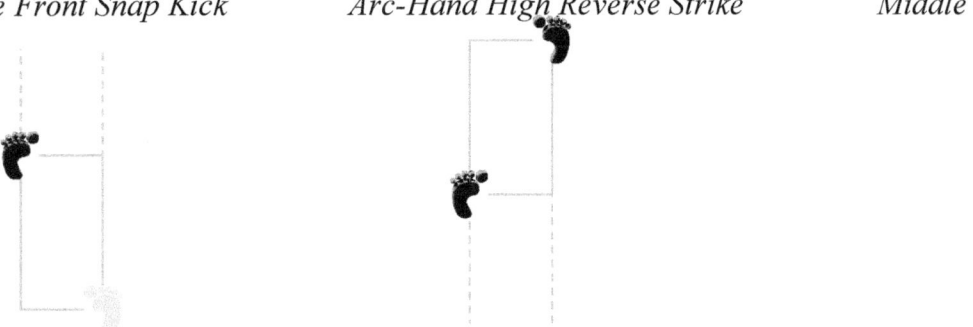

43. Execute a *Middle Front Snap kick* with your Right leg, maintain Arc-Hand position as you execute the kick.

44. Following the previous kick, lower your Right foot to form a Right Walking Stance and execute an *Arc-Hand High Reverse Strike* with your Left hand.

45. Execute a *Middle Front Snap kick* with your Left leg, maintain Arc-Hand position as you execute the kick.

Side View Of Moves 42 to 45

  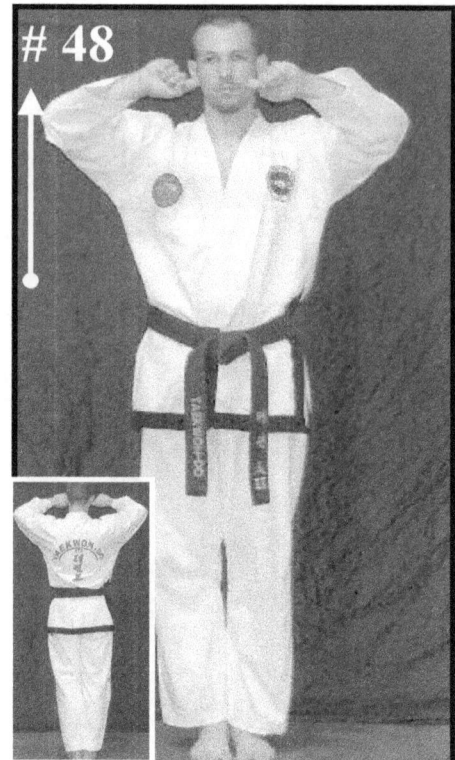

Kaunde Bandae Ap Joomok Jirugi	**Kaunde Baro Ap Joomok Jirugi**	**Nopunde Sang Inji Joomok Bandal Jurugi**
Middle Reverse Forefist Punch	*Middle Obverse Forefist Punch*	*High Twin Fore-Knuckle Fist Crescent Punch*

ITF Note: Movements 46 & 47 are performed in *'Fast Motion'*

46. After the previous kick, lower your Left foot to form a *Left Walking Stance* and execute a *Middle Reverse Forefist Punch* with your Right fist.

47. Maintain your stance and execute a *Middle Obverse Forefist Punch* with your Left fist.

48. Move forwards into a *Closed Stance* and execute a *Twin Fore-Knuckle Fist Crescent Punch*.

   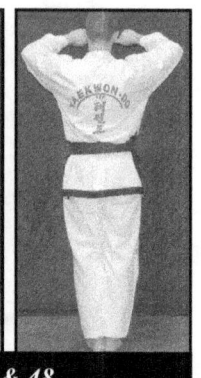

Previous — *Moves 46, 47 & 48*

Najunde Sonkal Makgi
Low Knifehand Block

**Pyon Joomok
Nopunde Bandae Jirugi**
Open Fist High Reverse Punch

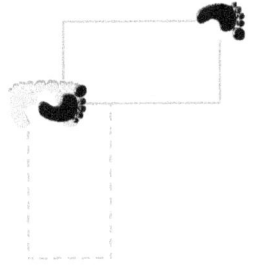

49. Pivot anti-clockwise on your Right foot to 90 degrees (around to your right), to form a *Left Walking Stance* and execute a *Low Knifehand Block* with your Left hand.

50. Maintain your stance and execute an *Open Fist High Reverse Punch* with your Right hand.

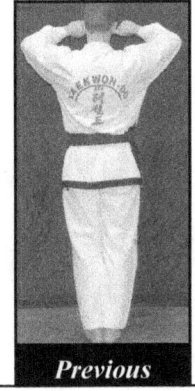

Previous | *Moves 49 & 50*

51

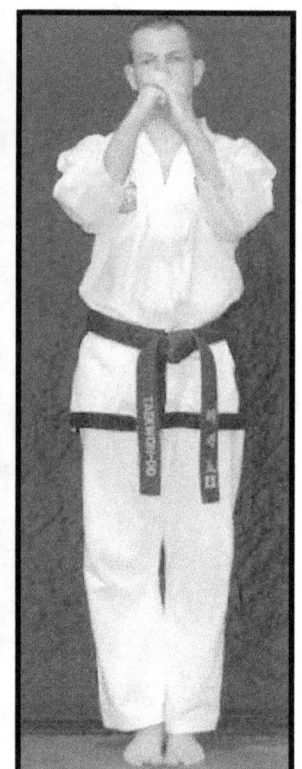

52

Najunde Sonkal Makgi
Low Knifehand Block

Pyon Joomok Nopunde Bandae Jirugi
Open Fist High Reverse Punch

Moa Junbi Sogi 'A'
Closed Ready Stance 'A'

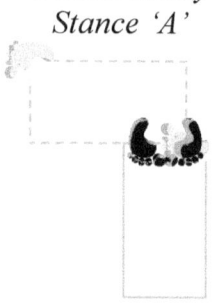

51. Perform a centre-line turn to form a *Right Walking Stance* and execute a *Low Knifehand Block* with your Right hand.

52. Maintain your stance and execute an *Open Fist High Reverse Punch* with your Left hand.

Return. Upon completion of the pattern, bring your left leg forwards to *Closed Ready Stance 'A'*.

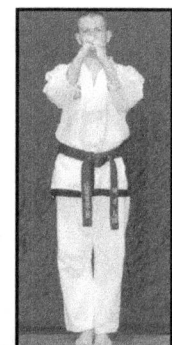

Previous | *Moves 51 & 52 and Return to Ready Posture*

Tips For Choong-Jang Tul

1. Choong-Jang has many turns and pivots, as well as 180 degree turns using only one leg rather than a centre-line turn. It is well work taking the time to memorise these.

2. Move #41 (Twin Knifehand Horizontal Strike) feels weird at first, but you will get used to it. Try not to let the Knifehands go further back than their POI (Point of Impact) which is in-line with the side of your body.

3. Though you may see it at tournaments, moves #43 and #45 (Middle Front Snap Kicks) do not kick through the previous Arc-hand Strikes. The Arc-hands are targeted at the opponents throat, with the kicks attacking the Solar Plexus whilst the hand is still at the throat.

4. Again, though you see it at many tournaments, moves #51 and ##52 are Open Fist Punches not Palm Strikes, as such the fingers should be bent inwards and the palm pushed forwards, as opposed to the fingers remaining vertical i.e. Pointing upwards.

Juche
Man is the master of everything

주 체 틀

Juche has 45 movements. Juche is a philosophical idea that man is the master of everything and decides everything. In other words, the idea that man is the master of the world and his own destiny. It is said that this idea was rooted in Baekdu Mountain which symbolizes the spirit of the Korean people. The diagram represents the Baekdu mountain.

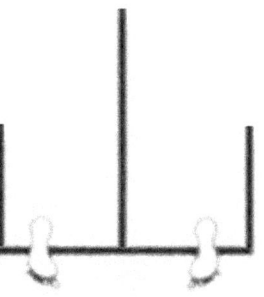

Narani Sogi *with* Sang Yop Palkup
Parallel Stance with Twin Side Elbow

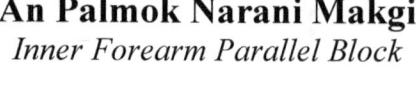

An Palmok Narani Makgi
Inner Forearm Parallel Block

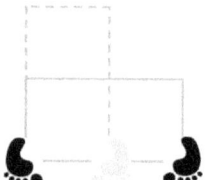

1. From the ready posture *(Parallel Stance with Twin Side Elbow)*, move your left foot into a *Sitting Stance* while executing an *Inner Forearm Parallel Block*.

Kaunde Sonbadak Golcha Makgi
Middle Palm Hooking Block

Kaunde Ap Joomok Jirugi
Middle Forefist Punch

2. Raise up and execute a *Middle Palm Hooking Block* with your Right palm.

3. Drop down back into your *Sitting Stance* and execute a *Middle Forefist Punch*.

From the ready posture to moves 1, 2 & 3

Bakat Palmok Narani Makgi
Outer Forearm Parallel Block

Kaunde Yop Cha Jirugi
Middle Side Piercing Kick
(slow motion)

4. Raise your Right leg to form a *Left One-Leg Stance* while executing an *Outer Forearm Parallel Block*.

5a. Slowly chamber and execute a *Middle Side Piercing Kick* to your Right (keep kick extended).

Previous — *Moves 4 & 5a*

Nopunde Bandae Dollyo Goro Chagi
High Reverse Hooking Kick
(slow motion)

Note: Movements 5a & 5b are performed as *'Consecutive Kicks'*

**Dung Joomok
Naeryo Taeragi**
Back Fist Downward Strike

5b. Raise the kicking leg slightly and slowly execute a *High Reverse Hooking Kick*, pivoting 180 degrees clockwise.

6. Lower kick and jump into a *Right X-Stance* while executing a *Back Fist Downward Strike* with your Right fist.

Previous — *Moves 5b & 6*

Kaunde Golcha Chagi
Middle Hooking Kick

Nopunde Yop Cha Jirugi
High Side Piercing Kick

Nopunde Bakuro Gutgi
High Outward Cross-Cut

Note: Movements 7a & 7b are performed as *'Consecutive Kicks'*

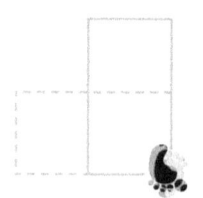
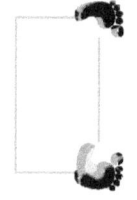

7a. Execute a *Middle Hooking Kick* using your Left leg, targeting the kick 90 degrees anti-clockwise from your previous *Backfist*.

7b. Without placing your foot down, consecutively execute a *High Side Piercing Kick* with your Left leg.

8. Stamp your Left foot into a *Sitting Stance* and execute a *High Outward Cross-Cut* with your Left hand.

Previous — *Moves 7a, 7b & 8*

Nopunde Palkup Taeragi
High Elbow Strike

Sonkal Dung Najunde Ap Makgi
Reverse Knifehand Low Front Block

Kaunde Sonkal Daebi Makgi
Middle Knifehand Guarding Block

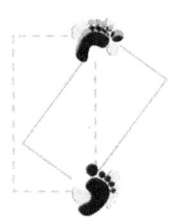  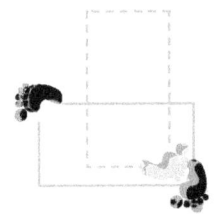

9. Pivot to form an angled (45 degree) *Left Walking Stance* and execute a *High Elbow Strike* with your Right elbow, grabbing the side of your Right fist just prior to execution (hold throughout).

10. Move your Left foot backwards across the front of your Right foot, to form a *Right X-Stance*, while executing a *Reverse Knifehand Low Front Block* with your Left hand, bringing the finger belly of your Right hand to the back of your forearm.

11. Pivot 180 degrees clockwise on your Left foot to form a *Left L-Stance* while executing a *Middle Knifehand Guarding Block*.

  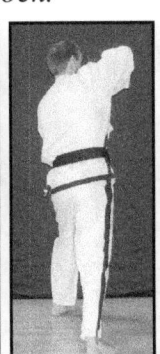    

Previous — *Moves 9, 10 & 11*

Sonkal Twio Dolmyo Taeragi
Knifehand Mid-Air Strike

Landing Position
From Knifehand Mid-Air Strike

12a. Jump and spin 180 degrees anti-clockwise, tucking your knees up and executing a *Knifehand Mid-Air Strike* with your Left hand.

12b. Land in a *Right L-Stance*, keeping the previous striking arm extended in the Knifehand position.

 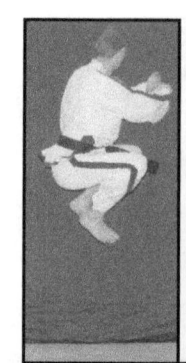  

Previous — *Moves 12a & 12b*

An Palmok Narani Makgi
Inner Forearm Parallel Block

Kaunde Sonbadak Golcha Makgi
Middle Palm Hooking Block

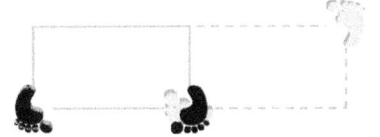

13. Move your Right foot to form a Sitting Stance while executing an *Inner Forearm Parallel Block*

14. Raise up and execute a *Middle Palm Hooking Block* with your Left palm.

Previous — *Moves 13, 14 & 15*

Kaunde Ap Joomok Jirugi
Middle Forefist Punch

Bakat Palmok Narani Makgi
Outer Forearm Parallel Block

---

15. Drop down back into your *Sitting Stance* and execute a *Middle Forefist Punch*.

16. Raise your Left leg to form a *Right One-Leg Stance* while executing an *Outer Forearm Parallel Block*.

Previous 　　　　　　　　　　　　　　　　　　　　　*Moves 15, 16 & 17a*

Kaunde Yop Cha Jirugi
Middle Side Piercing Kick
(slow motion)

17a. Slowly chamber and execute a *Middle Side Piercing Kick* to your Left (keep kick extended).

Nopunde Bandae Dollyo Goro Chagi
High Reverse Hooking Kick
(slow motion)

**Dung Joomok
Naeryo Taeragi**
Back Fist Downward Strike

Note: Movements 17a & 17b are performed as *'Consecutive Kicks'*

 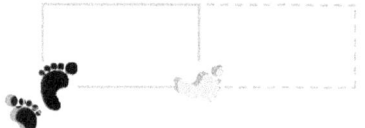

17b. Raise the kicking leg slightly and slowly execute a *High Reverse Hooking Kick*, pivoting 180 degrees anti-clockwise.

18. Lower kicking leg and jump into a *Left X-Stance* while executing a *Back Fist Downward Strike* with your Left fist.

Previous — *Move 18*

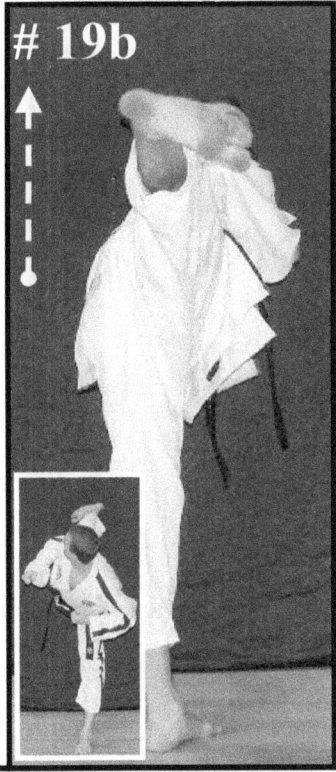

Kaunde Golcha Chagi
Middle Hooking Kick

Nopunde Yop Cha Jirugi
High Side Piercing Kick

Nopunde Bakuro Gutgi
High Outward Cross-Cut

Note: Movements 19a & 19b are performed as *'Consecutive Kicks'*

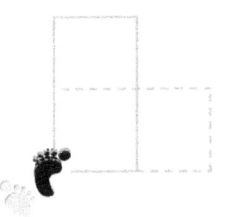
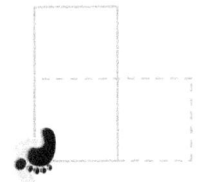

19a. Execute a *Middle Hooking Kick* using your Right leg, 90 degrees clockwise from your previous *Backfist*.

19b. Without placing your foot down, consecutively execute a *High Side Piercing Kick* with your Right leg.

20. Stamp your Right foot into a *Sitting Stance* and execute a *High Outward Cross-Cut* with your Right hand.

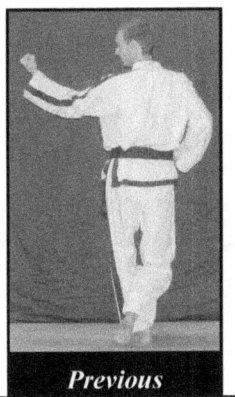

Previous — *Moves 19a, 19b & 20*

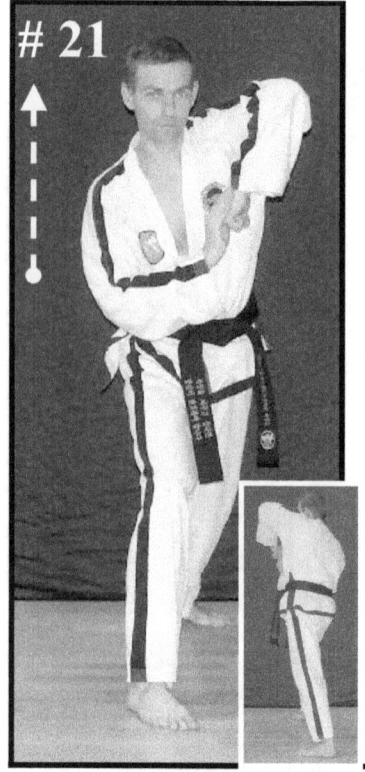

Nopunde Palkup Taeragi
High Elbow Strike

Sonkal Dung Najunde Ap Makgi
Reverse Knifehand Low Front Block

Kaunde Sonkal Daebi Makgi
Middle Knifehand Guarding Block

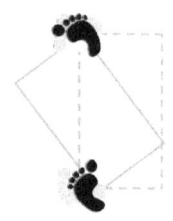
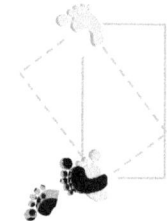
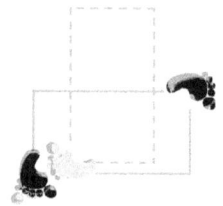

21. Pivot to form an angled (45 degree) *Right Walking Stance* and execute a *High Elbow Strike* with your Left elbow, grabbing the side of your Left fist just prior to execution (keep hold).

22. Move your Right foot backwards across the front of your Left foot, to form a *Left X-Stance,* while executing a *Reverse Knifehand Low Front Block* with your Right hand, bringing the finger belly of your Left hand to the back of your forearm.

23. Pivot 180 degrees anti-clockwise on your Right foot to form a *Right L-Stance* while executing a *Middle Knifehand Guarding Block*.

Previous — *Moves 21, 22 & 23*

Sonkal Twio Dolmyo Taeragi
Knifehand Mid-Air Strike

Landing Position
From Knifehand Mid-Air Strike

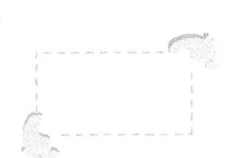

24a. Jump and spin 180 degrees clockwise, tucking your knees up and executing a *Knifehand Mid-Air Strike* with your Right hand.

24b. Land in a *Left L-Stance*, keeping the previous striking arm extended in the Knifehand position.

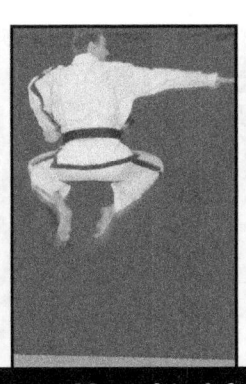

Previous — *Moves 24a & 24b*

Gokgaeng-i Chagi
Pick-Shape Kick

Kaunde Palmok Daebi Makgi
Middle Forearm Guarding Block

Moa Sogi Hanulson
Closed Stance with Heaven Hand
(slow motion)

25a. Execute a *Pick-Shape Kick* with your Left leg towards the direction you are facing.

25b. Following the kick, lower your foot to form a *Right Rear Foot Stance* while executing a *Middle Forearm Guarding Block*.

26. Bring your Right foot to your Left Foot forming a *Closed Stance with Heaven Hand*. Perform in slow motion.

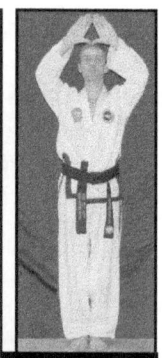

Previous — *Moves 25a, 25b & 26*

**Sun Palkup
Naerjo Tulgi**
*Straight Elbow
Downward Thrust*

**Nopunde Bandalson
Bandal Taeragi**
High Arc-Hand Crescent Strike

**Sun Palkup
Naerjo Tulgi**
*Straight Elbow
Downward Thrust*

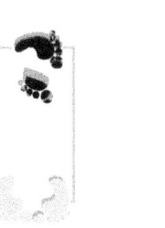
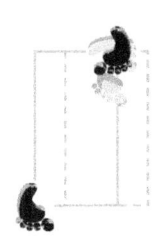
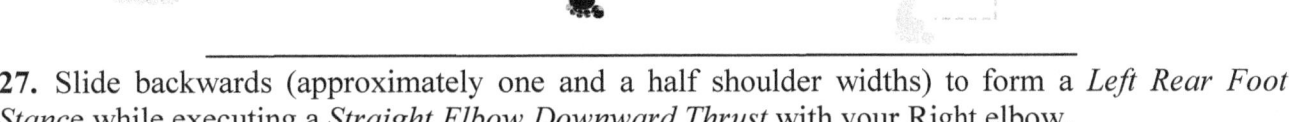

27. Slide backwards (approximately one and a half shoulder widths) to form a *Left Rear Foot Stance* while executing a *Straight Elbow Downward Thrust* with your Right elbow.

28. Slip your Right foot forwards again, to form a *Right Walking Stance* while executing an *High Arc-Hand Crescent Strike* with your Left hand.

29. Slide backwards (approximately one and a half shoulder widths) to form a *Right Rear Foot Stance* while executing a *Straight Elbow Downward Thrust* with your Left elbow.

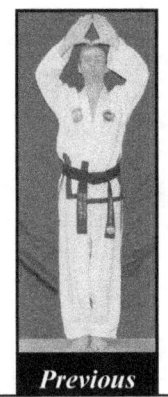

Previous — Moves 27, 28 & 29

Nopunde Bandalson Bandal Taeragi
High Arc-Hand Crescent Strike

Nopunde Sang Sonkal Anuro Taeragi
High Twin Knifehand Inward Strike

Naeryo Jirugi
Downward Punch

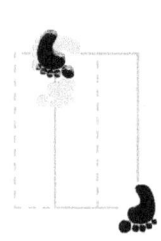
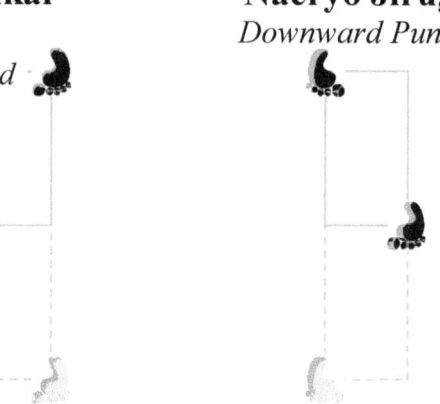

30. Slip your Left foot forwards again, to form a *Left Walking Stance* while executing an *High Arc-Hand Crescent Strike* with your Right hand.

31. Move your Left foot backwards to form a *Right Walking Stance* while executing a *High Twin Knifehand Inward Strike*.

32. Move your Right foot backwards to form a *Left Walking Stance* while executing a *Downward Punch* with your Right hand.

Previous — *Moves 30, 31 & 32*

Bakat Palmok Naeryo Makgi
Outer Forearm Downward Block

Pihamyo Bandae Dollyo Chagi
Dodging Reverse Turning Kick

Kaunde Palmok Daebi Makgi
Middle Forearm Guarding Block

ITF Note: ITF-C now perform move #34a as a *Flying Reverse Hooking Kick*

33. Take a double step and slide backwards *(Dwiro Ibo Omgyo Didimyo Mikulmyo)* by moving your Left foot just past your Right foot, then sliding your Right foot back to form a *Right L-Stance* and executing an *Outer Forearm Downward Block* with your Left arm.

34a. Jump up and backwards while executing a *(Dodging) Reverse Turning Kick* with your Right leg.

34b. Land in a *Left L-Stance* while executing a *Middle Forearm Guarding Block*.

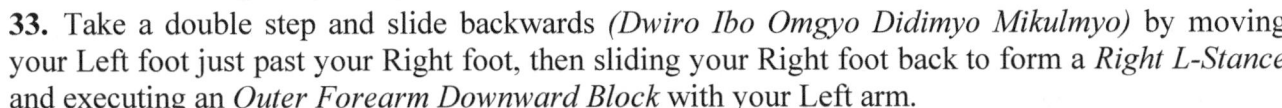

Previous — *Moves 33, 34a & 34b*

Bakat Palmok Naeryo Makgi
Outer Forearm Downward Block

Pihamyo Bandae Dollyo Chagi
Dodging Reverse Turning Kick

Kaunde Palmok Daebi Makgi
Middle Forearm Guarding Block

> **ITF Note:** ITF-C now perform move #36a as a *Flying Reverse Hooking Kick*

35. Take a double step backwards by moving your Right foot just past your Left foot, then sliding your Left foot backwards to form a *Left L-Stance* backwards *(Dwiro Ibo Omgyo Didimyo Mikulmyo)*, executing an *Outer Forearm Downward Block* with your Right arm.

36a. Jump up and backwards while executing a *(Dodging) Reverse Turning Kick* with your Left leg.

36b. Land in a *Right L-Stance* while executing a *Middle Forearm Guarding Block*.

Previous — Moves 35, 36a & 36b

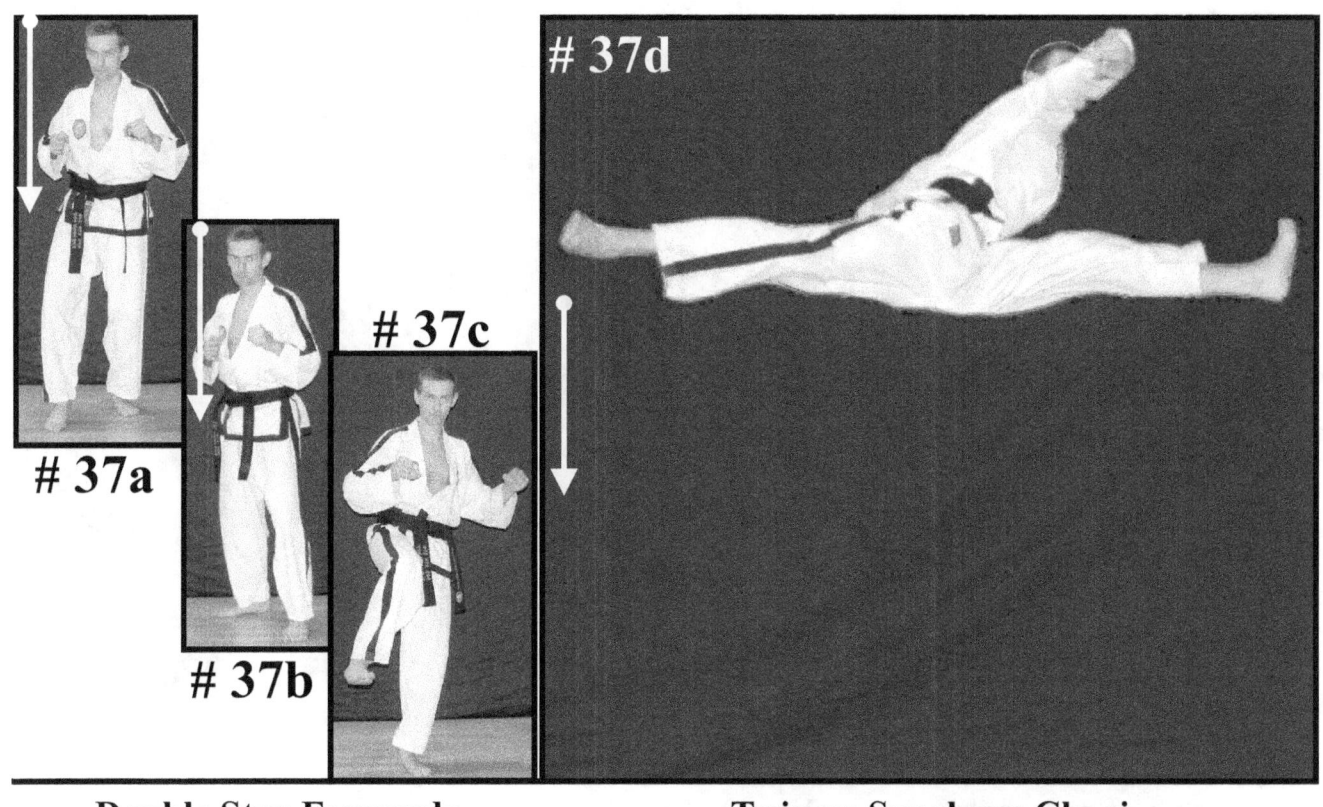

Double Step Forwards **Twimyo Sangbang Chagi**
Flying Two Directional Kick

37a & b. Take a double step forwards moving your Right foot, followed by your Left foot.

37c. Continuing from the steps, use your Right leg to help launch yourself into the air.

37d. Leap up and execute a *Flying Two Directional Kick* (with the Left leg forming a *Twisting Kick* and the Right leg forming a *Side Piercing Kick*). Land in *Diagonal Stance* (see #38).

Sang Sonbadak Chookyo Makgi
Twin Palm Rising Block

Yop Palkup Tulgi
Side Elbow Thrust

Goburyo Junbi Sogi 'B'
Bending Ready Stance 'B'
(slow motion)

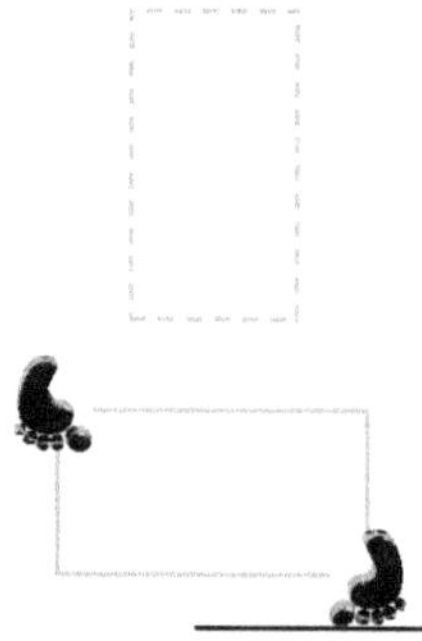

38. From the Flying Two Directional Kick, land in a *Left Diagonal Stance* while executing a *Twin Palm Rising Block*.

39. Taking your weight on your Left foot, pivot (anti-clockwise, 180 degrees) and slide into a *Right Rear Foot Stance* while executing a *Side Elbow Thrust* with your Right elbow.

40a. Take your weight on your Right leg and execute a *Bending Ready Stance 'B'* (Looking over your Left shoulder). Perform in slow motion.

Moves 38, 39 40a

Kaunde Dwitcha Jirugi
Middle Back Piercing Kick
(slow motion)

Dung Joomok Soopyong Taeragi
Back Fist Horizontal Strike

Nopunde Anuro Gutgi
High Inward Cross-Cut

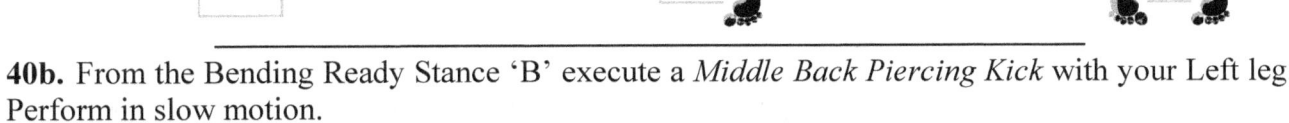

40b. From the Bending Ready Stance 'B' execute a *Middle Back Piercing Kick* with your Left leg. Perform in slow motion.

41. Following the Back Piercing Kick, land in a *Right L-Stance* stamping your Left foot as you do so and execute a *Back Fist Horizontal Strike* with your Left fist.

42. Move your Right foot in-line with your Left foot to form a *Parallel Stance* while executing a *High Inward Cross-Cut* with your Right hand.

Twimyo Yonsok Jirugi
Flying Consecutive Punch

43a, b & c. Jump forwards and execute a *Flying Consecutive Punch* with your Right fist. While in the air execute a Front Punch (# 43a) and an Upset Punch (# 43b) with your Right hand, landing in a *Closed Stance*, with the fist extended (# 43c) in the Upset Punch position.

  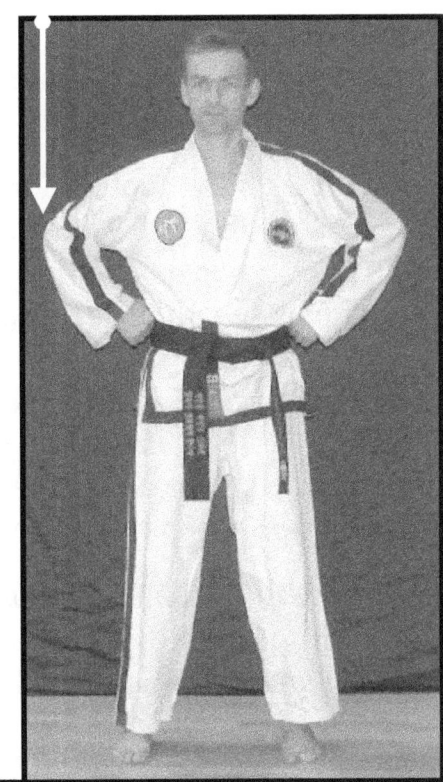

Sonkal Naerjo Taeragi
Knifehand Downward Strike

Kaunde Bandae Ap Joomok Jirugi
Middle Reverse Forefist Punch

Narani Sogi *with* Sang Yop Palkup
Parallel Stance with Twin Side Elbow

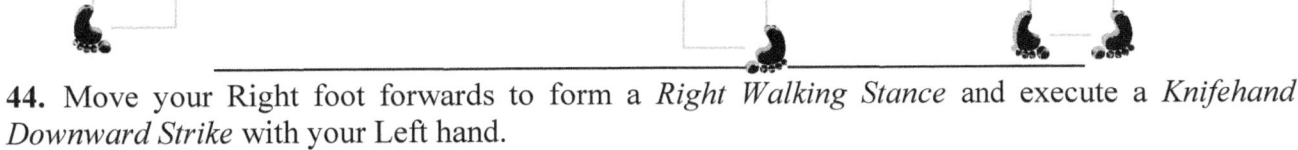

44. Move your Right foot forwards to form a *Right Walking Stance* and execute a *Knifehand Downward Strike* with your Left hand.

45. Move forwards with your Left foot to form a *Left Walking Stance* while executing a *Middle Reverse Forefist Punch* with your Right hand.

Return. Bring your Right foot forwards to the Ready Posture.

Previous | *Moves 44 & 45 and Return to Ready Posture*

Tips For Juche Tul

1. With its slow motion kicks, dodging kicks and the Flying Two Directional Kick Juche is possibly the most difficult pattern to perform in Ch'ang Hon Taekwon-Do. To make your performance better it is suggested your practice the following techniques separately as well as within the pattern:

- Moves #5a and #17a - Middle Side Piercing Kicks in slow motion

Practice these to improve your leg muscles. Performing them with an ankle weight on may help, but always execute them slowly. Don't forget to raise the kick up to high section when its fully extended!

- Moves #5b and #17b - High Reverse Hooking Kick

As with the Side Kicks practice these on their own to achieve the muscle strength that is required to perform them.

- Moves #34a and #36a - Dodging Reverse Turning Kicks

To practice these in isolation, grab a training partner and a focus pad. Assume the previous posture and ask your training partner to stand so the focus pad is above your front foot, then perform the technique. Once that can be done successfully, ask your training partner to stand just in front of your front foot (without the pad) and execute the technique so you successfully kick just in front of them as opposed to hitting them with it!

- Move 37d - Flying Two Directional Kick

First practice this by having two training partners hold focus pads opposite to each other and try to perform the kick to the pads. Once this is achieved a number of times, remove the pads and practice the technique with the training partners just standing there (opposite each other). As the kick is performed in thin air, this helps to train the positioning of the kick as its easier the kick hitting pads, as opposed to placing the kick accurately as the pattern requires. Try to land in Diagonal stance each time.

2. The sequence at the beginning of the pattern, moves #1 to #5a are easily remembered by memorising that you step 'Left' first and simply change sides each time i.e. (step) *Left* (and block), *Right* (Palm Hooking Block), *Left* (Punch), *Right* (Side Piercing Kick). This is reversed when the moves are repeated in the pattern, so you starts with 'Right' first.

3. When executing the slow Middle Side Piercing Kick, remember that the foot raises before executing the slow High Reverse Hooking Kick. At the end of the movement, some perform the *'hook'* part with speed, while other organisations require it to remain in slow motion.

4. Remember that the strike in moves #12a and #24a (Knifehand Mid-Air Strike) are executed whilst in the air, not when or as you land.

5. On move #37 (Flying Two Directional Kick), time your steps so you are not too fast and not too slow. The steps are to help with the kick, not to gain distance as if you run to fast you will finish too far forwards.

6. When performing move #37 (Flying Two Directional Kick), jump up as high as you can by using your Right knee to gain height, but quickly raise your Left knee and kick out. Execute the kick quickly and tuck the legs back in so you can land in Diagonal stance properly.

7. Remember, to be 100% correct, you execute move #38 (Twin Palm Rising Block) as you land from the previous kick, not after you have landed - this takes a lot of practice!

8. For move #43 (Flying Consecutive Punch) both of the punches should ideally be executed in the air - you simply land with the fist in the 'Upset Punch' position - this is fairly hard to achieve and takes some practice.

Ko-Dang
Cho Man Sik

Ko-Dang is the pseudonym of the patriot Cho Man Sik, who dedicated his life to the Korean Independence Movement and to the education of his people. Kodang has 39 movements which signify his times of imprisonment and his birthplace on the 39th parallel.

Moa Junbi Sogi 'C'
Closed Ready Stance 'C'

Kaunde Sonbadak Miro Makgi
Middle Palm Pushing Block

Kaunde Ap Joomok Jirugi
Middle Forefist Punch

1. From the ready posture *(Closed Ready Stance 'C')*, move your Right foot out and backwards to form a *Sitting Stance* at a 45 degree angle while executing a *Middle Palm Pushing Block* with your Left hand.

2. Maintain your stance and execute a *Middle Forefist Punch* with your Right fist.

From the ready posture to moves 1 & 2

Kaunde Palmok Daebi Makgi
Middle Forearm Guarding Block

Najunde Bakat Palmok Magki / Kaunde An Palmok Yop Makgi
Low Outer Forearm Block / Middle Inner Forearm Side Block

Kaunde Sonbadak Miro Makgi
Middle Palm Pushing Block

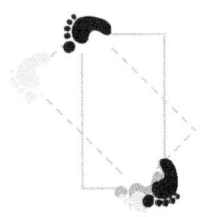 

3. Move your Right foot back to form a *Right L-Stance* while executing a *Middle Forearm Guarding Block*.

4. Maintain your stance and execute a *Low Outer Forearm Block* with your Right arm and an *Middle Inner Forearm Side Block* with your Left arm at a 45 degree angle.

5. Move your Left foot out and backwards to form a *Sitting Stance* at a 45 degree angle while executing a *Middle Palm Pushing Block* with your Right hand.

Previous — *Moves 3, 4 & 5*

Kaunde Ap Joomok Jirugi
Middle Forefist Punch

Kaunde Palmok Daebi Makgi
Middle Forearm Guarding Block

Najunde Bakat Palmok Magki / Kaunde An Palmok Yop Makgi
Low Outer Forearm Block / Middle Inner Outer Forearm Side Block

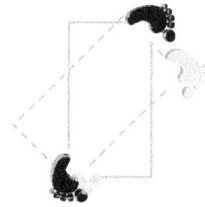
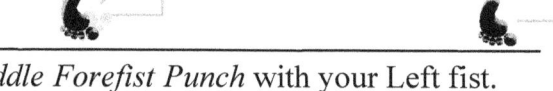

6. Maintain your stance and execute a *Middle Forefist Punch* with your Left fist.

7. Move your Left foot back another 45 degrees to form a *Left L-Stance* while executing a *Middle Forearm Guarding Block*.

8. Maintain your stance and execute a *Low Outer Forearm Block* with your Left arm and a *Middle Inner Forearm Side Block* with your Right arm at a 45 degree angle.

Previous | *Moves 6, 7 & 8*

Goburyo Junbi Sogi 'B'
Bending Ready Stance 'B'

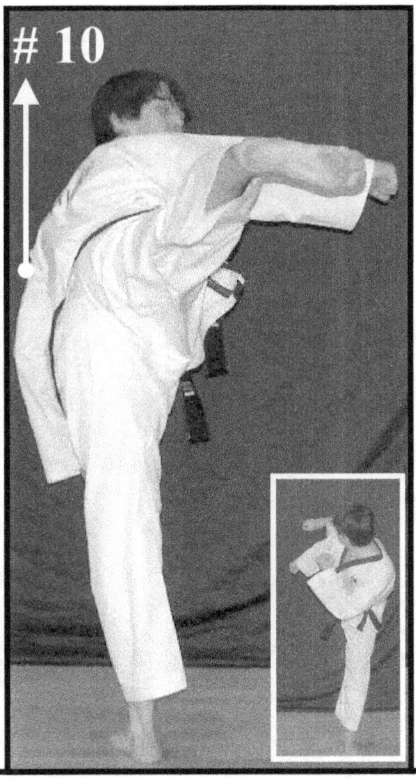

Kaunde Dwitcha Jirugi
Middle Back Piercing Kick

Kaunde Sonkal Makgi
Middle Knifehand Block

9. Bring your Right foot back towards your Left foot and execute a Left *Bending Ready Stance 'B'*.

10. From the Bending Ready Stance 'B', execute a *Middle Back Piercing Kick* with your Right leg.

11. Following the kick, lower your Right foot to form a *Right L-Stance* and execute a *Middle Knifehand Block* with your Left hand.

Moves 9, 10 & 11

Goburyo Junbi Sogi 'B'
Bending Ready Stance 'B'

Kaunde Dwitcha Jirugi
Middle Back Piercing Kick

Kaunde Sonkal Makgi
Middle Knifehand Block

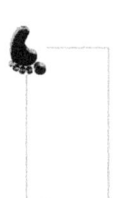
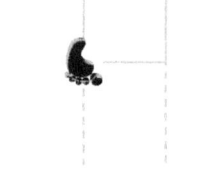

12. Bring your Left foot back towards your Right foot and execute a Right *Bending Ready Stance 'B'*

13. From the Bending Ready Stance 'B', execute a *Middle Back Piercing Kick* with your Left leg.

14. Following the kick, lower your Left foot to form a *Left L-Stance* and execute a *Middle Knifehand Block* with your Right hand.

Previous — *Moves 12, 13 & 14*

Sun Palkup Naeryo Tulgi
Straight Elbow Downward Thrust

Sun Palkup Naeryo Tulgi
Straight Elbow Downward Thrust

Sonbadak Noollo Makgi
Palm Pressing Block

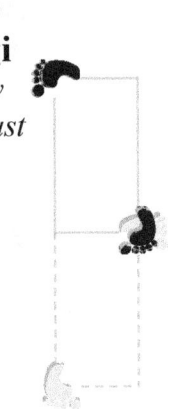 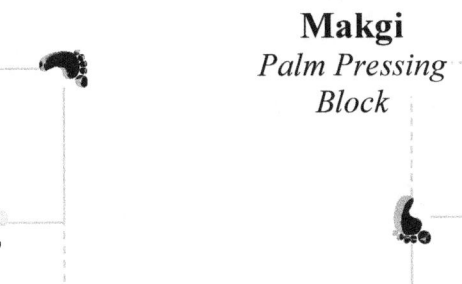

15. Move your Right foot back to form a *Right L-Stance* executing a *Straight Elbow Downward Thrust* with your Left elbow.

16. Move your Left foot back to form a *Left L-Stance* executing a *Straight Elbow Downward Thrust* with your Right elbow.

17. Move your Left foot forwards into a *Left Walking Stance* while executing a *Right Palm Pressing Block*. Perform in slow motion.

Previous — *Moves 9, 10 & 11*

Sonbadak Noollo Makgi	**Bakat Palmok Naeryo Makgi**	**Bakat Palmok Naeryo Makgi**
Palm Pressing Block	*Outer Forearm Downward Block*	*Outer Forearm Downward Block*

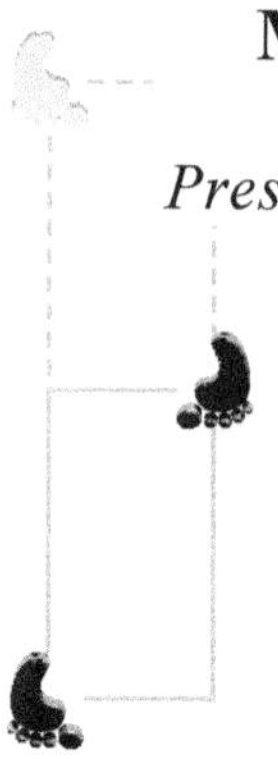

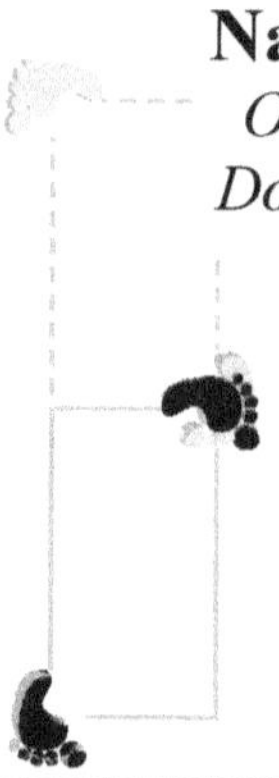

18. Move your Right foot forwards into a *Right Walking Stance* while executing a *Left Palm Pressing Block*. Perform in slow motion.

19. Move your Right foot backwards to form a *Right L-Stance* while executing an *Outer Forearm Downward Block* with your Left arm.

20. Move your Right foot forwards to form a *Left L-Stance* while executing an *Outer Forearm Downward Block* with your Right arm.

Moves 18, 19 & 20

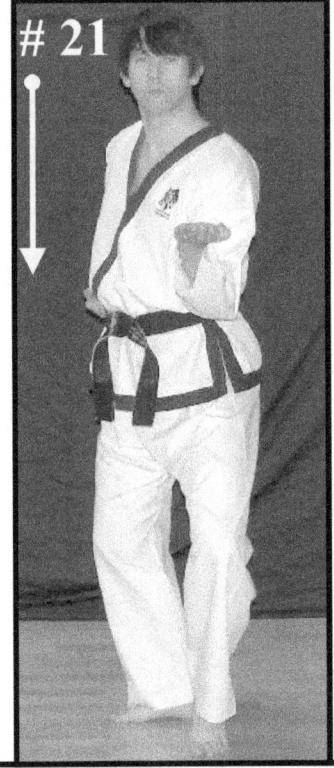  

Sonbadak Ollyo Makgi
Palm Upward Block

Sonbadak Ollyo Makgi
Palm Upward Block

Kaunde Ap Cha Busigi
Middle Front Snap Kick

21. Move your Left foot forwards to form a *Right Rear Foot Stance* while executing a *Palm Upward Block* with your Left palm.

22. Move your Right foot forwards to form a *Left Rear Foot Stance* while executing a *Palm Upward Block* with your Right palm.

23. Move your Right foot backwards just past your Left foot, then execute a *Middle Front Snap Kick* with your Left leg.

Previous — *Moves 21, 22 & 23*

Sang Sonkal Anuro Taeragi
Twin Knifehand Inward Strike

Sonkal Chookyo Makgi
Knifehand Rising Block

Najunde Sonkal Daebi Makgi
Low Knifehand Guarding Block

Note: Movements 24 & 25 are performed as *'Continuous Motion'*

24. Following the kick, lower your Left foot in front to form a *Left Walking Stance* while executing a *Twin Knifehand Inward Strike*.

25. Maintain your stance and execute a *Knifehand Rising Block* with your Left hand.

26. Without stepping forwards, move your Left foot to form a *Right L-Stance* while executing a *Low Knifehand Guarding Block*.

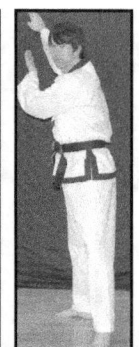

Previous — *Moves 24, 25 & 26*

Naeryo Jirugi
Downward Punch

Kaunde Sonkal Daebi Makgi
Middle Knifehand Guarding Block

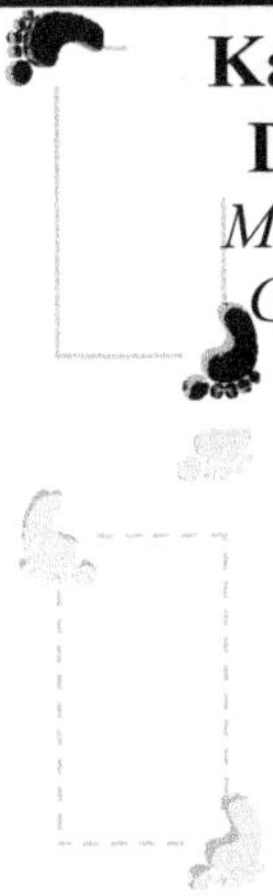

Jump
(Straight Up)

27. Without stepping forwards, move your Left foot to form a *Left Walking Stance* while executing a *Downward Punch* with your Left fist.

28. Move your Left foot backwards, just past your Right foot, then move your Right foot backwards and slide to form a *Right L-Stance* while executing a *Middle Knifehand Guarding Block*.

29a. Jump straight up (with no forward or backwards motion).

Previous — Moves 27, 28, 29a & 29b

Kaunde Sonkal Daebi Makgi
Middle Knifehand Guarding Block

Dung Joomok Nopunde Yop Taeragi
Back Fist High Side Strike

Nopunde Bakat Palmok Yop Makgi
High Outer Forearm Side Block

29b. Following the jump, land in the same stance (*Right L-Stance*) while executing a *Middle Knifehand Guarding Block*.

30. Jump forwards to form a *Right X-Stance* while executing a *Back Fist High Side Strike* with your Right fist.

31. Pivot 180 degrees anti-clockwise on your Right foot, before stepping your Left foot forwards to form a *Left Walking Stance* executing a *High Outer Forearm Side Block* with your Left arm.

Previous | *Moves 30 & 31*

Nopunde Bakat Palmok Yop Makgi
High Outer Forearm Side Block

Dwijibo Jirugi
Upset Punch

Kaunde Golcha Chagi
Middle Hooking Kick

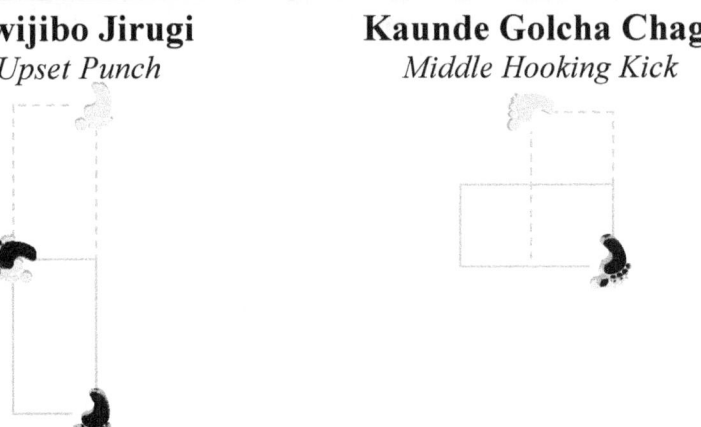

32. Move your Left foot back and inwards so it is in-line with your Left foot and pivot 180 degrees clockwise, moving your Right foot forwards to form a *Right Walking Stance* while executing a *High Outer Forearm Side Block* with your Right arm.

33. Move your Left foot forwards to form a *Right L-Stance* while executing an *Upset Punch* with your Right fist, bringing your Left fist to your Right shoulder.

34. Execute a *Middle Hooking Kick* with your Right leg to your Right-hand side.

Previous   *Moves 32, 33 & 34*

Nopunde Bakuro Gutgi
High Outward Cross-Cut

Kaunde Golcha Chagi
Middle Hooking Kick

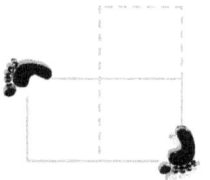

35. Following the kick, lower your Right foot to form a *Left L-Stance* (so you are 90 degrees from your previous position) and execute a *High Outward Cross-cut* with your Right hand.

36. Move your Right foot back towards your Left foot, placing next to your Left foot before executing a *Middle Hooking Kick* with your Left leg to your Left hand side.

Previous — *Moves 35 & 36*

Nopunde Bakuro Gutgi
High Outward Cross-Cut

Nopunde Sonkal Daebi Makgi
High Knifehand Guarding Block

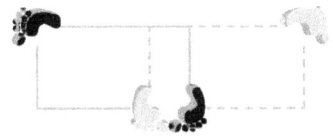

37. Following the kick, lower your Left foot to form a *Right L-Stance* and execute a *High Outward Cross-cut* with your Left hand.

38. Move foot to foot (Left foot to Right foot), turn and move your Right foot forward to form a *Left L-Stance* while executing a *High Knifehand Guarding Block*.

Previous | *Moves 37 & 38*

Nopunde Sonkal Daebi Makgi
High Knifehand Guarding Block

Moa Junbi Sogi 'C'
Closed Ready Stance 'C'

39. Move foot to foot (Right foot to Left foot) turning 180 degrees, then move your Left foot to form a *Right L-Stance* while executing a *High Knifehand Guarding Block*.

Return. Bring your Left foot back to the Ready Posture (*Closed Ready Stance 'C'*)

Previous | *Move 39 & Return*

Tips For Ko-Dang Tul

1. When you perform the Downward Elbow be careful to raise your arm sufficiently high enough and fully drop into the technique in order to gain the full power. Ensure the drop is combined with the drop in the stance.

2. Same a #1 for the Downward Blocks, ensure you raise your arm sufficiently high enough and fully drop into the technique in order to gain the full power. Ensure the drop is combined with the drop in the stance.

3. When performing the jump try to lift your knees whilst keeping your back straight. Practice this with a mirror if possible.

4. Remember, when you perform the cross-cut that it is not a knife hand strike, there is no twist and you need to create a whipping motion.

5. Movements #27 and #33 are often seen performed in two different ways. Move #27 (Downward Punch) can see the performer keeping the back straight as the punch is executed or bending the back so the punch is closer to the ground. Move #33 is termed 'Upset Punch' and some perform it that way; almost horizontal to the floor, while others perform it more as in an 'Upwards Punch' motion. The correct way is how your instructor or organisation requires them to be executed.

Examples of
#27 Naeryo Jirugi
Downward Punch

Examples of
#33 Dwijibo Jirugi
Upset Punch

Jook-Am
Grandmaster Park, Jung Tae

Jook-Am is the pseudonym of Grandmaster Park, Jung Tae. *'Jook'* means a bamboo which shoots up straight without any curvature, its roots intertwining to form an inseparable force. *'Am'* is an immovable rock, on which the bamboo strikes its roots to form an unshakable foundation. This pattern represents the life of Grandmaster Park, Jung Tae and his striving for perfection. The diagram symbolize the bamboo, which grows high from the rock. Jook-Am has 95 movements which symbolize the year 1995, in which Jook-Am was created.

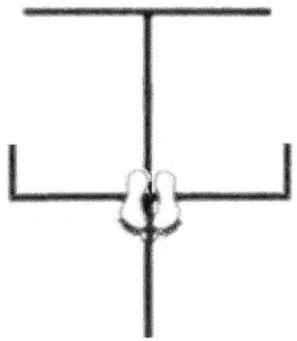

Moa Sogi
Closed Stance with Fists Above Head

Sang Joomok Kaunde Ap Jirugi
Twin Fist Middle Front Punch (slow motion)

Goburyo Junbi Sogi 'B'
Bending Ready Stance 'B' (slow motion)

1. From the ready posture *(Closed Stance with Fist Above head)*, slide your Left foot backwards to form a *Right Walking Stance* while executing a *Twin Fist Middle Punch*. Perform in slow motion.

2a. Withdraw your Right leg to form a *Left Bending Ready Stance 'B'*. Perform in slow motion.

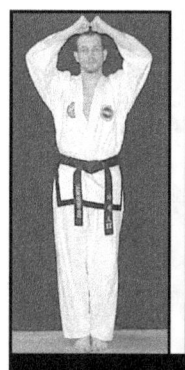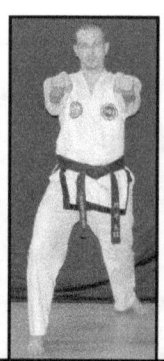

From the ready posture to moves 1 & 2a

Kaunde Dwitcha Jirugi
Middle Back Piercing Kick
(slow motion)

Nopunde Dwitcha Jirugi
High Back Piercing Kick

Kaunde Sonkal Makgi
Middle Knifehand Block

Note: Movements 2b & 3 are performed as *'Consecutive Kicks'*

2b. Execute a *Middle Back Piercing Kick* with your Right leg. Perform in slow motion.

3. Re-chamber your Right leg and execute a *High Back Piercing Kick* with your Right leg.

4. Following the kick, place your Right leg down behind to form a *Right L-Stance* while executing a *Middle Knifehand Block* with your Left hand.

Previous — *Moves 2b, 3 & 4*

Goburyo Junbi Sogi 'B'
Bending Ready Stance 'B'
(slow motion)

Kaunde Dwitcha Jirugi
Middle Back Piercing Kick
(slow motion)

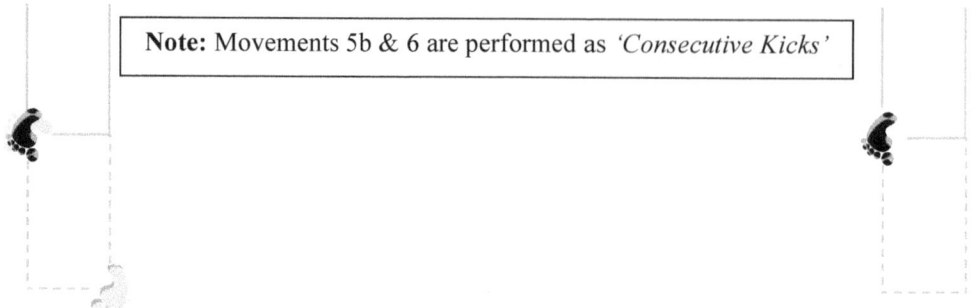

Note: Movements 5b & 6 are performed as *'Consecutive Kicks'*

5a. Withdraw your Left leg to form a *Right Bending Ready Stance 'B'*. Perform in slow motion.
5b. Execute a *Middle Back Piercing Kick* with your Left leg. Perform in slow motion.

Previous — *Moves 5a & 5b*

Nopunde Dwitcha Jirugi
High Back Piercing Kick

Kaunde Sonkal Makgi
Middle Knifehand Block

Sang Yop Palkup Tulgi
Twin Side Elbow Thrust (slow motion)

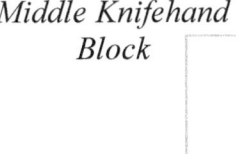 

6. Re-chamber your Left leg and execute a *High Back Piercing Kick* with your Left leg.

7. Following the kick, place your Left leg down behind to form a *Left L-Stance* while executing a *Middle Knifehand Block* with your Right hand.

8. Withdraw your Right leg to form a *Closed Stance* while executing a *Twin Side Elbow Thrust*. Perform in slow motion.

Previous — *Moves 6, 7 & 8*

Kyocha Sogi
X-Stance

Kaunde Yop Cha Jirugi
Middle Side Piercing Kick
(slow motion)

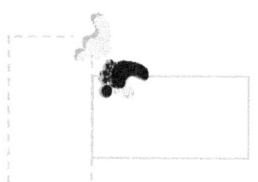

9a. Move your Right foot across the front of your Left foot to form an *X-Stance*, keeping your hands in their previous position.

9b. Execute a *Middle Side Piercing Kick* with your Left leg, keeping your hands in their previous position (on hips). Perform in slow motion.

Previous — *Moves 9a & 9b*

Nopunde Yop Cha Jirugi
High Side Piercing Kick

Sang Soopyong Palkup Tulgi
Twin Horizontal Elbow Thrust

Note: Movements 9b & 10 are performed as *'Consecutive Kicks'*

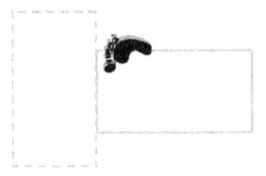
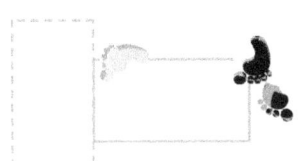

10. Without placing your foot down, consecutively execute a *High Side Piercing Kick* with your Left leg.

11. Following the kick, lower your Left foot in front, then move your Right foot across the front of your Left foot to form an *X-Stance* while executing a *Twin Horizontal Elbow Thrust*.

Previous　　　　　　　　　　　　　　　　　　　　*Moves 10 & 11*

Nopunde Bandae Dollyo Goro Chagi
High Reverse Hooking Kick

Gokgaeng-i Chagi
Pick-Shape Kick

---

12. Taking your weight on your Right foot, pivot 180 degrees anti-clockwise and execute a *High Reverse Hooking Kick* with your Left leg.

13. Execute a *Pick-Shape Kick* with your Right leg.

Kaunde Palmok Daebi Makgi
Middle Forearm Guarding Block

Sang Yop Palkup Tulgi
Twin Side Elbow Thrust

Kyocha Sogi
X-Stance

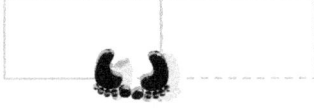
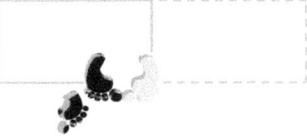

14. Following the kick, lower your Right foot in front to form a *Left Rear Foot Stance* while executing a *Middle Forearm Guarding Block*.

15a. Pivot 90 degrees anti-clockwise and move your Left foot inwards to form a *Closed Stance* while executing a *Twin Side Elbow Thrust*. Perform in slow motion.

15b. Move your Left foot across the front of your Right foot to form an *X-Stance*, keeping your hands in their previous position.

Previous — *Moves 14, 15 & 16a*

Kaunde Yop Cha Jirugi
Middle Side Piercing Kick
(slow motion)

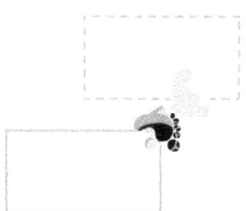

16. Execute a *Middle Side Piercing Kick* with your Right leg, keeping your hands in their previous position (on hips). Perform in slow motion.

Previous

Move 16b

Nopunde Yop Cha Jirugi
High Side Piercing Kick

Note: Movements 16b & 17 are performed as *'Consecutive Kicks'*

Sang Soopyong Palkup Tulgi
Twin Horizontal Elbow Thrust

17. Without placing your foot down, consecutively execute a *High Side Piercing Kick* with your Right leg.

18. Following the kick, lower your Right foot in front, then move your Left foot across the front of your Right foot to form an *X-Stance* while executing a *Twin Horizontal Elbow Thrust*.

Nopunde Bandae Dollyo Goro Chagi
High Reverse Hooking Kick

Gokgaeng-i Chagi
Pick-Shape Kick

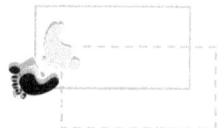
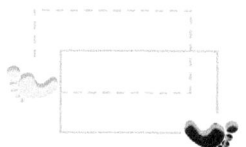

19. Taking your weight on your Left foot, pivot 180 degrees anti-clockwise and execute a *High Reverse Hooking Kick* with your Right leg.

20. Execute a *Pick-Shape Kick* with your Left leg.

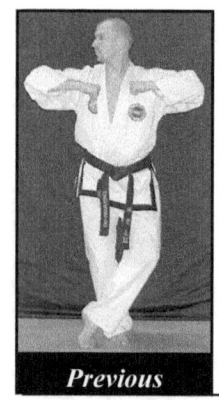

Previous — *Move 19 & 20*

Kaunde Palmok Daebi Makgi
Middle Forearm Guarding Block

Moa Sogi Hanulson
Close Stance with Heaven Hand
(slow motion)

Dung Joomok Nopunde Yop Taeragi
Back Fist High Side Strike

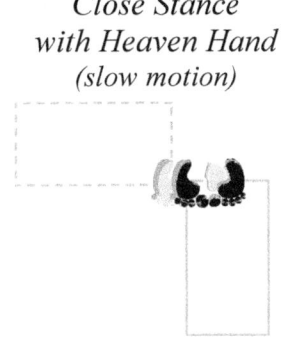

21. Following the kick, lower your Right foot in front to form a *Right Rear Foot Stance* while executing a *Middle Forearm Guarding Block*.

22. Pivot 90 degrees clockwise and move your Right foot inwards to form a *Closed Stance* while executing *Heaven Hand*. Perform in slow motion.

23. Jump forwards to form a *Right X-Stance* while executing a *Back Fist High Side Strike* with your Right fist, bringing the finger belly of your Left hand to the side of your Right fist.

Previous — *Moves 21, 22 & 23*

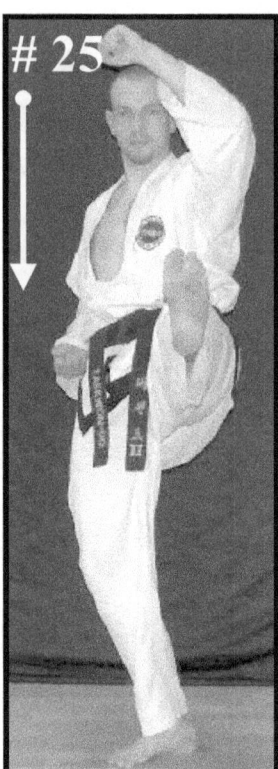
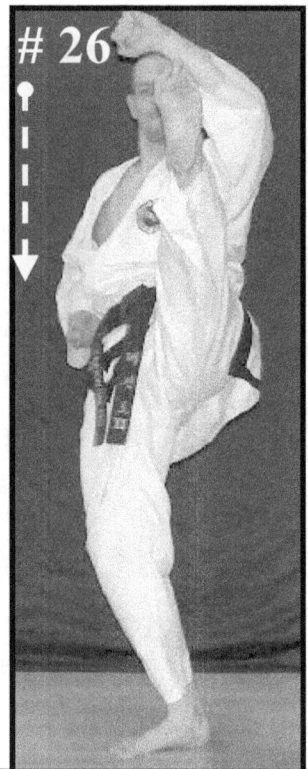

Bandae Palmok Chookyo Makgi
Reverse Forearm Rising Block

Kaunde Ap Cha Busigi
Middle Front Snap Kick (slow motion)

Nopunde Ap Cha Busigi
High Front Snap Kick

Note: Movements 25 & 26 are performed as *'Consecutive Kicks'*

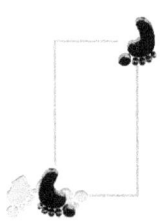

24. Move your Left foot backwards to form a *Right Walking Stance* while executing a *Reverse Forearm Rising Block* with your Left arm.

25. Keeping your arms in their previous positions, execute a *Middle Front Snap Kick* with your Left leg. Perform in slow motion.

26. Without placing your Left foot down, re-chamber and execute a *High Front Snap Kick* with your Left foot at normal/fast speed.

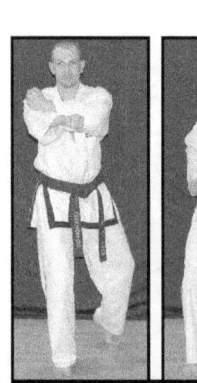

Previous — Moves 24, 25 & 26

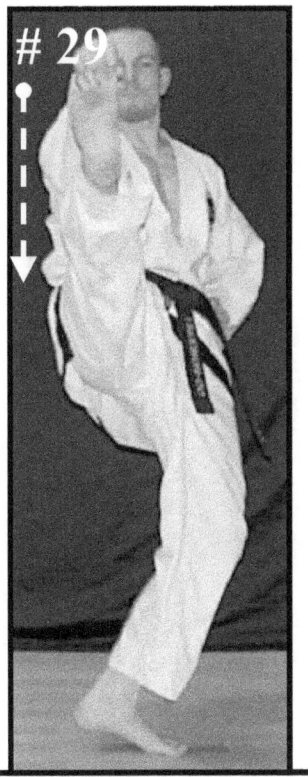

Nopunde Bandae Ap Joomok Jirugi
High Reverse Forefist Punch

Kaunde Ap Cha Busigi
Middle Front Snap Kick (slow motion)

Nopunde Ap Cha Busigi
High Front Snap Kick

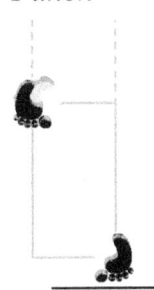

Note: Movements 28 & 29 are performed as *'Consecutive Kicks'*

27. Following the kick, place your Left foot in front to form a *Left Walking Stance* while executing a *High Reverse Forefist Punch* with your Right fist.

28. Keeping your arms in their previous positions, execute a *Middle Front Snap Kick* with your Right leg. Perform in slow motion.

29. Without placing your Right foot down, re-chamber and execute a *High Front Snap Kick* with your Right foot at normal/fast speed.

      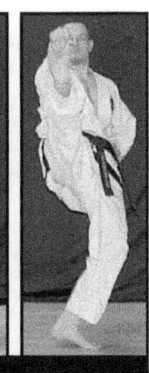

Previous — *Moves 27, 28 & 29*

Nopunde Bandae Ap Joomok Jirugi
High Reverse Forefist Punch

Narani Sogi, Kyocha Paldung
Parallel Stance with Forearms Crossed
(slow motion)

Najunde Bakat Palmok Makgi
Low Outer Forearm Block

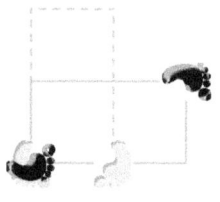

30. Following the kick, place your Right foot in front to form a *Right Walking Stance* while executing a *High Reverse Forefist Punch* with your Left fist.

31. Bring your rear (Left) foot forwards to form a *Parallel Stance* while *crossing both back Forearms* (known as the *cross-out ready position*). Perform in slow motion.

32. Turn and step to your Left, moving your Left leg to form a *Left Walking Stance* while executing a *Low Outer Forearm Block* with your Left arm.

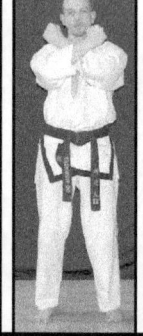

Previous — *Moves 30, 31 & 32*

Nopunde Anuro Bandal Chagi
High Inward Crescent Kick

Twimyo Anuro Bandal Chagi
Flying Inward Crescent Kick

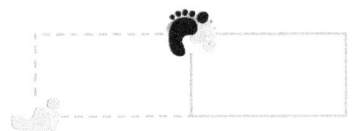

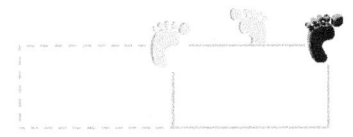

Note: This diagram shows the stepping & landing positions of the feet

---

33. Execute a *High Inward Crescent Kick* with your Right leg.

34. Following the kick, lower your Right foot across your centre line then jump and spin anti-clockwise, executing a *Flying Inward Crescent Kick* with your Right leg. This is performed in '*double motion*' (aka bicycle motion) by raising your Left knee into the air as you spin, to help pull your weight up into the air, then kicking with the Right leg.

Previous — *Moves 33 & 34*

Dung Joomok Naerjo Taeragi
Back Fist Downward Strike

Kaunde Bakuro Sewo Cha Momchugi
Middle Outward Vertical Checking Kick

Nopunde Yop Cha Jirugi
High Side Piercing Kick

Note: Movements 36 & 37 are performed as *'Consecutive Kicks'*

35. Following the kick, lower the Right foot and (before it touches the ground) jump forwards into a *Right X-Stance*, executing a *Back Fist Downward Strike* with your Right fist.

36. Execute a *Middle Outward Vertical Checking Kick* with your Left leg, 90 degrees anti-clockwise from your current position..

37. Following the kick, re-chamber and without placing your foot down, consecutively execute a *High Side Piercing Kick* with your Left leg.

Previous — *Moves 35, 36 & 37*

Nopunde Bakuro Gutgi
High Outward Cross-Cut

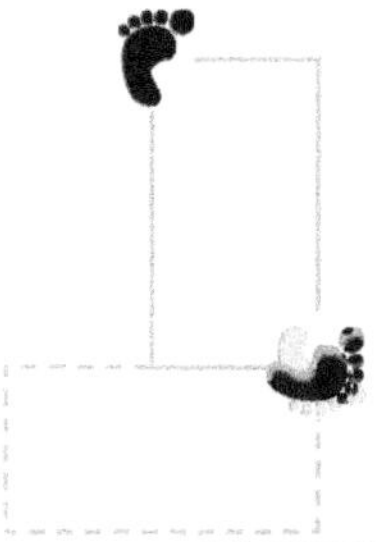

Kaunde Bituro Chagi
Middle Twisting Kick

Kyocha Joomok Noollo Makgi
X-Fist Pressing Block

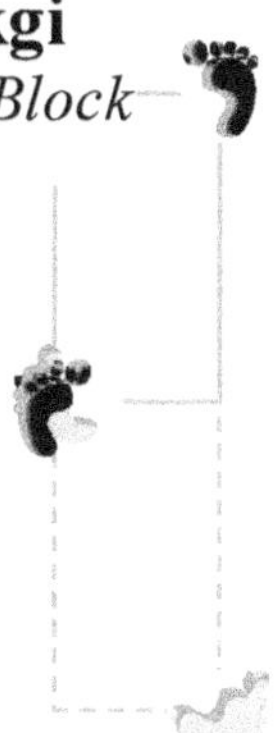

38. Following the kick, stamp your Left foot to form a *Right L-Stance* while executing a *High Outward Cross-Cut* with your Left hand.

39. Execute a *Middle Twisting Kick* with your Right foot.

40. Following the kick, lower your Right foot into a *Right Walking Stance* and execute an *X-Fist Pressing Block*.

Kyocha Sonkal Chookyo Makgi
X-Knifehand Rising Block

Nopunde Bandae Ap Joomok Jirugi
High Reverse Forefist Punch

Dollimyo Makgi
Circular Block

41. Maintain your stance and immediately execute an *X-Knifehand Rising Block*.

42. Maintain your stance and execute a *High Reverse Forefist Punch* with your Left fist, rotating your hands clockwise and slipping your Right palm above your Left elbow joint as you execute the punch.

43. Without stepping, pivot 135 degrees anti-clockwise forming a 45 degree *Left Walking Stance* and execute an *Inner Forearm Circular Block* with your Right arm.

Previous — Moves 41, 42 & 43

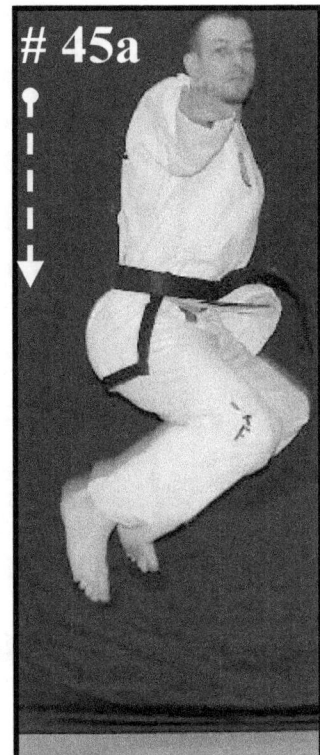

**Nopunde Bandae
Ap Joomok Jirugi**
High Reverse Forefist Punch

Sonkal Twio Dolmyo Taeragi
Knifehand Mid-Air Strike

44. Maintain your stance and execute a *High Reverse Forefist Punch* with your Left fist.

45a. Jump and spin 315 degrees clockwise in the air, executing a *Knifehand Mid-Air Strike* with your Right Hand.

45b. Following the jump, land with your *Knifehand extended* in a *Left L-Stance*.

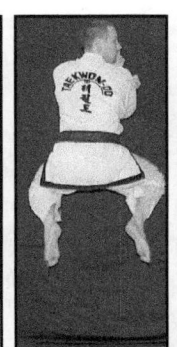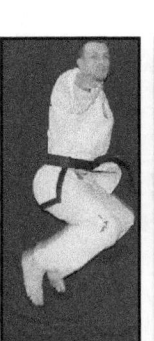

Previous — *Moves 44, 45a & 45b*

Sonbadak Ollyo Makgi	**Sang Sonbadak Noollo Makgi**	**Sang Dwijibo Jirugi**
Palm Upward Block	*Twin Palm Pressing Block*	*Twin Upset Punch*

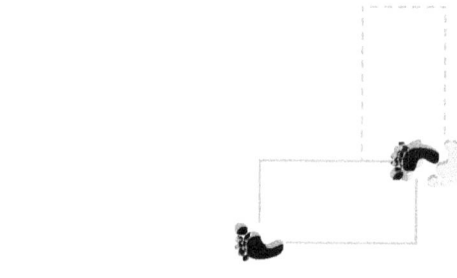

46. Move your Left leg forwards to form a *Right Rear Foot Stance* while executing a *Palm Upwards Block* with your Left hand.

47. Pivoting on your Left foot, move your Right foot 90 degrees to your Right, into a *Left Rear Foot Stance* while executing a *Twin Palm Pressing Block*.

48. Stamp your Left foot forwards into a *Left Walking Stance* while executing a *Twin Upset Punch*.

Previous — Moves 46, 47 & 48

Najunde Bakat Palmok Makgi
Low Outer Forearm Block

Nopunde Anuro Bandal Chagi
High Inward Crescent Kick

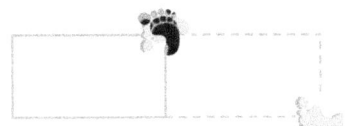

49. Move forwards to form a *Right Walking Stance* while executing a *Low Outer Forearm Block* with your Right Arm.

50. Execute a *High Inward Crescent Kick* with your Left leg.

Previous — *Moves 49 & 50*

Twimyo Anuro Bandal Chagi
Flying Inward Crescent Kick

Dung Joomok Naerjo Taeragi
Back Fist Downward Strike

Note: This diagram shows the stepping & landing positions of the feet

---

51. Following the kick, lower your Left foot across your centre line then jump and spin clockwise, executing a *Flying Inward Crescent Kick* with your Left leg. This is performed in '*double motion*' (aka bicycle motion) by raising your Right knee into the air as you spin, to help pull your weight up into the air, then kicking with the Left leg.

52. Following the kick, lower the Left foot and (before it touches the ground) jump forwards into a Left X-Stance, executing a *Back Fist Downward Strike* with your Left fist.

Previous   *Moves 51 & 52*

Kaunde Bakuro Sewo Cha Momchugi
Middle Outward Vertical Checking Kick

Nopunde Yop Cha Jirugi
High Side Piercing Kick

Nopunde Bakuro Gutgi
High Outward Cross-Cut

Note: Movements 53 & 54 are performed as *'Consecutive Kicks'*

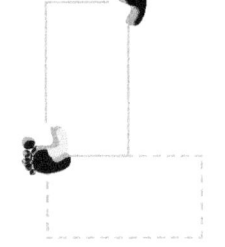

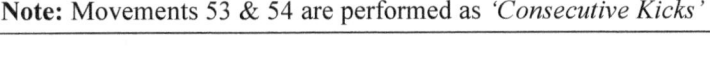

53. Execute a *Middle Outward Vertical Checking Kick* with your Right leg, 90 degrees clockwise from your current position..

54. Following the kick, re-chamber and without placing your foot down, consecutively execute a *High Side Piercing Kick* with your Right leg.

55. Following the kick, stamp your Right foot to form a *Left L-Stance* while executing a *High Outward Cross-Cut* with your Right hand.

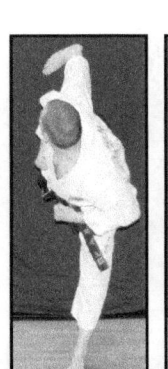

Previous — *Moves 53, 54 & 55*

Kaunde Bituro Chagi
Middle Twisting Kick

Kyocha Joomok Noollo Makgi
X-Fist Pressing Block

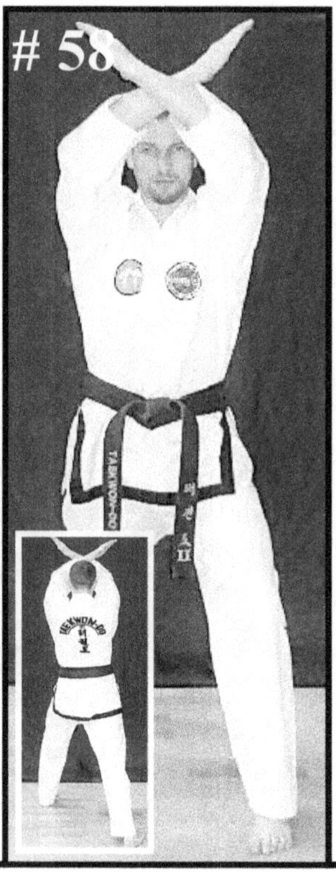

Kyocha Sonkal Chookyo Makgi
X-Knifehand Rising Block

56. Execute a *Middle Twisting Kick* with your Left foot.

57. Following the kick, lower your Right foot into a *Right Walking Stance* and execute an *X-Fist Pressing Block*.

58. Maintain your stance and immediately execute an *X-Knifehand Rising Block*.

Moves 56, 57 & 58

| **Kaunde Bandae Ap Joomok Jirugi** *Middle Reverse Forefist Punch* | **Dollimyo Makgi** *Circular Block* | **Nopunde Ap Joomok Jirugi** *High Forefist Punch* |

59. Maintain your stance and execute a *Middle Reverse Forefist Punch* with your Right fist, rotating your hands anti-clockwise and slipping your Left palm above your Right elbow joint as you execute the punch.

60. Without stepping, pivot 135 degrees clockwise forming a 45 degree *Left Walking Stance* and execute an *Inner Forearm Circular Block* with your Left arm.

61. Maintain your stance and execute a *High Forefist Punch* with your Right fist.

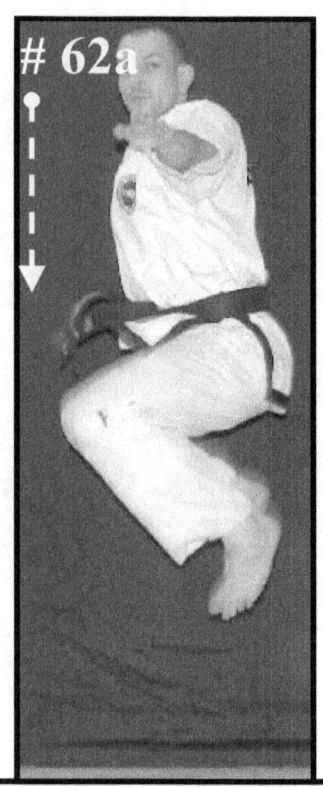  

Sonkal Twio Dolmyo Taeragi
Knifehand Mid-Air Strike

Sonbadak Ollyo Makgi
Palm Upward Block

62a. Jump and spin 315 degrees anti-clockwise in the air, executing a *Knifehand Mid-Air Strike* with your Left Hand.

62b. Following the jump, land with your Knifehand extended in a *Right L-Stance*.

63. Move your Right leg forwards to form a *Left L-Stance* while executing a *Palm Upwards Block* with your Right hand.

  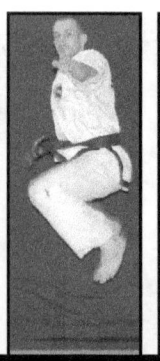   

Previous — *Moves 62a, 62b & 63*

Sang Sonbadak Nollo Makgi
Twin Palm Pressing Block

Sang Dwijibo Jirugi
Twin Upset Punch

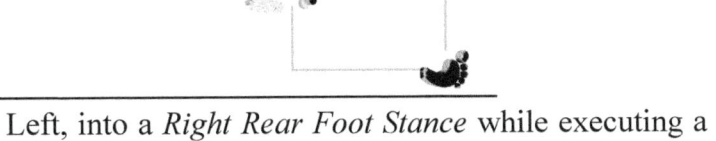

64. Move your Left foot 90 degrees to your Left, into a *Right Rear Foot Stance* while executing a *Twin Palm Pressing Block*.

65. Stamp your Right foot forwards into a *Right Walking Stance* while executing a *Twin Upset Punch*.

Previous — *Moves 64 & 65*

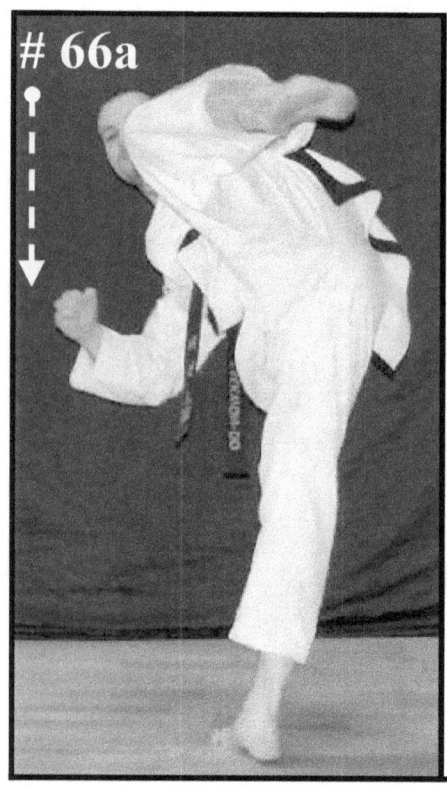

Nopunde Bandae Dollyo Goro Chagi
High Reverse Hooking Kick

Nopunde Dollyo Chagi
High Turning Kick

Kaunde Bandae Ap Joomok Jirugi
Middle Reverse Forefist Punch

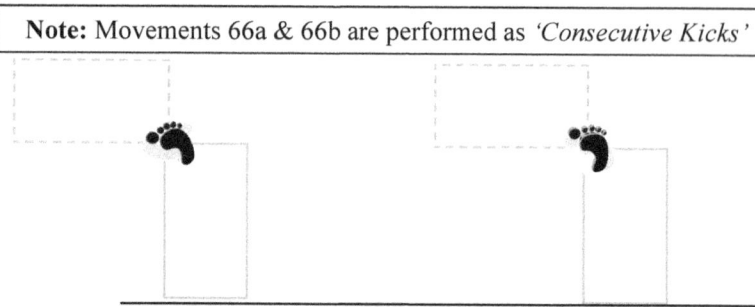

Note: Movements 66a & 66b are performed as *'Consecutive Kicks'*

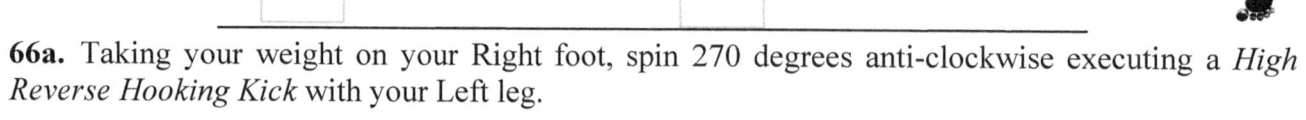

66a. Taking your weight on your Right foot, spin 270 degrees anti-clockwise executing a *High Reverse Hooking Kick* with your Left leg.

66b. Without placing your Left leg down, immediately execute a *High Turning Kick* with your Left leg.

67. Following the previous kick, lower your Left foot to form a *Right L-Stance* while executing a *Middle Reverse Forefist Punch* with your Left fist.

Previous   *Moves 66a, 66b & 67*

Nopunde Anuro Gutgi
High Inward Cross-Cut

Twimyo Yonsok Jirugi
Flying Consecutive Punch

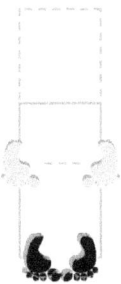

68. Bring your Right foot forwards to form a *Parallel Stance* while executing a *High Inward Cross-Cut* with your Right hand.

69a, b & c. Jump forwards about a stance length, while executing a *Flying Consecutive Punch* with your Left fist. The first strike being a *Forefist Punch* and the second an *Upset Punch*.

Note: GTF students chamber for the second punch (see small pictures at bottom of page). Both punches should be executed in the air, landing in *Closed Stance* with the *Upset Punch* still extended.

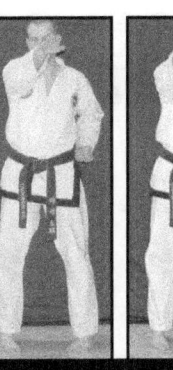

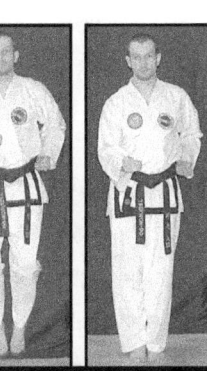

Previous — *Moves 68, 69a, 69b & 69c*

Sonkal Naeryo Taeragi
Knifehand Downward Strike

Twimyo Dwit Cha Jirugi
Flying Back Piercing Kick

Kaunde Palmok Daebi Makgi
Middle Forearm Guarding Block

70. Move your Left leg forwards to form a *Left Walking Stance* while executing a *Knifehand Downwards Strike* with your Right hand.

71a. Jump up, spinning 180 degrees clockwise and execute a *Flying Back Piercing Kick* with your Right leg. **Note:** This is sometimes called a *180° Flying Side Kick* in the GTF.

71b. Following the kick, land in a *Left L-Stance* while executing a *Middle Forearm Guarding Block*.

Previous — *Moves 70, 71a & 71b*

 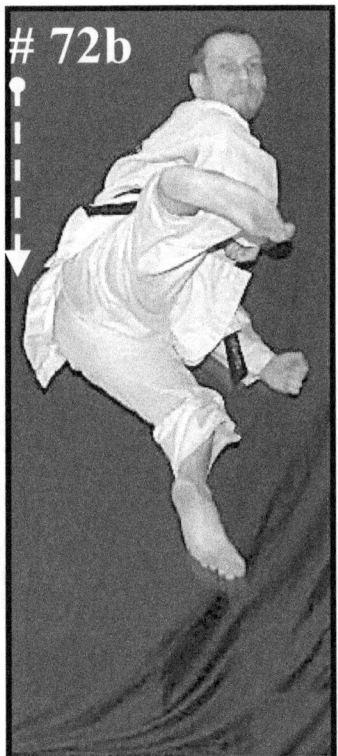 

360° Twimyo Dwit Cha Jirugi
360° Flying Back Piercing Kick

Kaunde Sonkal Daebi Makgi
Middle Knifehand Guarding Block

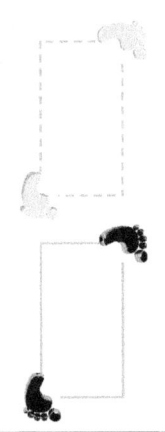

72a & b. Spin 360 degrees in the direction you are facing, raising your Left knee as you start to spin and executing a *(360 degree) Flying Back Piercing Kick* with your Right leg. **Note:** This is sometimes called a *360° Flying Side Kick* in the GTF.

72c. Following the Kick, land in a *Left L-Stance* while executing a *Middle Knifehand Guarding Block*.

 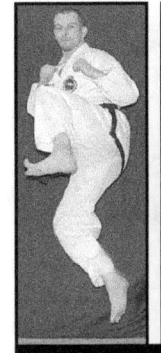   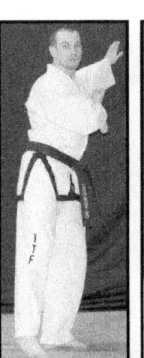 

Previous — *Moves 72a, 72b & 72c*

Twimyo Bandae Dollyo Chagi
Flying Reverse Turning Kick

Kaunde Palmok Daebi Makgi
Middle Forearm Guarding Block

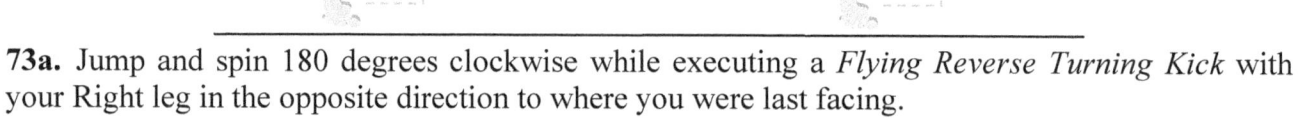

73a. Jump and spin 180 degrees clockwise while executing a *Flying Reverse Turning Kick* with your Right leg in the opposite direction to where you were last facing.

73b. Following the kick, land in a *Right L-Stance* while executing a *Middle Forearm Guarding Block*.

Previous — *Moves 73a & 73b*

Twimyo Bandae Dollyo Goro Chagi
Flying Reverse Hooking Kick

Kaunde Sonkal Daebi Makgi
Middle Knifehand Guarding Block

74a. Jump and spin 180 degrees anti-clockwise while executing a *Flying Reverse Hooking Kick* with your Left leg.

74b. Following the kick, land in a *Right L-Stance* while executing a *Middle Knifehand Guarding Block*.

Previous — *Moves 74a & 74b*

To show steps, this these pictures have not been reversed

Twimyo Sambang Chagi
Flying Three Directional Kick
'Left Twisting Kick & Right Side Piercing Kick'

75a, b & c. Take two steps forwards (running to gain speed), first with your Right leg, then your Left leg before using your Right leg again to launch yourself up into the air and execute a *Flying Three Directional Kick*, performing a *Side Piercing Kick* with your Right leg and a *Twisting Kick* with your Left leg before executing a *Turning Kick* with your Right leg (75d).

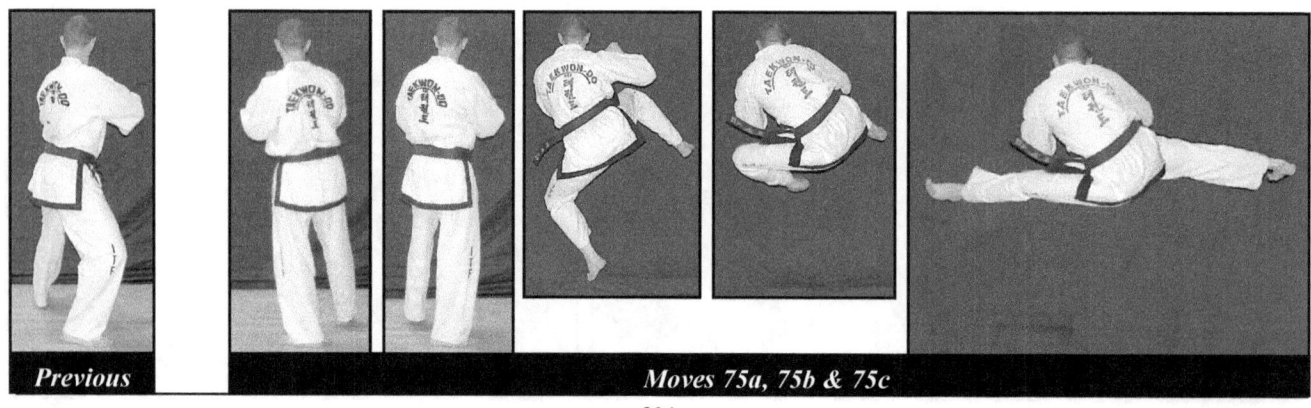

Previous   *Moves 75a, 75b & 75c*

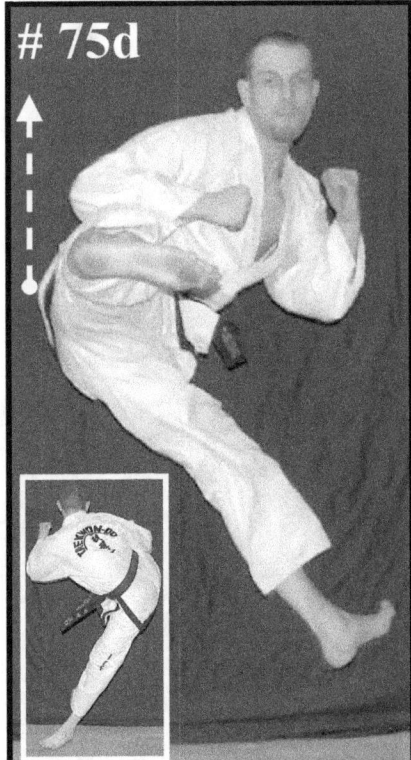

Twimyo Sambang Chagi
Flying Three Directional Kick
'Right Turning Kick'

Yop Palkup Tulgi
Side Elbow Thrust

75d. Following the first part of the *Flying Three Directional Kick*, execute a *Turning Kick* with your Right leg before landing.

76. Following the previous kick, land in the direction your were travelling to form a *Right L-Stance* (facing away) while executing a *Side Elbow Thrust* with your Right elbow, looking behind.

Previous

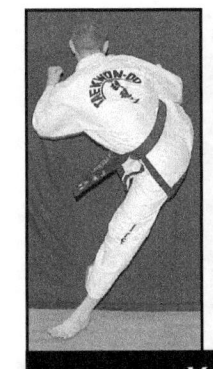
Moves 75d & 76

Twimyo Nopi Chagi
Flying High Kick

Sonkal Dung Nopunde Daebi Makgi
High Reverse Knifehand Guarding Block

Doo Bandalson Nopunde Makgi
Double Arc-Hand High Block

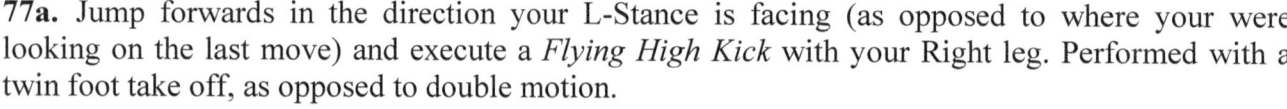

77a. Jump forwards in the direction your L-Stance is facing (as opposed to where your were looking on the last move) and execute a *Flying High Kick* with your Right leg. Performed with a twin foot take off, as opposed to double motion.

77b. Following the previous kick, land in a *Left L-Stance* while executing a *High Reverse Knifehand Guarding Block*.

78. Without stepping, move your Left foot to form a Right Walking Stance while executing a Double Arc-hand High Block (to your Left side).

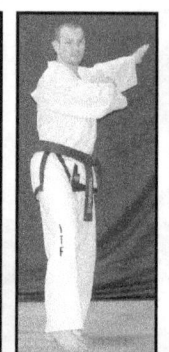

Previous — *Moves 77a, 77b & 78*

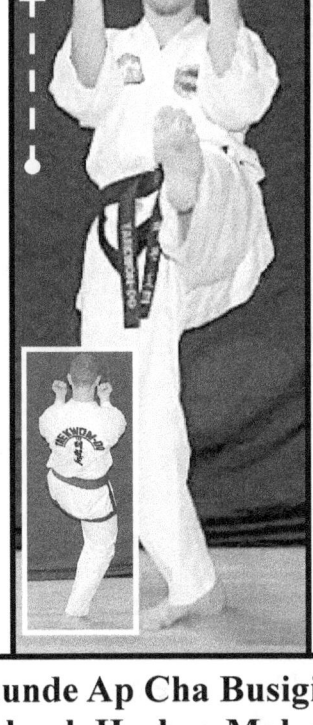

Dwijibo Jirugi
Upset Punch

Kaunde Kyocha Sonkal Monchau Makgi
Middle X-Knifehand Checking Block

Kaunde Ap Cha Busigi / Palmok Hechyo Makgi
Middle Front Snap Kick / Forearm Wedging Block

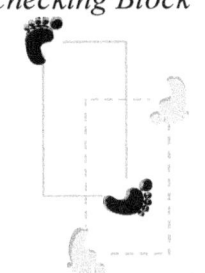
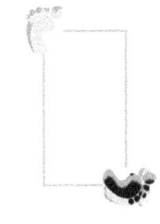

79. Maintain your stance and execute an *Upset Punch* with your Left fist.

80. Perform a centre-line turn to form a *Right L-Stance* while executing a *Middle X-Knifehand Checking Block*.

81. Taking your weight on your rear (Right) leg, execute a *Left Middle Front Snap Kick* and *Middle Forearm Wedging Block* together.

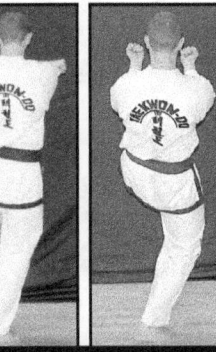

Previous — *Moves 79, 80 & 81*

Nopunde Sang Sewo Jirugi
High Twin Vertical Punch

Sang Palmok Makgi
Twin Forearm Block

Nopunde Sonkal Anuro Taeragi
High Knifehand Inward Strike

Gojang Sogi, Kaunde Jirugi
Fixed Stance, Middle Punch

Note: Movements 83a & 83b are performed in *'Consecutive Motion'*

82. Following the previous kick (and block), lower your Left foot to form a *Left Walking Stance* while executing a *High Twin Vertical Punch*.

83a. Without stepping, shift your Left foot to form a *Right L-Stance* while executing a *Twin Forearm Block*.

83b. Following the last block, immediately execute a *High Knifehand Inward Strike* with your Right hand, bringing your Left fist to your Right Shoulder.

84. *Slide* forwards to form a *Left Fixed Stance* while executing a *Middle Forefist Punch* with your Left Fist.

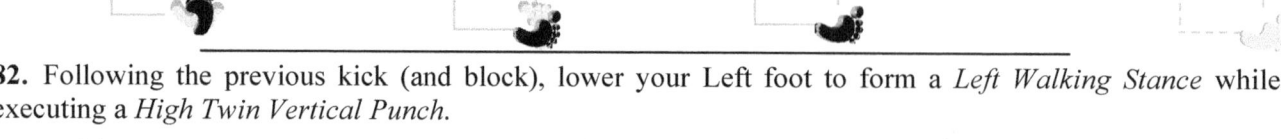

Previous — Moves 82, 83a, 83b & 84

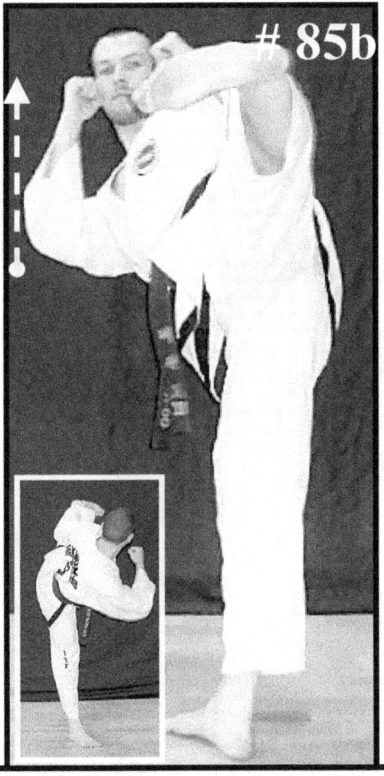
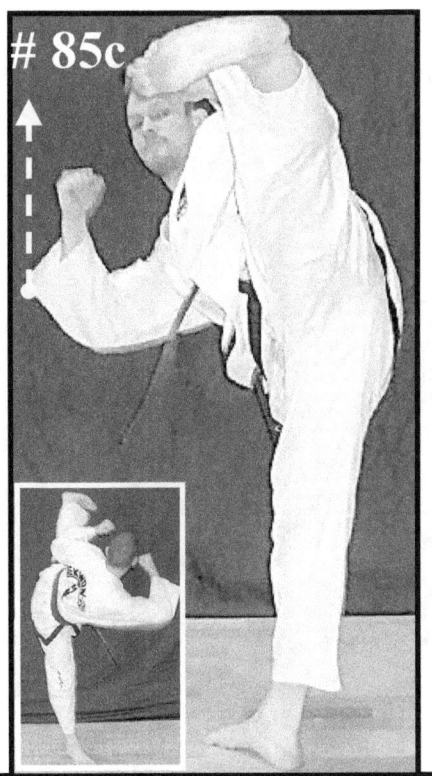

Najunde Dollyo Chagi　　**Kaunde Dollyo Chagi**　　**Nopunde Dollyo Chagi**
Low Turning Kick　　　　*Middle Turning Kick*　　　*High Turning Kick*
(slow motion)　　　　　　*(slow motion)*　　　　　　*(slow motion)*

Note: Movements 85a, 85b & 85c are performed as *'Consecutive Kicks'* in slow motion

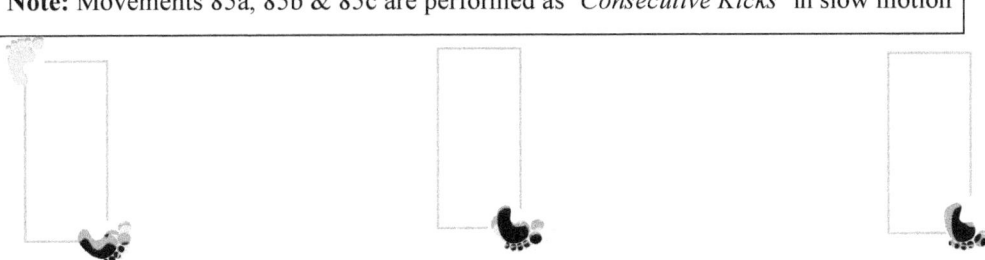

85a. Taking your weight on your Right foot, execute a *Low Turning Kick* with your Left leg. Perform in slow motion.

85b. Following the last kick, without placing your foot down, re-chamber and execute a *Middle Turning Kick* with your Left leg. Perform in slow motion.

85c. Following the last kick, without placing your foot down, re-chamber and execute a *High Turning Kick* with your Left leg. Perform in slow motion.

Previous　　　　　　　　　　　　　　*Moves 85a, 85b & 85c*

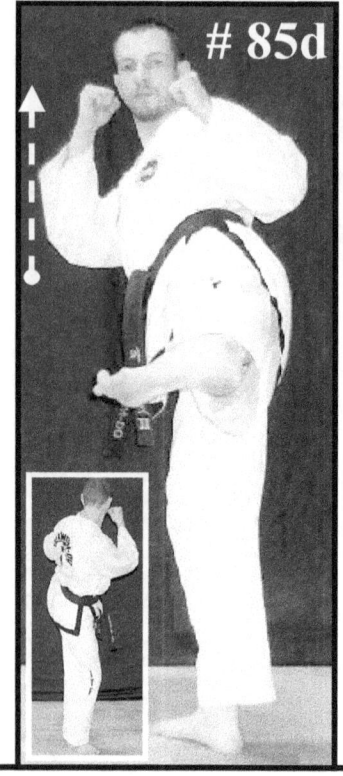

Najunde Dollyo Chagi
Low Turning Kick

Kaunde Dollyo Chagi
Middle Turning Kick

Nopunde Dollyo Chagi
High Turning Kick

> **Note:** Movements 85d, 85e & 85f are performed as *'Consecutive Kicks'* in fast motion, without pacing the foot down between 85a to 85f

85d. Following the last kick, without placing your foot down, re-chamber and execute a *Low Turning Kick* with your Left leg. Perform in normal (fast) motion.

85e. Following the last kick, without placing your foot down, re-chamber and execute a *Middle Turning Kick* with your Left leg. Perform in normal (fast) motion.

85f. Following the last kick, without placing your foot down, re-chamber and execute a *High Turning Kick* with your Left leg. Perform in normal (fast) motion.

Previous — *Moves 85d, 85e & 85f*

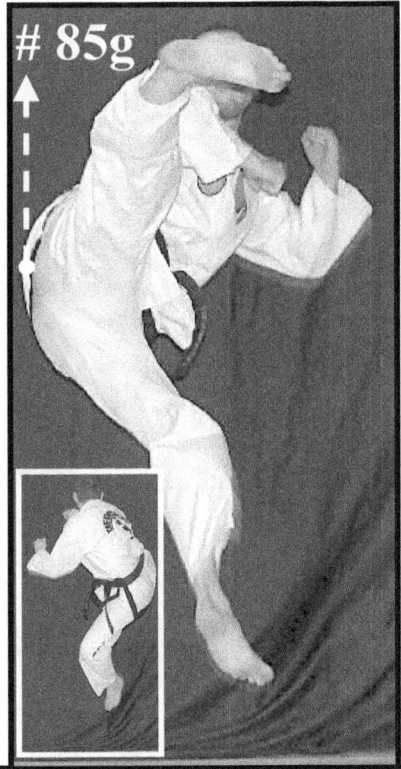

360° Twimyo Bandae Dollyo Chagi
360° Flying Reverse Turning Kick

Note: Kihap on movement 85g

Kaunde Palmok Daebi Makgi
Middle Forearm Guarding Block

Bandae Nopunde Bakat Palmok Anuro Makgi
Reverse High Outer Forearm Inward Block

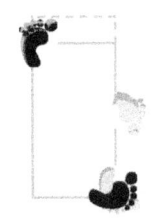

85g. Following the previous kick, lower your Left foot next to your Right foot, then jump and execute a *360° Flying Reverse Turning Kick* with your Right Leg. Kihap as you execute the kick.

85h. Following the last kick, land to form a *Right L-Stance* while executing a *Middle Forearm Guarding Block*.

86. Shift your Right foot to form a *Left Walking Stance* while executing a *Reverse High Outer Forearm Inward Block* with your Right arm.

Previous — *Moves 85g, 85h & 86*

Kaunde Ap Joomok Jirugi	**Najunde Sonkal Daebi Makgi**	**Naeryo Jirugi**	**Goburyo Junbi Sogi 'A'**
Middle Forefist Punch	*Low Knifehand Guarding Block*	*Downward Punch*	*Bending Ready Stance 'A'*

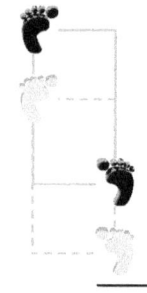   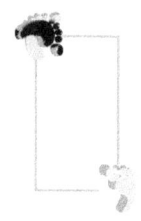

87. *Slide* forwards (approximately half a stance) maintain your *Left Walking* Stance while executing a *Middle Forefist Punch* with your Left fist.

88. Without stepping forwards, move your Left foot to form a *Right L-Stance* while executing a *Low Knifehand Guarding Block*.

89. Without stepping, move your Right foot to form a *Left Walking Stance* while executing a *Downward Punch* with your Right fist.

90. Pivot 180 degrees clockwise on your Left foot, pulling your Right foot inwards to form a *Left Bending Ready Stance 'A'*.

        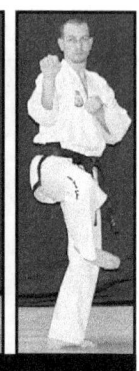

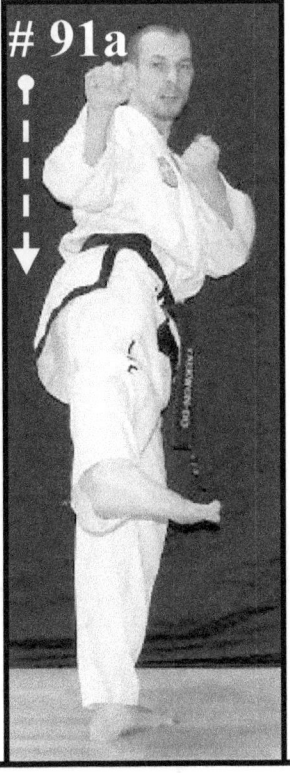
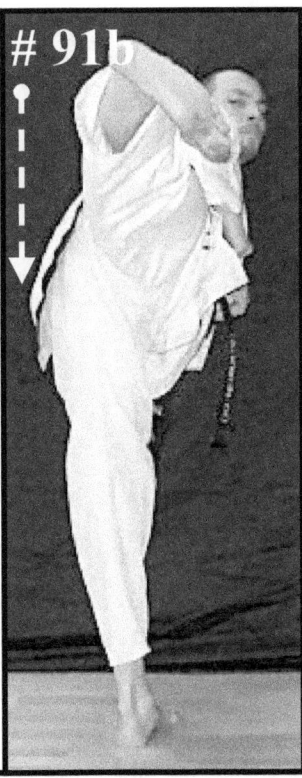
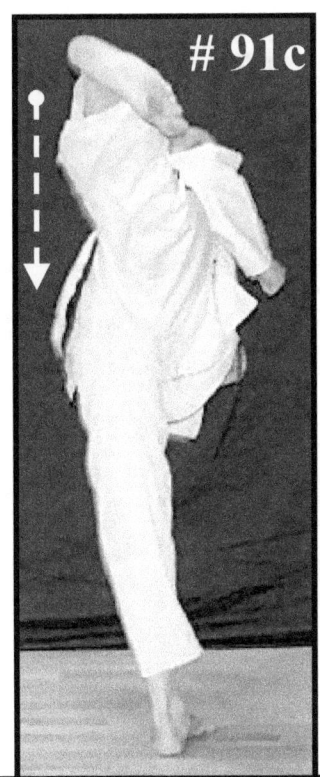

Najunde Yop Cha Jirugi
Low Side Piercing Kick
(slow motion)

Kaunde Yop Cha Jirugi
Middle Side Piercing Kick
(slow motion)

Nopunde Yop Cha Jirugi
High Side Piercing Kick
(slow motion)

Note: Movements 91a, 91b & 91c are performed as *'Consecutive Kicks'* in slow motion

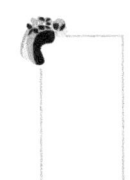

91a. From the Bending Ready Stance 'A' execute a *Low Side Piercing Kick* with your Right leg. Perform in slow motion.

91b. Following the last kick, without placing your foot down, re-chamber and execute a *Middle Side Piercing Kick* with your Right leg. Perform in slow motion.

91c. Following the last kick, without placing your foot down, re-chamber and execute a *High Side Piercing Kick* with your Right leg. Perform in slow motion.

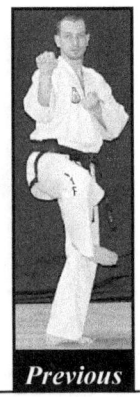

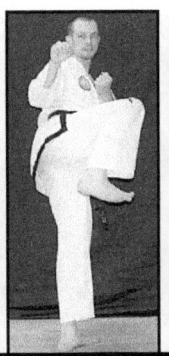

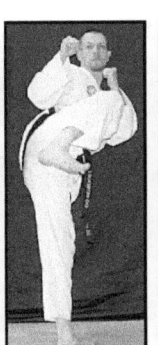

Previous — *Moves 91a, 91b & 91c*

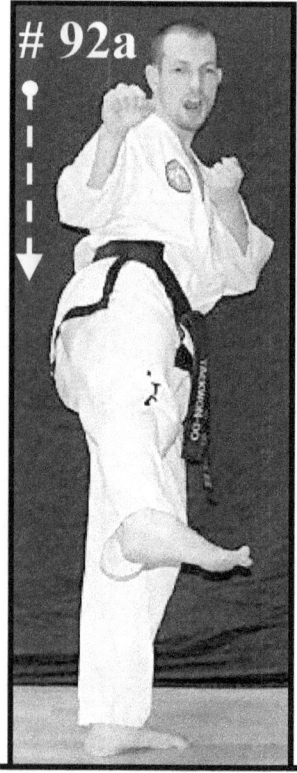  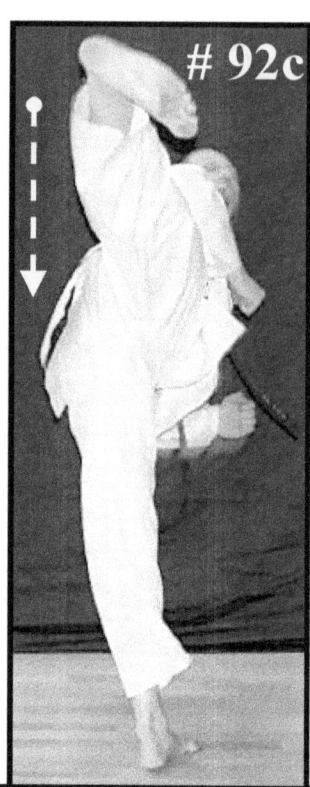

Najunde Yop Cha Jirugi
Low Side Piercing Kick

Kaunde Yop Cha Jirugi
Middle Side Piercing Kick

Nopunde Yop Cha Jirugi
High Side Piercing Kick

Note: Movements 92a, 92b & 92c are performed as *'Consecutive Kicks'* in fast motion, without pacing the foot down between 91c. **GTF students** should shout the letters 'G' 'T' 'F' on each kick (92a, 92b & 92c)

92a. Following the last kick, without placing your foot down, re-chamber and execute a *Low Side Piercing Kick* with your Right leg. Perform in normal (fast) motion, shouting 'G' as you kick.

92b. Following the last kick, without placing your foot down, re-chamber and execute a *Middle Side Piercing Kick* with your Right leg. Perform in normal (fast) motion, shouting 'T' as you kick.

92c. Following the last kick, without placing your foot down, re-chamber and execute a *High Side Piercing Kick* with your Right leg. Perform in normal (fast) motion, shouting 'F' as you kick.

 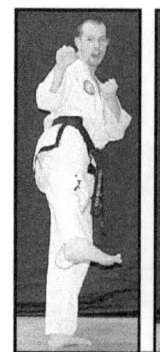 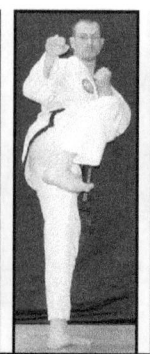   

Previous — *Moves 92a, 92b & 92c*

Kaunde An Palmok Makgi
Middle Inner Forearm Block

Nopunde Ap Cha Busugi
High Front Snap Kick

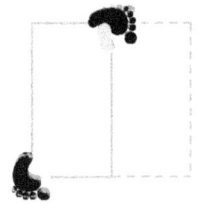

93. Following the last kick, lower your Right foot to form a *Left L-Stance* while executing a *Middle Inner Forearm Block* with your Right Arm.

94a. Taking your weight on to your Left foot, pivot 90 degrees anti-clockwise and execute a *High Front Snap Kick* with your Right leg. Perform in normal (fast) motion, shouting 'Tae' as you kick.

Previous — *Moves 93 & 94a*

Nopunde Dollyo Chagi
High Turning Kick

Nopunde Dollyo Goro Chagi
High Hooking Kick

Note: Movements 94a, 94b & 94c are performed as *'Consecutive Kicks'*.
GTF students should shout the words 'Tae' 'Kwon' 'Do' on each kick

94b. Following the last kick, without placing your foot down, re-chamber and pivot 90 degrees anti-clockwise then execute a *High Turning Kick* with your Right leg. Perform in normal (fast) motion, shouting 'Kwon' as you kick.

94c. Following the last kick, without placing your foot down, re-chamber and pivot 90 degrees anti-clockwise then execute a *High Hooking Kick* with your Right leg. Perform in normal (fast) motion, shouting 'Do' as you kick.

Previous — *Moves 94b & 94c*

Nopunde Doo Palmok Makgi
High Double Forearm Block

Moa Sogi
Closed Stance with Fists Above Head

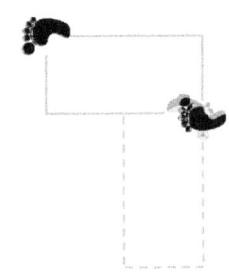
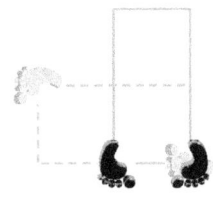

95. Following the last kick, lower your Right foot to form a *Right Walking Stance* while executing a *High Double Forearm Block*.

Return. Turning 90 degrees anti-clockwise, bring your Right foot back to the Ready Posture.

Previous *Move 95 & Return To Ready Posture*

Tips For Jook-Am Hyung

Jook-Am is possibly the hardest pattern GTF students have to perform. Though it contains many elements from 2nd, 3rd and 4th degree patterns that will serve you well as you progress up the Dan ranks, its not so useful now, so like Juche many of the movements should be taken out of the pattern and practiced in isolation. Practice these with a partner and a focus pad at first, but remember, ultimately they are performed without a target to hit making them much harder to execute correctly. The following moves that need to be isolated are:

- ***The Middle and High Back Piercing Kicks*** (from Bending Ready Stance) as these are performed consecutively in slow and fast/normal motion and require good balance.

- ***The Middle and High Side Piercing Kicks*** as these are performed consecutively in slow and fast/normal motion and require good balance as well as strong muscles.

- ***The Middle and High Front Snap Kicks*** as these are performed consecutively in slow and fast/normal motion and require good balance as well as strong muscles.

- the ***High Inward Crescent Kick and Flying Crescent Kick*** combinations.

- The ***High Reverse Punch following the X-Knifehand Rising Block*** if you are to get the rotation of the hands correct, although some simply slip the non-punching over the fist and on top of the elbow joint.

- The ***High Reverse Hooking Kick and High Turning Kick*** combinations as these are performed consecutively and require excellent balance.

- The ***Flying Back Piercing Kick*** from a Walking Stance (move #71a) as the hips make this move difficult to execute, rather than executing it from a standard L-Stance.

- The ***360° Flying Back Piercing Kick*** (move#72) as it uses a bicycle motion, which is new to many students for this technique.

- The ***Flying Reverse Turning Kick*** (move #73a) may need to be isolated and practice as some find it 'weird' executing it in the opposite direction to where you are facing.

- The ***Flying Reverse Hooking Kick*** is not actually too hard to execute with a little practice, but deserves to be isolated none the less, for those that have difficulty with this technique.

- The ***Flying Three Directional Kick*** (move #75c) is an extremely difficult technique to execute properly. Practice this with three fellow students as 'virtual' targets (i.e. you don't actually hit them).

- ***The consecutive Turning kicks*** and ***Side Piercing Kicks*** may require a bit of isolated practice by some, especially as they are performed in slow motion, then normal/fast motion.

- ***The 360° Flying Reverse Turning Kick*** may warrant practice in isolation, but in reality many will not find it that difficult to perform at this level as really it's the way most of us performed it when we first learned it and we were unable to stop the kick in mid air!

- ***Move #94*** needs isolated practice due to the fact that you change direction by 90 degrees with each of the kicks.

2. Remember that the strike in moves #45a and #62a (Knifehand Mid-Air Strike) are executed whilst in the air, not when or as you land.

3. To remember which way round the arms should be following the Middle Twisting Kick (moves #39 and #56), so that the X-Fist Pressing Block (moves #40 and #57), X-Knifehand Rising Block (moves #41 and #58) and following High Reverse Punch combination (moves #42 and #59) are executed correctly just remember, the leg that performs the Twisting Kick is the same as the arm that goes 'underneath' on the X-Fist Downward Block, so remains underneath on the X-Knifehand Rising Blocks and *'slips'* around the arm for the High Reverse Forefist punch., so that it end up on top of the elbow joint.

4. For move #69a (Flying Consecutive Punch) both of the punches should ideally be executed in the air - you simply land with the fist in the 'Upset Punch' position - this is fairly hard to achieve and takes some practice. GTF students have the added problem of using a *'reaction hand'* between the movements - something ITF students do not need to do.

5. Move 75 (c and d), the Flying Three Directional Kick, needs to be executed with a lot of speed to perform it successfully - practice, practice, practice and don't *'over extend'* on the kicks involved.

Sam-Il
33 Patriots

Sam-Il denotes the historical date of the independence movement of Korea which began throughout the country on 1st March, 1919. Sam-Il has 33 movements which stand for the 33 patriots who planned the movement.

Moa Junbi Sogi 'C'
Closed Ready Stance 'C'

Kaunde Palmok Daebi Makgi
Middle Forearm Guarding Block

Nopunde Doo Palmok Makgi
High Double Forearm Block

1. From *Closed Ready Stance 'C'*, slide forwards approximately half a stance to form a *Right L-Stance* while executing a *Middle Forearm Guarding Block*.

2. Move your Right leg forwards into a *Right Walking Stance* while executing a *High Double Forearm Block*.

From the ready posture to moves 1 & 2

Sonkal Nopunde Bandae Yop Makgi
Knifehand High Reverse Side Block

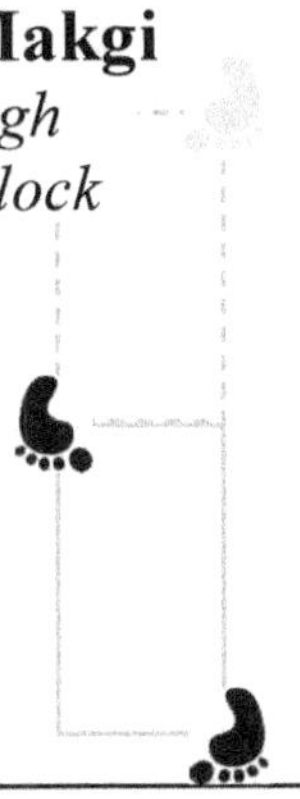

Kaunde Bituro Chagi
Middle Twisting Kick

Kaunde Ap Joomok Jirugi
Middle Forefist Punch

3. Move your Left leg forwards into a *Left Walking Stance* and execute a *Knifehand High Reverse Side Block* with your Right hand, placing your Left palm on the back of your Right forearm.

4. Execute a *Middle Twisting Kick* with your Right leg.

5. Place the Right leg down to form a *Right Walking Stance* while executing a *Right Middle Forefist Punch*.

Previous   Moves 3, 4 & 5

Sonkal Dung Hechyo Makgi
Reverse Knifehand Wedging Block

Dwijibun Sonkut Tulgi
Upset Fingertip Thrust

Bakat Palmok Nopunde Bakuro Makgi / Naujunde Palmok Makgi
Outer Forearm High Outward Block / Low Forearm Block

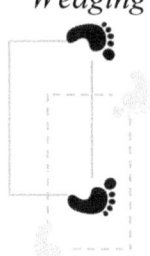
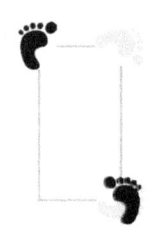

6. Withdraw your Right foot slightly, then pivot 90 degrees anti-clockwise by moving your Left foot backwards, to form a *Sitting Stance* and execute a *Reverse Knifehand Wedging Block*.

7. Move your Left foot 90 degrees anti-clockwise to form a *Left Walking Stance* and execute an *Upset Fingertip Thrust* with your Right hand.

8. Maintain your position but shift your Right foot to form a *Left L-Stance* while executing an *Outer Forearm High Outward Block* with your Right arm and a *Low Forearm Block* with your Left arm.

Previous — Moves 6, 7 & 8

Sonkal Dung Hechyo Makgi
Reverse Knifehand Wedging Block

Doo Joomok Najunde Jirugi
Double Fist Low Punch

Doo Bandalson Nopunde Makgi
Double Arc-Hand High Block

9. Pivot 90 degrees anti-clockwise by moving your Right foot to form a *Sitting Stance* and execute a *Reverse Knifehand Wedging Block*.

10. Move your Right foot to form a Left L-Stance (facing 90 degrees clockwise from last position) and execute a *Double Fist Low Punch*.

11. Move your Left leg forwards into a *Left Walking Stance* while executing a *Double Arc-Hand High Block* (to your Right side).

   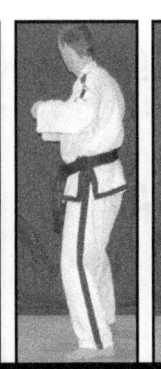   

Previous — *Moves 8, 9 & 10*

Kaunde Bandae Ap Joomok Jirugi
Middle Reverse Forefist Punch

Doo Joomok Najunde Jirugi
Double Fist Low Punch

Nopunde Sonkal Dung Daebi Makgi
High Reverse Knifehand Guarding Block

12. Move your Right leg forwards into a *Right Walking Stance*, executing a *Middle Reverse Forefist Punch*.

13. Perform a centre-line turn into a *Right L-Stance* and execute a *Double Fist Low Punch*.

14. Pivot 90 degrees anti-clockwise on your Right foot, moving your Left foot to form a *Right L-Stance* and execute a *High Reverse Knifehand Guarding Block*.

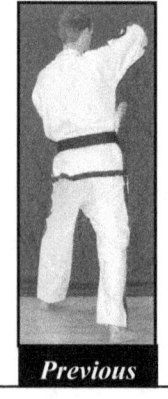     

Previous — *Moves 12, 13 & 14*

Sang Bandalson Digutja Makgi
Twin Arc-hand U Shape Block

Suroh Chagi
Sweeping Kick

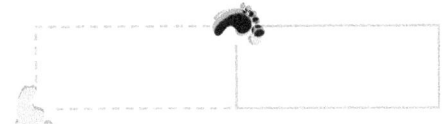

---

15. Do not move forwards but shift your Left foot to form a *Left Fixed Stance* while executing a *Twin Arc-hand U Shape Block*.

16a. Execute a *Sweeping Kick* with your Right foot (sole).

Previous — *Moves 15, 16a & 16b*

Sang Bandalson Digutja Makgi
Twin Arc-hand U Shape Block

360° Twigi
360° Degree Jump

Kaunde Sonkal Daebi Makgi
Middle Knifehand Guarding Block

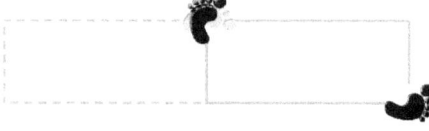

16b. Lower the Right foot into a Right Fixed Stance while executing a *Twin Arc-hand U Shape Block*.

17a. Jump up and spin 360 degrees anti-clockwise, chambering for the next block (Knifehand Guarding block).

17b. Land from the jump in a *Left L-Stance* while executing a *Middle Knifehand Guarding Block*.

Previous — *Moves 17a & 17b*

Kaunde Yop Cha Jirugi
Middle Side Piercing Kick

Ap Palkup Taeragi
Front Elbow Strike

18. Taking your weight onto your Left leg, execute a *Middle Side Piercing Kick* with your Right (front) leg in the direction you are facing, maintaining your previous hand position as they were in move #17.

19. Following the kick, lower your Right foot next to your Left foot, then step forwards 180 degrees in the opposite direction into a *Left Walking Stance* while executing a *Front Elbow Strike* with your Right elbow to your Left palm.

Previous — *Moves 18 & 19*

Dwit Palkup Tulgi
Back Elbow Thrust

Kyocha Joomok Noollo Makgi
X-Fist Pressing Block

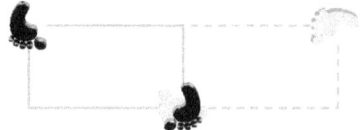

20. In an anti-clockwise motion, move your Right foot forwards to form a *Left Diagonal Stance* while executing a *Left Back Elbow Thrust*. Look behind and place your Right palm on top of your closed fist as you execute the technique.

21. Without stepping, pivot 45 degrees clockwise to form an angled *Right Walking Stance* while executing an X-*Fist Pressing Block*.

Previous — *Moves 20 & 21*

San Makgi
W Block

Kaunde Yop Cha Jirugi
Middle Side Piercing Kick

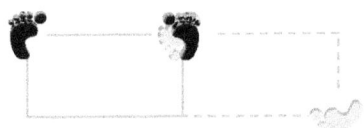

22. Stamp your Right foot into a *Sitting Stance* while executing an *Outer Forearm W Block*.

23. Taking your weight onto your Right leg, execute a *Middle Side Piercing Kick* with your Left (front) leg to your Left side, forming a *Forearm Guarding Block* as you execute the kick.

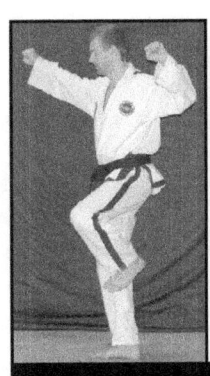

Previous — *Moves 22 & 23*

Najunde Sonkal Daebi Makgi
Low Knifehand Guarding Block

Sonbadak Ollyo Makgi
Palm Upward Block

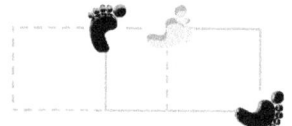

24. Lower your kicking foot approximately 1 shoulder width from your Right foot and shift Right foot forwards in the opposite direction to form a *Left L-Stance* while executing a *Low Knifehand Guarding Block*.

25. Move your Left foot forwards to form a *Right Rear Foot* Stance and execute a *Left Palm Upward Block*.

Previous — *Moves 24 & 25*

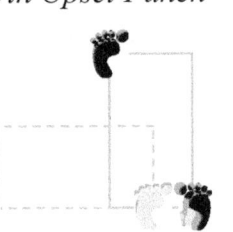

Sang Sonbadak Noollo Makgi
Twin Palm Pressing Block

Sang Dwijibo Jirugi
Twin Upset Punch

Najunde Bakat Palmok Makgi
Low Outer Forearm Block

26. Move your Right leg forwards to form a *Left Rear Foot Stance* and execute a *Twin Palm Pressing Block*.

27. Pivot 90 degrees anti-clockwise on your Right foot, stamping your Left foot forwards to form a *Left Walking Stance* while executing a *Twin Upset Punch*.

28. Move your Right leg forwards to form a *Left L-Stance* while executing a *Low Outer Forearm Block* with your Right arm, pulling your Left fist under your Left armpit as you execute the block.

Previous — Moves 26, 27 & 28

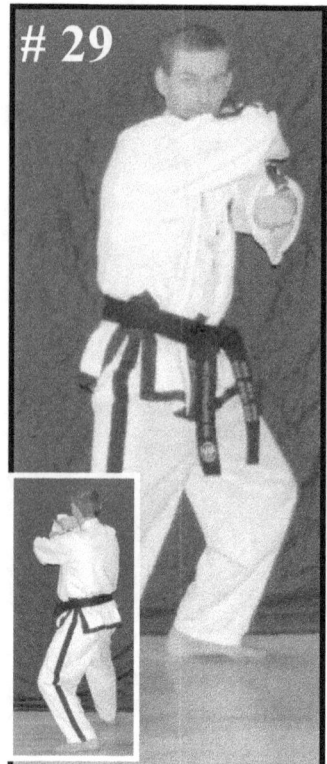

Kaunde Jirugi
Middle Punch

An Palmok Kaunde Ap Makgi
Inner Forearm Middle Front Block

Nopunde Ap Joomok Jirugi
High Forefist Punch

ITF Note: Movements 30 & 31 are performed in *'Continuous Motion'*

29. Maintain your stance and execute a *Middle Punch* with your Left fist, bringing your Right fist over your Left shoulder as you execute the punch.

30. Pivot 180 degrees anti-clockwise on your Right foot, moving your Left foot to form a *Left Walking* Stance while executing an *Inner Forearm Middle Front Block* with your Right arm.

31. Maintain your stance and execute a *High Forefist Punch* with your Left fist.

Previous — Moves 29, 30 & 31

Najunde Ap Cha Busigi
Low Front Snap Kick

Nopunde Sang Sewo Jirugi
High Twin Vertical Punch

Moa Junbi Sogi 'C'
Closed Ready Stance 'C'

32. Execute a *Low Front Snap Kick* with your Left (front) Leg, *keeping your hands in their previous position*.

33. Lower the kicking foot about 1 shoulder width in front, then stamp forwards again into a *Right Walking Stance* while executing a *High Twin Vertical Punch*.

Return. Bring your Left foot back to the Ready Posture (*Closed Ready Stance 'C'*)

Tips For Sam-Il Tul

1. Sam-Il has a number of moves that are contrary to your training so far and only appear in this pattern, so they should be practiced carefully. These are:

A. Move #3 *(Knifehand High Reverse Side Block)* - This is due to the fact that the same hand is used for the Knifehand as the previous technique, while stepping forwards - this can be confusing at first.

B. Move #8 (*Outer Forearm High Outward Block / Low Forearm Block*) - This is due to the way the Right (rear) hand is facing palm, unlike similar Backfist motions where the palm is usually upwards facing - this takes a little getting use to.

C. Move #28 *(Low Outer Forearm Block)* - This is due to where you bring the reaction arm, which is high up under your armpit, as opposed to the usual hip placement.

D. Move #29 *(Middle Punch)* - As with the previous technique, it is not the main technique but the application hand placement that is unusual, due to the fact it covers your face by travelling over the punch so it ends up above your Left shoulder, at the side of your head.

Side View Of Moves #28 & #29

2. Attention should be given to the stepping motion following move #5 (from Middle Punch to Knifehand Wedging Block) as it's a two step motion, performed by withdrawing your Right foot then moving your Left as you pivot 90 degrees. It is not the same when the move is repeated laster in the pattern (move #9)

3. Following the Front Leg Side Kicks (moves #18 and #23) don't forget that you lower the kicking leg to your opposite foot, before moving the other leg forwards again, in the opposite direction to the kick.

Yoo-Sin
General Kim Yoo Sin

유 신 틀

Yoo-Sin is named after General Kim Yoo Sin, a commanding general during the Silla Dynasty. Yoo-Sin has 68 movements which refer to the last two figures of 668 A.D., the year Korea was united. The ready posture signifies a sword drawn on the right rather than left side, symbolizing Yoo Sin's mistake of following his King's orders to fight with foreign forces against his own nation.

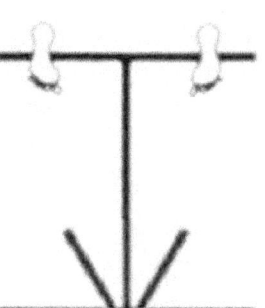

Moosa Junbi Sogi 'B'
Warrior Ready Stance 'B'

Annun Sogi Baegi
Sitting Stance Pull Out (Release) Motion

Kyockja Jirugi
Angle Punch

1. From *Warrior Ready Stance 'B'*, move your Left foot to the side to form a *Sitting Stance*, raising both elbow horizontally in a release motion.

2. Slide to your Right maintaining your stance, as you do so execute a *Left Angle Punch*, bringing your fist to the side of your head, above your Right shoulder.

Hand Position — *From the ready posture to moves 1 & 2*

Kyockja Jirugi
Angle Punch

Kaunde Sonbadak Golcha Makgi
Middle Palm Hooking Block

ITF Note: Movements 2 & 3 are performed in *'Fast Motion'*

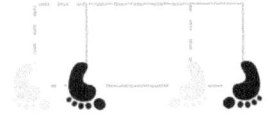

3. Slide to your Left maintaining your stance, as you do so execute a *Right Angle Punch*, bringing your fist to the side of your head, above your Left shoulder.

4. Raise up from your stance and execute a *Middle Palm Hooking Block* with your Right hand.

Previous — *Moves 3 & 4*

Kaunde Ap Joomok Jirugi
Middle Forefist Punch

Kaunde Sonbadak Golcha Makgi
Middle Palm Hooking Block

5. Drop back into your *Sitting Stance* and execute a *Middle Forefist Punch* with your Left fist.

6. Raise up from your stance and execute a *Middle Palm Hooking Block* with your Left hand.

Kaunde Ap Joomok Jirugi
Middle Forefist Punch

Nopunde Bakat Palmok Yop Makgi
High Outer Forearm Side Block

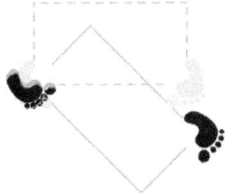

7. Drop back into your *Sitting Stance* and execute a *Middle Forefist Punch* with your Right fist.

8. Pivot 45 degrees to your Left, moving your Left foot to form a *Left Walking Stance* while executing a High Outer Forearm Side Block with your Left arm.

Previous — *Moves 5, 6, 7 & 8*

Dollimyo Makgi
Circular Block

Sonbadak Duro Makgi
Palm Scooping Block

   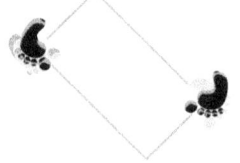

9. Maintain your stance and execute a *Circular Block* with your Right arm.

10. Without stepping, pivot clockwise to form a *Sitting Stance* while executing a *Palm Scooping Block* with your Left palm.

Previous — *Moves 9 & 10*

Kaunde Ap Joomok Jirugi
Middle Forefist Punch

Nopunde Bakat Palmok Yop Makgi
High Outer Forearm Side Block

ITF Note: Movements 10 & 11 are performed in *'Connecting Motion'*

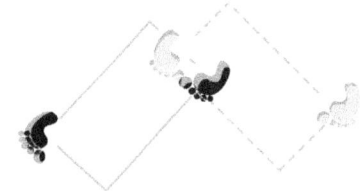

11. Maintain your stance and execute a *Middle Forefist Punch* with your Right fist.

12. Move your Left foot to your Right foot, then move your Right foot 45 degrees to your Right to form a *Right Walking Stance* and execute a *High Outer Forearm Side Block* with your Right arm.

Previous — *Moves 11 & 12*

Dollimyo Makgi
Circular Block

Sonbadak Duro Makgi
Palm Scooping Block

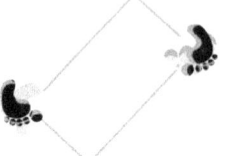

13. Maintain your stance and execute a *Circular Block* with your Left arm.

14. Without stepping, pivot anti-clockwise to form a *Sitting Stance* while executing a *Palm Scooping Block* with your Right palm.

Previous — *Moves 13 & 14*

Kaunde Ap Joomok Jirugi
Middle Forefist Punch

ITF Note: Movements 14 & 15 are performed in *'Connecting Motion'*

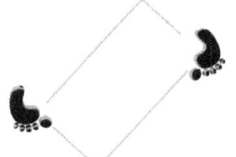

Nopunde Sonbadak Golcha Makgi
High Palm Hooking Block

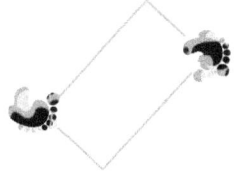

15. Maintain your stance and execute a *Middle Forefist Punch* with your Right fist.

16. Without stepping, form a *Left Walking Stance* by pivoting on the balls of your feet and execute a *High Palm Hooking Block* with your Right palm.

Previous — *Moves 15, 16, 17 & 18*

Kaunde Ap Joomok Jirugi
Middle Forefist Punch

Nopunde Sonbadak Golcha Makgi
High Palm Hooking Block

ITF Note: Movements 16, 17, 18 & 19 are performed as *'Continuous Motion'*

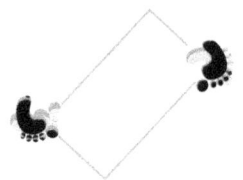 

17. Pivot back into the previous *Sitting Stance* and execute a *Middle Forefist Punch* with your Left fist.

18. Without stepping, form a *Right Walking Stance* by pivoting on the balls of your feet and execute a *High Palm Hooking Block* with your Left palm.

Kaunde Ap Joomok Jirugi
Middle Forefist Punch

Kyocha Joomok Noollo Makgi
X-Fist Pressing Block

Kyocha Sonkal Chookyo Makgi
X-Knifehand Rising Block

ITF Note: Movements 20 & 21 are performed as *'Continuous Motion'*

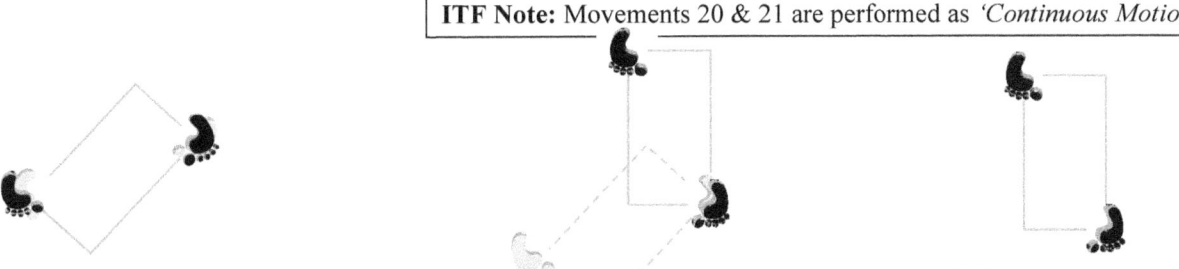

19. Pivot back into the previous *Sitting Stance* execute a *Middle Forefist Punch* with your Left fist.

20. Move your Right foot backwards to form a *Left Walking Stance* (facing forwards) while executing an *X-Fist Pressing Block*.

21. Without stepping, execute an *X-Knifehand Rising Block*. Ensure Left Knifehand is in front.

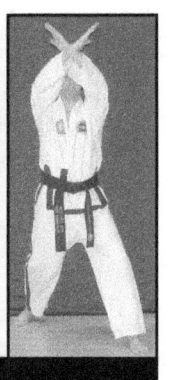

Previous — *Moves 19, 20 & 21*

Kaunde Ap Joomok Jirugi
Middle Forefist Punch

Najunde Ap Cha Busigi
Low Front Snap Kick

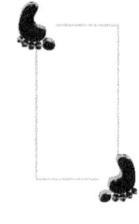

22a & b. Maintain your stance and execute a *Middle Forefist Punch* with your Right fist, rotating your hands anti-clockwise and slipping your Left palm above your Right elbow joint as you execute the punch.

23. Execute a *Low Front Snap Kick* with your Right leg, while keeping your arms in their previous position.

Detailed view of moves 21 to 22

Kaunde Bandae Ap Joomok Jirugi
Middle Reverse Forefist Punch

Kyocha Joomok Noollo Makgi
X-Fist Pressing Block

Kyocha Sonkal Chookyo Makgi
X-Knifehand Rising Block

ITF Note: Movements 25 & 26 are performed as *'Continuous Motion'*

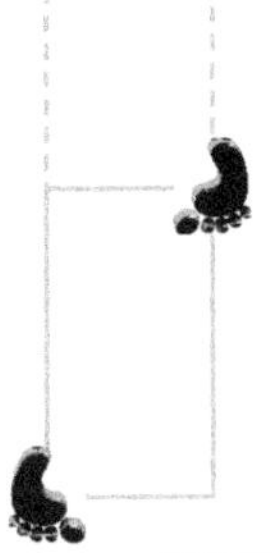

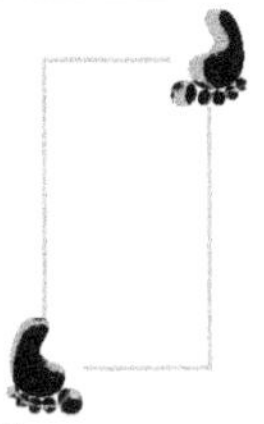

24. From the previous kick, lower your foot to form a *Right Walking Stance* while executing a *Middle Reverse Forefist Punch* with your Left fist.

25. Maintain your Stance and execute a *X-Fist Pressing Block*.

26. Without stepping, execute a *X-Knifehand Rising Block*. Ensure Right Knifehand is in front.

Previous — Moves 22a, 22b, 23, 24, 25 & 26

Kaunde Ap Joomok Jirugi
Middle Forefist Punch

Najunde Ap Cha Busigi
Low Front Snap Kick

27a & b. Maintain your Stance and execute a *Middle Forefist Punch* with your Left fist, rotating your hands clockwise and slipping your Right palm above your Left elbow joint as you execute the punch.

28. Execute a *Low Front Snap Kick* with your Left leg, while keeping your arms in their previous position.

Detailed view of moves 26 to 27

Kaunde Bandae Ap Joomok Jirugi
Middle Reverse Forefist Punch

Kaunde Sonkal Daebi Makgi
Middle Knifehand Guarding Block

Kaunde Sonkal Daebi Makgi
Middle Knifehand Guarding Block

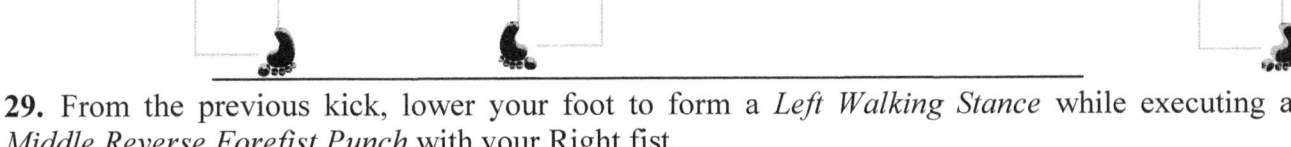

29. From the previous kick, lower your foot to form a *Left Walking Stance* while executing a *Middle Reverse Forefist Punch* with your Right fist.

30. Move your Right foot forwards to form a *Left L-Stance* while executing a *Middle Knifehand Guarding Block*.

31. Move your Left foot forwards to form a *Right L-Stance* while executing a *Middle Knifehand Guarding Block*.

Previous — Moves 27a, 27b, 28, 29, 30 & 31

Kaunde Sonkal Daebi Makgi
Middle Knifehand Guarding Block

Kaunde Sonkal Daebi Makgi
Middle Knifehand Guarding Block

Nopunde Doo Palmok Makgi
High Double Forearm Block

32. Move your Left foot backwards to form a *Left L-Stance* while executing a *Middle Knifehand Guarding Block*.

33. Move your Right foot backwards to form a *Right L-Stance* while executing a *Middle Knifehand Guarding Block*.

34. Move your Right foot forwards to form a *Right Walking Stance* while executing a *High Double Forearm Block*.

Previous — *Moves 32, 33 & 34*

Bandae Najunde Bakat Palmok Makgi
Reverse Low Outer Forearm Block

ITF Note: Movements 34 & 35 are performed in *'Fast Motion'*

Nopunde Doo Palmok Makgi
High Double Forearm Block

Bandae Najunde Bakat Palmok Makgi
Reverse Low Outer Forearm Block

ITF Note: Movements 36 & 37 are performed in *'Fast Motion'*

35. Maintain your stance and execute a *Reverse Low Outer Forearm Block* with your Left arm, keeping the Right arm in its previous position.

36. Move your Left foot forwards to form *a Left Walking Stance* while executing a *High Double Forearm Block*.

37. Maintain your stance and execute a *Reverse Low Outer Forearm Block* with your Right arm, keeping the Left arm in its previous position.

Previous — *Moves 35, 36 & 37*

Kaunde Ap Joomok Jirugi
Middle Forefist Punch

Sonkal Dung Nopunde Makgi
Reverse Knifehand High Block

Moa Junbi Sogi 'C'
Closed Ready Stance 'C'

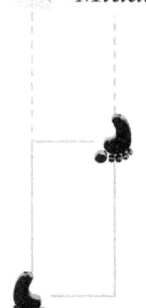
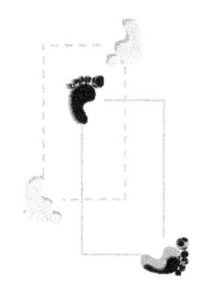

38. Move your Right foot forwards to form a *Right Walking Stance* while executing a *Middle Forefist Punch* with your Right fist.

39. Bring your back leg (Left) 6 inches towards your Right foot and pivot 180 degrees anti-clockwise, moving your Right foot backwards to form a *Right L-Stance* while executing a *Reverse Knifehand High Block* with your Left hand.

40. Bring your Right foot to your Left foot to form a *Closed Ready Stance 'C'*.

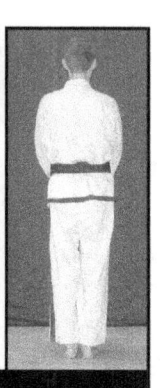

Sang Dwijibo Jirugi
Twin Upset Punch

Sang Dwijibo Jirugi
Twin Upset Punch

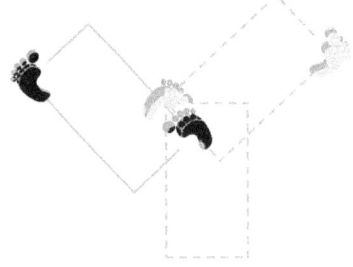

41. *Stamp* your Right foot at a 45 degree angle to your Right, forming a *Right Walking Stance* as you execute a *Twin Upset Punch*.

42. Bring your Right foot back to your Left foot (foot to foot), then stamp your Left foot at a 45 degree angle to your Left, forming a *Left Walking Stance* as you execute a *Twin Upset Punch*.

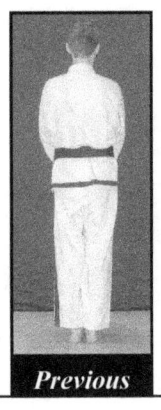

Previous — *Moves 41 & 42*

Kaunde An Palmok Makgi
Middle Inner Forearm Block

Kaunde Ap Joomok Jirugi
Middle Forefist Punch

Kyockja Jirugi
Angle Punch
(slow motion)

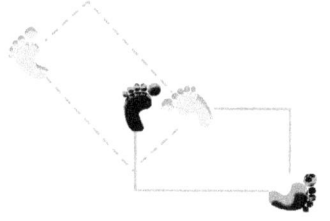

43. Bring your Left foot back to your Right foot (foot to foot), then move your Right foot 90 degrees to your Right to form a *Left L-Stance* while executing a *Right Middle Inner Forearm Block*.

44. Maintain your stance and execute a *Middle Forefist Punch* with your Left hand.

45. Bring your Left foot to your Right foot to form a *Closed Stance* while executing an *Angle Punch* with your Right hand. Perform in slow motion.

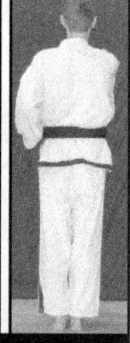

Previous — *Moves 43, 44 & 45*

Kaunde An Palmok Makgi
Middle Inner Forearm Block

Kaunde Ap Joomok Jirugi
Middle Forefist Punch

Kyockja Jirugi
Angle Punch
(slow motion)

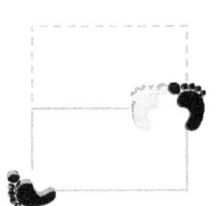

46. Move your Left foot 90 degrees to form a *Right L-Stance* while executing a *Left Middle Inner Forearm Block*.

47. Maintain your stance and execute a *Middle Forefist Punch* with your Right hand.

48. Bring your Right foot to your Left foot to form a *Closed Stance* while executing an *Angle Punch* with your Left hand. Perform in slow motion.

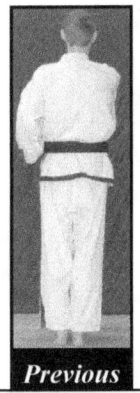

Previous | Moves 46, 47 & 48

Digutja Jirugi
U-Shape Punch

Digutja Jirugi
U-Shape Punch

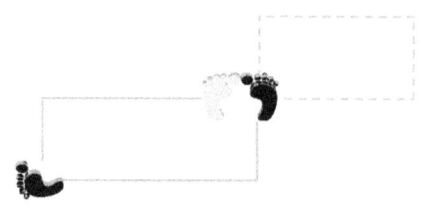
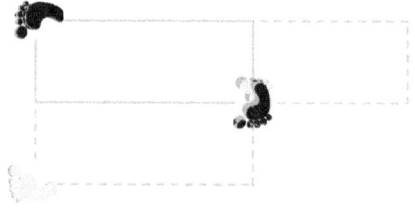

49. Move your Left foot to your Left to form a *Left Fixed Stance* while executing a *U-Shape Punch*.

50. Bring your Left foot back to your Right foot, then move your Right foot forwards to form a *Right Fixed Stance* while executing a *U-Shape Punch*.

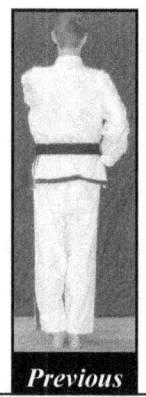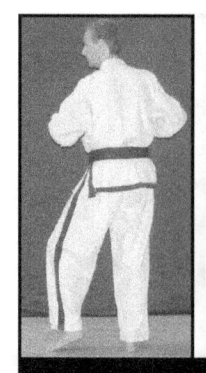

Previous | Moves 49 & 50

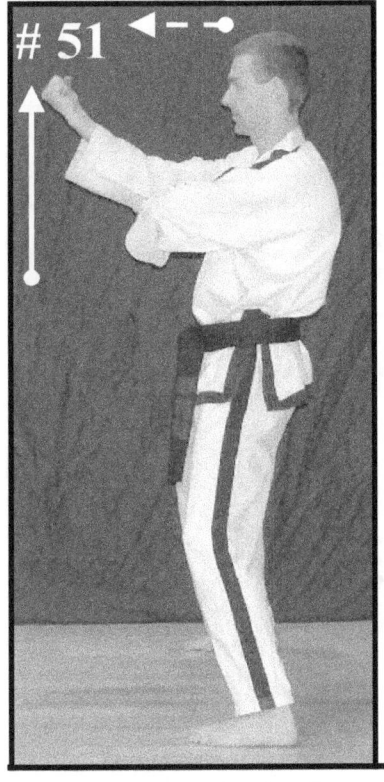 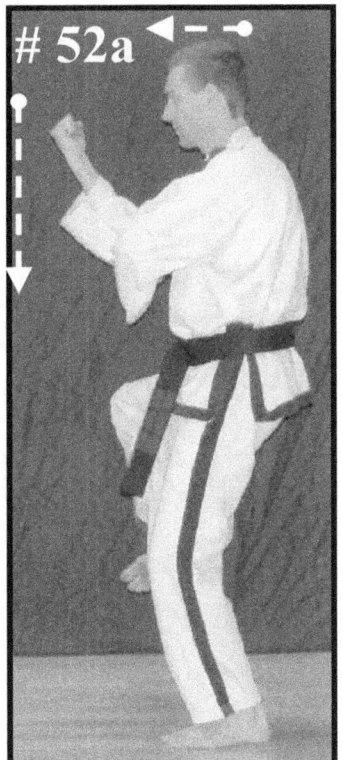 

**Dung Joomok
Ap Taeragi**
Back Fist Front Strike

Doro Chagi
Waving Kick

**Nopunde Bakat
Palmok Bakuro Makgi**
*High Outer Forearm
Outward Block*

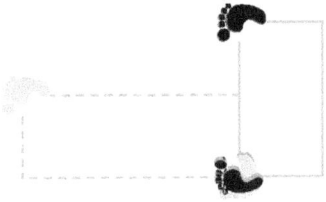  

51. Bring your Right foot inline with your Left foot in a stamping motion, to form a *Sitting Stance* while executing a *Back Fist Front Strike* with your Right fist.

52a. Maintain your arm positions and execute a *Waving Kick* with your Right leg.

52b. As you step down from the Waving Kick into a *Sitting Stance*, simultaneously execute a *High Outer Forearm Outward Block* with your Right arm, keeping your Left arm underneath your Right elbow.

  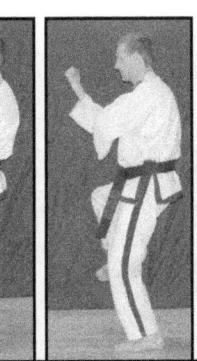   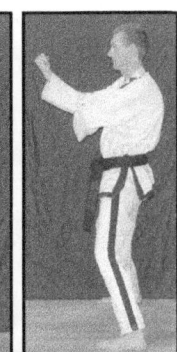

Previous — *Moves 51, 52a, 52b, 53a & 53b*

Doro Chagi
Waving Kick

Nopunde Bakat Palmok Bakuro Makgi
High Outer Forearm Outward Block

Sondung Soopyong Taeragi
Backhand Horizontal Strike

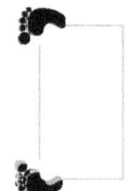

53a. Maintain your arm position and execute a *Waving Kick* with your Left leg.

53b. As you step down from the Waving Kick into a *Sitting Stance*, simultaneously execute a *High Outer Forearm Outward Block* with your Right arm, keeping your Left arm underneath your Right elbow.

54. Maintain your stance and execute a *Backhand Horizontal Strike* to your Right side with your Right hand.

Detailed view of the combination of moves that comprise 50 to 53

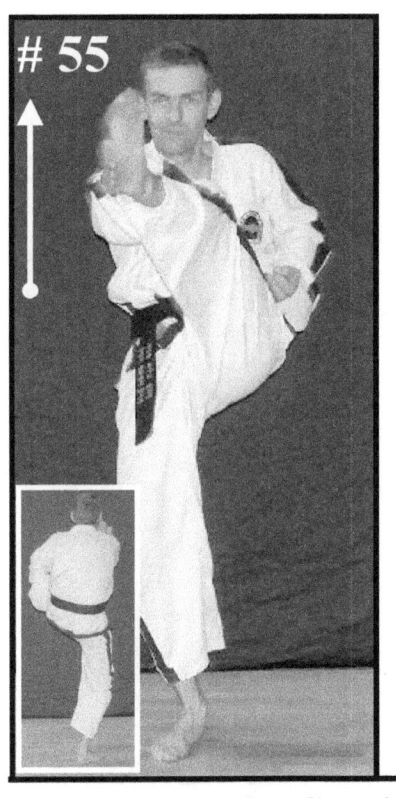
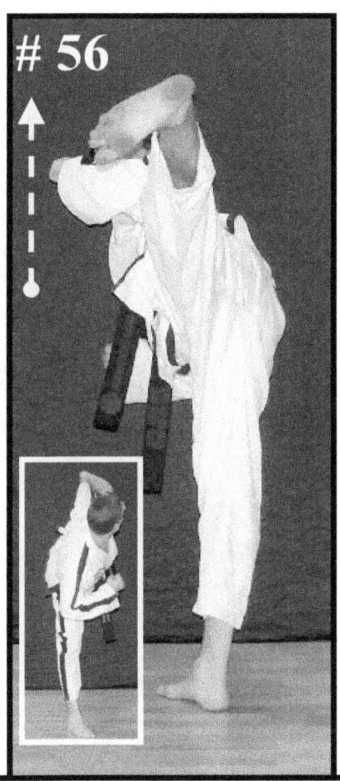

Kaunde Bandal Chagi
Middle Crescent Kick

Kaunde Yop Cha Jirugi
Middle Side Piercing Kick

Sondung Soopyong Taeragi
Backhand Horizontal Strike

Note: Movements 55 & 56 are performed as *'Consecutive Kicks'*

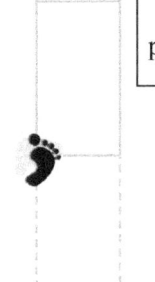

55. Execute a *Left Middle Crescent Kick* to the palm of your Right hand.

56. Without placing your foot down, re-chamber and execute a *Left Middle Side Piercing Kick*.

57. Following the kicks, place your Left foot down to form a Sitting Stance and execute a *Backhand Horizontal Strike* with your Left hand.

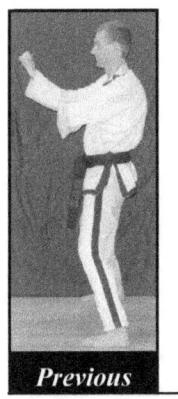

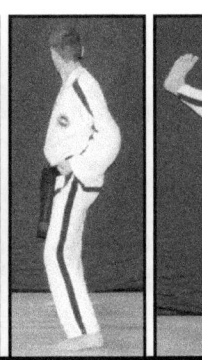
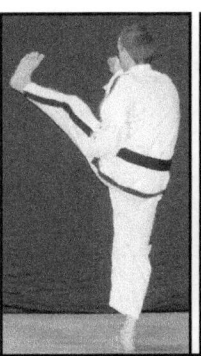
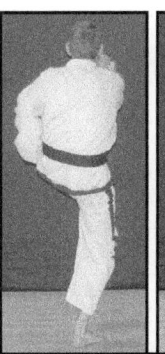

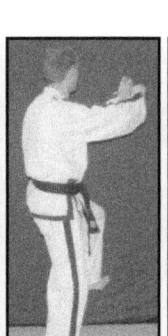

Previous — *Moves 54, 55, 56 & 57*

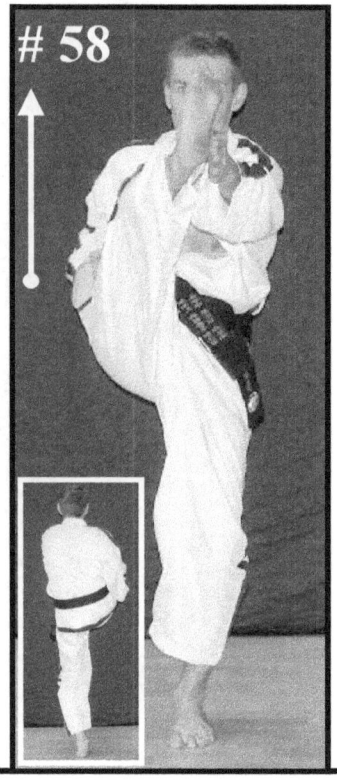

Kaunde Bandal Chagi
Middle Crescent Kick

Kaunde Yop Cha Jirugi
Middle Side Piercing Kick

Orun Gutja Makgi
Right 9-Shape Block

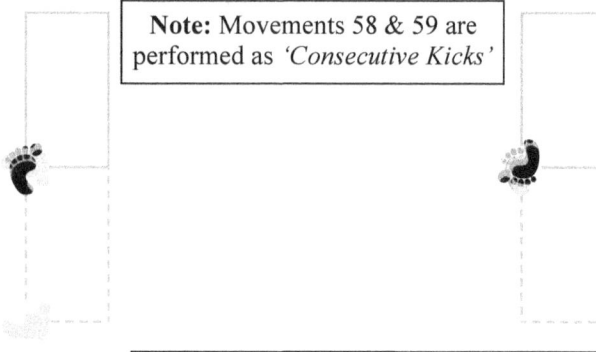

Note: Movements 58 & 59 are performed as *'Consecutive Kicks'*

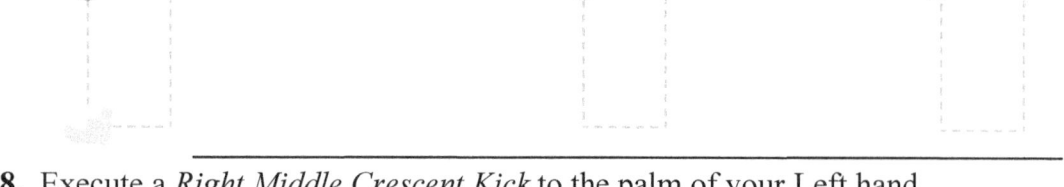

58. Execute a *Right Middle Crescent Kick* to the palm of your Left hand.

59. Without placing your foot down, re-chamber and execute a *Right Middle Side Piercing Kick*.

60. Following the kicks, place your Right foot down to form a *Sitting Stance* and execute a *Right 9-Shape Block*.

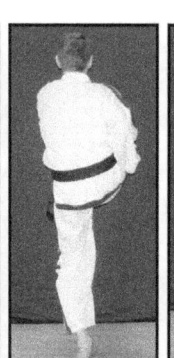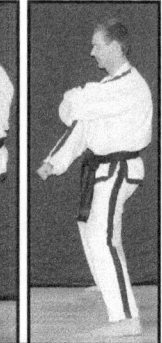

Previous — *Moves 58, 59, & 60*

# 61	# 62	# 63
Wen Gutja Makgi	**Orun Gutja Makgi**	**Wen Gutja Makgi**
Left 9-Shape Block	*Right 9-Shape Block*	*Left 9-Shape Block*

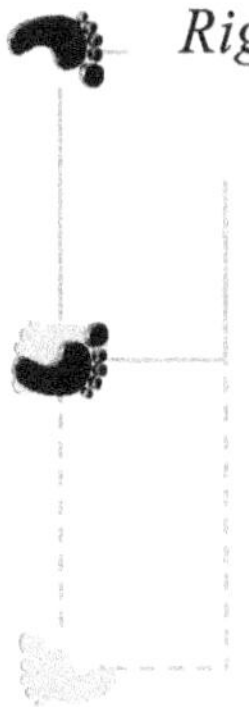

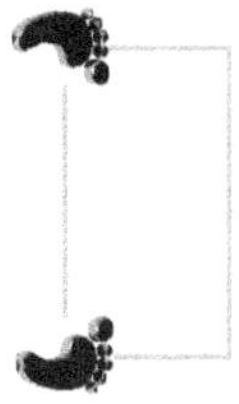

61. Maintain your stance and execute a *Left 9-Shape Block*..

62. Pivot 180 degrees clockwise on your Right foot (moving your Left foot), to form a Sitting Stance and execute a *Right 9-Shape Block*.

63. Maintain your stance and execute a *Left 9-Shape Block*.

Previous — Moves 61, 62 & 63

**Yop Joomok
Naerjo Taeragi**
*Side Fist
Downward Strike*

Nopunde Sang Sewo Jirugi
High Twin Vertical Punch

Nopunde Sang Sewo Jirugi
High Twin Vertical Punch

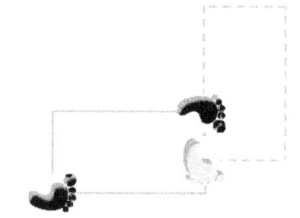
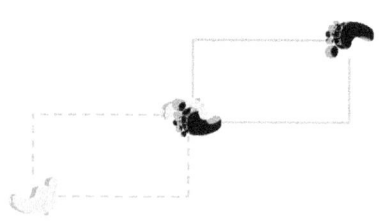

64. Draw your Left foot towards your Right foot to form a *Left Vertical Stance* while executing a *Side Fist Downward Strike* with your Right fist.

65. Move your Right foot back at 90 degrees from the way you are facing, to form a *Left Walking Stance* while executing a *High Twin Vertical Punch*.

66. Pivot 180 degrees anti-clockwise on your Left foot, to form a *Left Walking Stance* while executing a *Twin Vertical Punch*.

Previous *Moves 64, 65 & 66*

Kaunde Sonkal Daebi Makgi
Middle Knifehand Guarding Block

Kaunde Sonkal Daebi Makgi
Middle Knifehand Guarding Block

Moosa Junbi Sogi 'B'
Warrior Ready Stance 'B'

67. Bring your Right foot to your Left foot and turn 90 degrees (so you are facing forwards from the start position again) and move your Left foot 45 degrees to your Left, to form a *Right L-Stance* while executing a *Middle Knifehand Guarding Block*.

68. Bring your Left foot back to your Right foot then move your Right foot 45 degrees to your Right, to form a *Left L-Stance* while executing a *Middle Knifehand Guarding Block*.

Return. Bring your Right foot backwards to form *Warrior Ready Stance 'B'*.

Previous — *Moves 67, 68 & back to Ready Posture*

Tips For Yoo-Sin Tul

1. The sliding motions of moves #2 and #3 should be co-ordinated with the punches.

2. Your raise up on the Palm Hooking Blocks (moves #4 and #6) before dropping back into your Sitting Stance as you execute the Punches (moves #5 and #7), but you don't lock your legs straight when you do.

3. Although some simply teach to roll the palm around the fist, the full hand motions performed for moves #22 and #27 (just prior to the punch) needs some practice. It is vital that the preceding move (the X-Knifehand Rising Blocks), as well the move preceding those (the X-Fist Pressing Blocks) have the arms positioned the correct way round otherwise you will not be able to perfrom #22 or #27 correctly.

4. For the Low Reverse Outer Forearm Blocks (moves #35 and #37) try not to tilt the non-blocking arm as you execute the move from a Double Forearm Block. This is difficult but can be achieved by relaxing just prior to executing the techniques.

5. When executing the U-Shape Punch (moves #49 and #50) try to get a fellow student to check your fists are in-line vertically, as its hard to tell.

6. Moves #51 to #53 need to be given close attention as the arm position changes following the Waving Kicks but prior to placing your foot back down.

7. Remember the Waving Kicks (moves #52a and #53a) travel inline with the stationary foot as they are not a sweep, but an intercepting technique designed to block an attack to your scrotum.

8. Remember that when executing move #64 (the Side Fist Downward Strike in a Vertical Stance) you pull your Left foot towards your Right to form the stance, which is the opposite direction to the way you were currently travelling, so easily forgotten at fist.

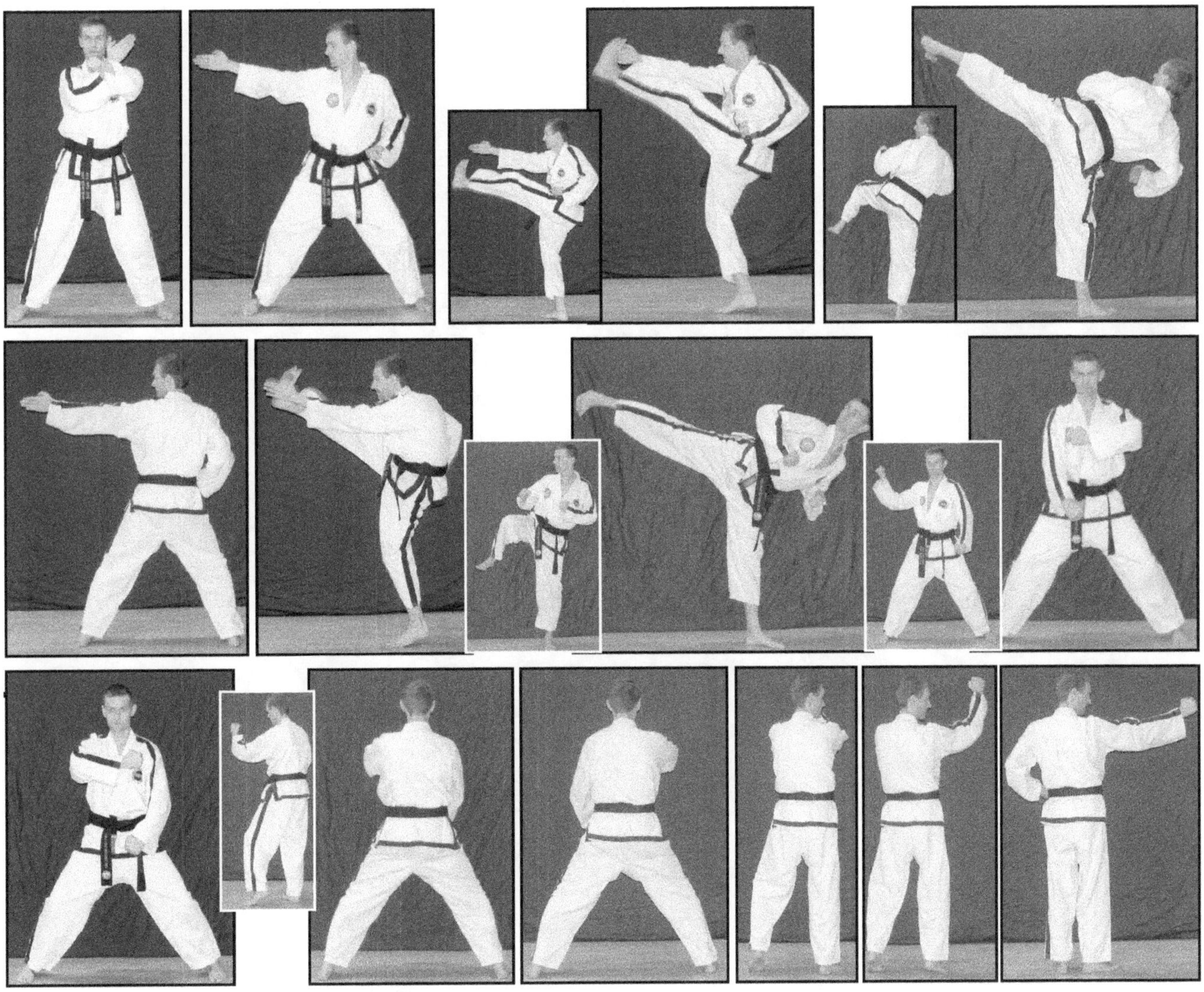

Yoo-Sin

Side view of moves #54 to #64

Appendices

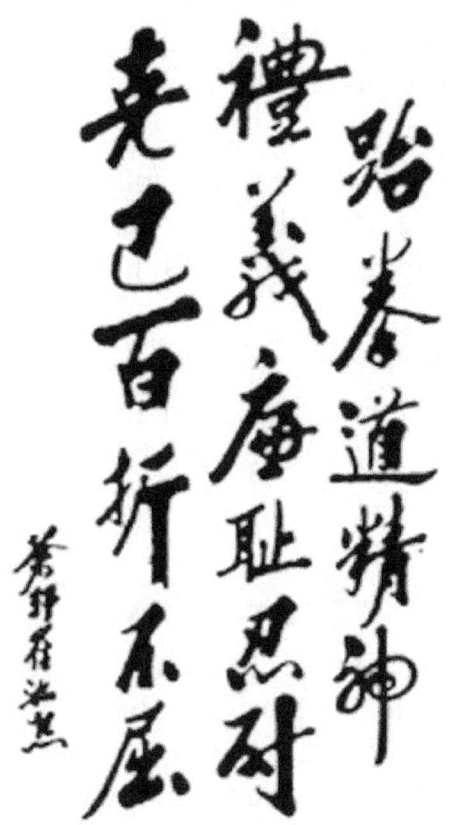

*'Glory is temporary.
Wisdom lasts forever.
Train for a deeper understanding of yourself'*

Appendix i

Pattern Speeds

By Master Paul McPhail, 7th Degree, ITFNZ

The follow is a study of the various speeds in patterns, such as fast and continuous motion, and how the ITF perform sine wave. "In the beginning", there was only *normal*, *fast* and *slow* motion. *Continuous* came later, then finally *connecting* with the publishing of the second edition of the 15 volume Encyclopedia in 1983.

There is generally no problem with understanding slow and connecting motion... *connecting* being two movements in the one sinewave and one breath...like hooking block/punch in Yul-Gok, scooping block/punch in Ge-Baek.

But what is the difference between fast and continuous motion?
Is it the sine wave? Is it the breathing? Is it the overall speed or time it takes to complete the movements? Is it the interval of time between the two movements? Let's look at these one by one:

Sine Wave

With the *continuous motion* in Dun-Gun, General Choi gave very clear instructions to drop down after the low block, then rise up, then down on the rising block. In other words, *full sine wave*. Down-up-down. In Po-Eun however, every *continuous* movement is NOT done with full sinewave - the final "down" of the preceding movement becomes the first "down" of the next. So there is no clear rule there. There is also the fast motion in Ul-Ji which is just one movement - dropping into x-stance...so how can we make a clear rule to do with sinewave? Then there is fast motion with kicks also - like in Hwa-Rang and Choong-Moo...

The ITF Technical Committee also offered this definition of *continuous motion* and *sine wave* at the seminar in New Zealand, August 2004: Movements in *continuous motion* should be completed using *full sine wave* (down-up-down) unless there are more than 2 movements (eg Po-Eun 6-12, 24-30 and Yoo-Sin 16-19), in which case perform a *2/3 sine wave*. This definition holds true on my chart in the Sine wave study displayed later.

Breathing

Both *fast* and *continuous* movements call for individual breaths...although the General tended to "merge" his breaths somewhat on continuous motion. The ITF

Technical Committee further explained *continuous motion* breathing as inhaling only once, then breathing out on each technique as you execute it. (NZ seminar, August 2004). *Connecting motion* has only one breath.

It should be noted (just to confuse things) that there appears to be a mistake in the Encyclopedia. It says in the *Theory of Power* section that each movement should have one breath except for *"continuous motion"*. This I think is an error, as it states in the Training Secret section *"except on connecting motion"*.

Over-all Speed or Time Taken

Sometimes *continuous* movements take longer to complete than *fast* - sometimes the other way around. For example, the two *fast motion* punches in Do-San are over and done with quicker than the low/rising blocks in Dan-Gun. Yet in Po-Eun, the *continuous motion* techniques are completed at a fast rate.

Interval Between Movements

There is a popular view that the difference between *normal*, *fast* and *continuous* is the interval, or gap BETWEEN the movements. The idea is that two movements performed at *normal speed* would have a natural count or gap between them, *fast* has this gap shortened, the *continuous* has no gap at all. This would fine except that this is not the way *fast motion* gets performed, either by seniors, Masters or General Choi himself. If you watch, there is no gap at all between the two punches in Do-san for example... as soon as the first is finished you spring straight up into the 2nd... almost in a *continuous-like* motion.

In my discussions with General Choi, I came across what I think it is all about. I asked him - *"why not just get rid of Continuous and just call everything Fast? Don't you mean just go fast - join them together - cut out the interval between movements?"*

"No no - fast motion is performed with urgency, - aggressive. Continuous motion is performed with grace and beauty - it must flow." he replied.

So I think then, we have to try and understand what his thoughts were when he introduced the terminology. He had *"fast motion"* already - but it didn't adequately describe the flowing, continuous nature by which he wanted certain other movements linked. I don't believe he gave that much thought to there being any confusion over the two terms, as in his mind they are totally different.

If you look then...continuous movements always involve defence - and the idea is to link them smoothly with a nice flow and rhythm. Fast techniques are normally attacks, nearly always punches and kicks (but not always - Yoo Sin 34-35).

Okay, that's all very well, until you have to teach your 1st dans Ge-Baek, where we have *fast* then *continuous* motion side by side. I tend to give a few guidelines, which make people feel more comfortable with the differences. This then is the general summary I use:

Conclusion

Slow Motion - movement is performed slowly with slow breathing. This is used to emphasize an important movement and to check balance and control.

Fast Motion - urgent and aggressive, normal breathing. Fast motion is nearly always attacks - mainly two punches. Short-cut your sine wave - spring straight from the first movement into the next.

Continuous Motion - link the movements together with no pause between the end of one movement and the start of the next. Breath in once then out in a continuous flow of air but emphasizing each movement. Try to link the moments smoothly, with grace and beauty. (Continuous movements always start with a block).

Connecting Motion - complete the two movements with one breath and one sine wave. Connecting motion is always with two movements using opposite arms.

There is also other terminology used in patterns like - ***"in a quick motion, a releasing motion, in a consecutive kick"*** etc. How is a *quick motion* different from a *fast motion*? I asked the General is it the same... he laughed and said *"no no"* ...but gave no explanation!

My thoughts with these are:

- ***"Releasing Motion",*** the General is telling us it is a releasing technique.

- ***"Consecutive Kick",*** the General is telling us *"do not put your foot on the ground after the first kick"*.

- ***"Quick"*** - used for single movements so means *"do it quickly"*, as opposed *to fast motion*, which describes how two or more movements should be performed together.

Appendix ii
Pattern Orders of Taekwon-Do Organisations

All organisations that have a link back to General Choi and the Ch'ang Hon patterns utilize them as part of their training and gradings. However, certain organisations have them in different orders due to the time they either left the ITF or for other reasons for example the way their Chief Instructor may have learned them. These lists represent the pattern orders of various big Taekwon-do organisations, with further breakaway groups usually following the exact same sequence.

The following organisational lists appear on the next few pages:

International Taekwon-Do Federation (ITF)
For ITF and Ch'ang Hon organisations that follow the ITF order of patterns.

Global Taekwon-Do Federation (GTF)
For GTF and other organisations that follow the patterns as directed by the late Grandmaster Park, Jung Tae.

Action International Martial Arts Association (AIMAA)
For AIMAA students and other organisations those that follow the patterns as directed by the Grandmaster Hee, Il Cho.

Grandmaster Jhoon Rhee
For students of Grandmaster Jhoon Rhee and organisations that follow the same order of patterns.

Grade	ITF	GTF
10th Kup	Saju Jirugi, Saju Makgi	Saju Jirugi, Saju Makgi
9th Kup	Chon-Ji	Chon-Ji
8th Kup	Dan-Gun	Dan-Gun, Jee-Sang
7th Kup	Do-San	Do-San
6th Kup	Won-Hyo	Won-Hyo, Dhan-Goon
5th Kup	Yul-Gok	Yul-Gok
4th Kup	Joong-Gun	Joong-Gun
3rd Kup	Toi-Gye	Toi-Gye
2nd Kup	Hwa-Rang, Saju-Tulgi	Hwa-Rang
1st Kup	Choong-Moo	Choong-Moo
1st Degree	Kwang-Gae, Po-Eun, Ge-Baek	Kwang-Gae, Po-Eun, Ge-Baek, Jee-Goo
2nd Degree	Eui-Am, Choong-Jang, Ko-Dang or Ju-Che	Eui-Am, Choong-Jang, Ko-Dang, Jook-Am
3rd Degree	Sam-Il, Yoo-Sin, Choi-Yong	Sam-Il, Yoo-Sin, Choi-Yong, Pyong-Hwa
4th Degree	Yong-Gae, Ul-Ji, Moon-Moo	Yong-Gae, Ul-Ji, Moon-Moo, Sun-Duk
5th Degree	So-San, Se-Jong	So-San, Se-Jong
6th Degree	Tong-Il	Tong-Il
7th Degree		
8th Degree		

Grade	AIMAA	GM Jhoon Rhee
10th Kup	Chon-Ji	
9th Kup	Dan-Gun	
8th Kup	Do-San	Chon-Ji
7th Kup	Won-Hyo	Dan-Gun
6th Kup	Yul-Gok	Do-San
5th Kup	Joong-Gun	Won-Hyo
4th Kup	Toi-Gye	Yul-Gok
3rd Kup	Hwa-Rang	Joong-Gun
2nd Kup	Choong-Moo	Toi-Gye, Hwa-Rang
1st Kup	Kwang-Gae	Choong-Moo, Chul-Gi*
1st Degree	Po-Eun	Kwang-Gae, Basai*
2nd Degree	Ge-Baek	Po-Eun, Sip-Soo*, Bo-Ichi* or Tonfa-Ichi*
3rd Degree	Yoo-Sin	Ge-Baek, Won-Kan*
4th Degree	Choong-Jang, Ul-Ji	Choi-Yong
5th Degree	Ko-Dang, Sam-Il	* Chul-Gi is Tekki Kata, Basai is Basai-Dai Kata, Sip-Soo is Jitte Kata - all found in Shotokan Karate, Won-Kan is an Okinawan Shorin-Ryu kata and Bo-Ichi/Tonfa-Ichi are Okinawan Kobudo kata's.
6th Degree	Choi-Yong	
7th Degree	Se-Jong	** The above list is based on the forms that Grandmaster Jhoon Rhee taught from 1968 onwards, he has since introduced new forms that he terms *'Martial Arts Ballet'* - these are Kyu-Yool, Kumsa, Jayoo, Chosang, Jung-Yee, Pyung-Fa, 'Might for Right' and 'Marriage of East to West' - *unfortunately, all the above are beyond the scope of these books*
8th Degree	Tong-Il	

Appendix iii
Kihaps In Patterns

Some, but not all Ch'ang Hon based Taekwon-Do organisations require students to Kihap (Spirit shout) at certain points within the patterns they are performing. The following charts list the various points within the patterns where Kihaps are executed, as detailed by very high ranking and respected Masters within Taekwon-Do and serve as a reference guide for those that practice patterns with Kihaps.

Cross-Referencing

The following charts have been compiled from research and cross-referencing the Kihap points used (or not) by the following Masters of Taekwon-Do:

General Choi, Hong Hi - As the founder of Ch'ang Hon Taekwon-Do and its patterns, research seems to indicate that *'unofficially'* Kihaps were allowed to be performed within the patterns. Despite this the General did not list any Kihap points at all in his books published between 1959 and 1999. Therefore Kihaps were never *'officially'* part of Ch'ang Hon Taekwon-Do or the ITF. It should be noted that, as far as I'm aware, it was always customary to Kihap on completion of a pattern (the last movement), possibly a *'knock on'* effect from Karate. This continued until some time in the early 1980's, when General Choi made it mandatory for those in the ITF to shout the name of the pattern instead of a Kihap, as well as formerly stating that there were to be no more Kihaps executed within the patterns.

Grandmaster Kang, Suh Chong - Originally a student under the Chung Do Kwan under its founder, Grandmaster Lee, Won Kuk and an instructor in the ROK army from 1960 to 1968. Vice president of the ITF from 1977 to 1983. As far as I am aware Grandmaster Kang is still teaching Taekwon-Do in the USA. Grandmaster Kang's Kihap points are referenced from Chon-Ji up to Tong-Il and include both Ko-Dang and Juche.

Grandmaster Kim, Bok Man - A military instructor with the ROK army from 1950 to 1962, Grandmaster Kim obtained the highest non-commissioned officer rank of Sgt. Major. He assisted General Choi in formulating at least 15 of the Ch'ang Hon patterns and further went on to formulate more patterns of his own. These patterns included weapons patterns and he developed his own system of martial art known as *'Chun Kuhn Do'*. Grandmaster Kim's Kihap points are referenced from Chon-Ji, up the 2nd degree patterns and include Ko-dang but not Juche.

Grandmaster Park, Jung Tae - Former ITF Secretary-General and Chairman of the ITF Instruction Committee from 1984 until he left to form the GTF in 1990.

Grandmaster Park played a major role in formulating the pattern *'Juche'* as well as being the main instructor chosen to teach Taekwon-Do in North Korea. He continued to develop his own patterns for the GTF until he passed away in 2002. Grandmaster Park did not teach any Kihap points for the Ch'ang Hon patterns. He has one Kihap point only and it appears in the GTF pattern *'Jook-Am'* (on the 360 degree Reverse Turning Kick). GTF students also shout the name on completion of a pattern, rather than Kihap. Grandmaster Park is an important inclusion in this research due to his former positions within the ITF as well as the fact that he knew and has taught all 25 Ch'ang Hon patterns and didn't teach any Kihaps in them at all.

Grandmaster Rhee, Jhoon Goo - Commonly recognised as the *'Father of American Taekwon-Do'*, he trained at the Chung Do Kwan under Grandmaster Nam, Tae Hi and moved to the USA in 1952. Grandmaster Rhee's Kihap points are referenced from Chon-Ji to Choong-Moo and it is unknown whether he included them in higher grade patterns.

Grandmaster Lim, Won Sup and Grandmaster Lee, Myung Woo - Two pioneering Taekwon-Do instructors who taught in Vietnam. Their combined list was supplied by my good friend Yi, Yun Wook who learned from them while training in Vietnam. Grandmaster Lim (who was part of the ITF until about 1984) replaced Grandmaster Park as the instructor for North Korea) and Grandmaster Lee's combined list references Kihap points from Chon-Ji up to the 1st degree patterns.

Grandmaster Hee, Il Cho - Grandmaster Cho is a well known and respected Taekwon-Do Grandmaster and pioneer. He has authored numerous books and videos on Taekwon-Do, as well as featuring in movies. Grandmaster Cho taught Taekwon-Do to Special Forces soldiers (Korea, India and US) during the 1960's before emigrating to the US in 1968. In the 1980's he was the black belt grading examiner for the TAGB, then in the 1990's he became the Black Belt grading examiner for the GTI. He runs his own organisation (AIMAA) which is respected worldwide. Grandmaster Cho's Kihap points are referenced for the 20 original patterns and do not include Eui-Am, Juche, Moon-Moo, Yon-Gae and So-San.

Grandmaster Choi, Jung Hwa - Grandmaster Choi is the son of the founder of Taekwon-Do (General Choi) and current President of ITF-Canada. He is thought to have helped Grandmaster Park formulate pattern Juche. Though not one of the original Pioneers, Grandmaster Choi is an important figure in Taekwon-Do, however his inclusion in this appendix is even more important as in 2008 he decided to re-introduce Kihaps back into the patterns performed by ITF-C members. Grandmaster Choi's Kihap points are referenced from Chon-Ji up to the 1st degree patterns only because, at the time of writing, the ITF-C has only issued points up to 1st degree, though more have been expected for a while now.

Note: Other ITF groups do not perform these Kihaps, but simply shout the name of the pattern on completion.

Pattern	GM Lim, Won Sup	GM Kim, Bok Man	GM Choi, Jung Hwa (ITF-C)	GM Hee, Il Cho (AIMAA)	GM Jhoon Rhee	GM Kang, Suh Chong
Chon-Ji	#17	#19	#17	#19	#1, #8, #19	#1, #17, #19
Dan-Gun	#8, #17	#8, #21	#8, #17	#8, #17	#1, #8, #21	#1 #8, #17, #19
Do-San	#6	#6, #24	#6, #22	#6, #24	#1, #6, #24	#2, #6, #22, #24
Won-Hyo	#12, #26	#12, #27	#12	#12, #26	#1, #12, #28	#1, #12, #26
Yul-Gok	#27, #36	#21, #36	#24, #27, #36	#24, #36	#21, #36, #38	#0*, #21, #36 #38
Joong-Gun	#12	#12	#12	None	#1, #12, #32	#1, #12, #32
Toi-Gye	#21	#21, #37	#29	#21, #37	#1, #21, #37	#1, #21, #29, #37
Hwa-Rang	#25	#14, #27	#14, #25	#14 & #25	#1, #14, #29	#0*, #12a, #25, #29
Choong-Moo	#9b	#9b, #30	#9b, #19	#9b, #30	#1, #9b, #19, #30	#9a, #12, #19, #32
Kwang-Gae	#31	#23, #27, #35, #39	#23, #27	None	NA	#0*, #12, #31, #39
Po-Eun	#12 & #30	#12 & #30	#12 & #30	None	NA	#1, #18, #36
Ge-Baek	#23, #28	#26, #44	#19, #28	#23, #28	NA	#1, #28, #44

#0* denotes a Kihap placement prior or during the first movement. For Yul-Gok and Hwa-Rang a Kihap is executed prior to the first move of the pattern, for Kwang-Gae a Kihap is performed at the first part of the first movement, when breaking from Heaven Hand with two Knifehand Strikes.

 # a or b denotes a Kihap placement during a move that has one count, but is actually two or more movements, such as the Flying Side Piercing Kick and landing with a Knifehand Guarding Block in Choong-Moo. Please reference the relevant pattern chapters for clarification.

Pattern	GM Lim, Won Sup	GM Kim, Bok Man	GM Choi, Jung Hwa (ITF-C)	GM Hee, Il Cho (AIMAA)	GM Jhoon Rhee	GM Kang, Suh Chong
Ko-Dang	None	#29	NA	None	NA	#27, #37, #39
Eui-Am	None	#45	None	NA	NA	#1, #45
Choong-Jang	None	#8, #50 & #52	None	None	NA	#1, #8, #12, #19, #41, #52
Juche	NA	NA	None	NA	NA	#12b, #24b, #37d, #45
Sam-Il	None	None	None	None	NA	#1, #12, #17b, #33
Yoo-Sin	None	None	None	None	NA	#1, #38, #68
Choi-Yong	None	None	None	None	NA	#1, #46
Yong-Gae	None	None	None	NA	NA	#1, #49
Ul-Ji	None	None	None	None	NA	#1, #6, #12, #17, #27, #33, #42
Moon-Moo	None	None	None	NA	NA	#58,
So-San	None	None	None	NA	NA	#1, #28, #51b, #56b, #72
Se-Jong	None	None	None	None	NA	#1, #7, #21, #24
Tong-Il	None	None	None	None	NA	#17, #19, #38, #56

Research

Further research into the Kihaps points in the Ch'ang Hon tul seems to indicate that rather than being formerly instituted by General Choi himself, the Kihaps used by most instructors are most likely to have been carried forward from previous Karate training and placed within the Ch'ang Hon tul by personal preference and sharing by various Masters. This seems to explain why some Kihaps are in the same place while others are not. I have come to this conclusion due to the discrepancies in their location from Master to Master (which you will see on the lists), as well as information from pioneering masters such as Master CK Choi. If they were *'officially'* instituted by General Choi himself, everyone would be performing them at the same point within each pattern.

Due to the lack of standardization in Taekwon-Do, which didn't occur until the late 1970's/early 80's, this simply carried on until Kihaps were officially removed from the patterns by General Choi once standardisation of the Ch'ang Hon patterns began. However many Masters kept them either because they had left General Choi by then or simply because of personal preference.

To further complicate matters, in interviews with Master George Vitale, Grandmaster CK Choi (who helped design Ge-Baek tul) said that when it was formulated it did not include Kihaps. Grandmaster Park, Jong Soo also has said that General Choi didn't teach Kihaps when instructing patterns. Grandmaster Park lived with General Choi (in his house) in 1965 when General Choi was finalizing his English version of his book and he worked on all the patterns and photographs within the book. Though some instructors did them due to their former karate training, Grandmaster Cho, Sang Min, a 5th dan in 1968 and instructor at the official ITF Instructors course at that time confirmed that Kihaps were used when a pattern finished. This coincides with changing the Kihap at the end to shouting the name of the pattern instead.

If you don't perform Kihaps and wish to know more about them, as well as 'Ki' itself and how it relates to Taekwon-Do there is a fantastic appendix in my first book *(Ch'ang Hon Taekwon-do Hae Sul)* written by my good friend Yi, Yun Wook that goes into a lot of detail about it.

Appendix iv
Sine Wave Study
By Master Paul McPhail, 7th Degree, ITFNZ

This is an analysis of how sine wave is performed in pattern movements in relation to *fast*, *continuous* and *connecting* motion. This is based on watching General Choi and others perform the movement at various seminars over the years. There seems to be 4 ways of moving from one movement on to the next, as listed below:

Full Sine Wave - This means once the first movement is complete, you then drop your weight down, up, then down again as you complete the next movement (down/up/down).

2/3 Sine Wave - This means completing the first movement, moving straight up then down to complete the next movement (up/down).

1/3 Sine Wave - This means you are already up at the completion of the first movement, so then drop down into the next (down).

Continuous Motion	Moves	Full	2/3	1/3	None
Dan-Gun	13-14 (low block/rising block)	X			
Toi-Gye	7-8 (pressing blk/vertical punch)	X			
Po-Eun	6-12, 24-30 (blocks-punches)		X		
Ge-Baek	5-6 (rising block, low block)	X			
Ge-Baek	37-38 (low guarding blocks)	X			
Eui-Am	5-6, 18-19 (down blk/rising blk)	X			
Sam-Il	30-31 (inward block/punch)	X			
Yoo-Sin	16-17, 18-19 (hook block/punch)		X		
Yoo-Sin	20-21, 25-26 (pressing blk/rising				
Ul-Ji	2-3 (pressing block/rising block)	X			
So-San	52-53, 57-58 (low block/punch)	X			
So-San	71-72 (knifehand guarding blk/	X			

Fast Motion	Moves	Full	2/3	1/3	None
Do-San	15-16, 19-20 (punches)		X		
Yul-Gok	2-3, 5-6 (punches)		X		
Yul-Gok	9-10,13-14 (punches)		X		
Joong-Gun	15-16,18-19 (release/punch)		X		
Hwa-Rang	18-19 (turn-kick/turn-kick/KHGB)	X (block)			X (kicks)
Choong-Moo	14-15 (turn-kick/back-kick)				X
Ge-Baek	3-4 (punches)		X		
Ge-Baek	22-23 (turn-kick/flying side kick)				X
Choong-Jang	46-47 (punches)		X		
Yoo-Sin	2-3 (angle punches)		X		
Yoo-Sin	34-35, 36-37 (dbl forearm/low blk)				X
Choi Yong	21-22 (pressing blocks)		X		
Ul-Ji	11 (X-stance drop)			X	
So-San	5-6, 7-8 (Knifehand Block/punch)		X		
So-San	39-40, 47-48 (punches)		X		
Tong-Il	5-6 (punches)		X		
Tong-Il	14-15 (punches)		X		
Tong-Il	20-21 (punches)		X		

Connecting	Moves	Full	2/3	1/3	None
Yul-Gok	16-17, 19-20 (hooking/punch)			X	
Ge Baek	9-10, 29-30 (scoop/punch)			X	
Yoo-Sin	10-11, 14-15 (scoop block/punch)			X	
Moon-Moo	28-29, 37-38 (scoop block/punch)			X	

It is apparent from studying this chart that there is no direct correlation between the speed of the movement (i.e. fast, continuous or connecting motion) and how the sine wave in the movement is performed.

Thanks to Mr Mark Banicevich, IV Dan, for his assistance with this study.

Appendix v
Performers Biographies

Gordon Slater, 6th Degree

Gordon started Taekwon-Do in February, 1983 with the UKTA (United Kingdom Taekwon-Do Association), gaining his 1st degree in August 1987 with the TAGB (Tae Kwon Do Association of Great Britain) after waiting a year longer to grade due to transferring associations.

Gaining his 6th degree with the GTI (Global Taekwon-Do International) in October, 2009 he has, on his journey been the 1995 GTI English patterns and destruction champion, as well as consistently winning gold medals in patterns and destruction throughout the 90's.

During his time in Taekwon-Do he has been part of various Taekwon-Do organisations such as the UKTA (United Kingdom Taekwon-Do Association), TAGB Tae Kwon Do Association of Great Britain), ITS (Independent Taekwondo Schools) but is happy with his current association the GTI (Global Taekwon-Do International) where he is Grading Examiner, qualified referee and umpire. He has also trained in Wing-Chun Kung Fu, Karate, Kick Boxing and Boxing.

I first met Gordon around 2003 at a tournament in Kent, UK, one that we went to many times over the years, both as instructors and competitors. Indeed we have both fielded students against each other in the various divisions, as well as competed against each other in patterns, sparring and destruction divisions over the years. I asked him to be part of these books because of my high regards for him, both as a person and due to his skills in Taekwon-Do.

Gordon demonstrates the patterns Yong-Gae, So-San, Se-Jong and Tong-Il. More information on Gordon can be found at *www.essextkd.co.uk*

Stuart Anslow, 5th Degree

Stuart started Taekwon-Do early in 1991 under David Bryan (now 6th degree) and

John Pepper (who has now retired from Taekwon-Do). He graded his kup grades with the BUTF (British United Taekwon-Do Federation), gaining his 1st degree in 1994. He continued with the BUTF (which rejoined the ITF for a period) through to 2nd degree before parting ways and going solo. During this solo period he established his school; *Rayners Lane Taekwon-do Academy* in 1999, as well as taking his 3rd degree in 2000, 4th degree in 2005, before finally achieving his current grade of 5th degree in 2010 under legendary Taekwon-Do pioneer, Master Willie Lim, 8th degree.

Having had a good career in competition, culminating in World gold and silver medals in 2000, his main focus has been running his school and promoting Taekwon-Do. Further information can be found in the 'About The Author' section of this book or at the academy web site *www.raynerslanetkd.com*

Stuart demonstrates the patterns Yul-Gok, Juche, Sam-Il, Yoo-Sin, Choi-Yong, Pyong-Hwa, Ul-Gi, Moon-Moo and Sun-Duk.

Elliott Walker, 3rd Degree

Elliott started Taekwon-Do in 1989, aged 15, where he trained with Mr Brian Williams (6th degree) the senior instructor for the TAGB clubs in the North West of England. When just a 7th kup he joined the British Army, but continued training whenever he could at various clubs around the UK gaining excellent experience of the various associations and clubs. He continued to grade through the kup ranks within the TAGB up to 2nd kup, being graded by such TAGB notables as Master Don Atkins, Master Ron Sergiew, Master Kenny Walton and Dorian Bytom, before taking his 1st kup with his original instructor Brian Williams, with the (then) newly formed North West TaeKwonDo.

Achieving his 1st degree in 1996, he then started instructing and continued to grade up to his present rank of 3rd degree, which he achieved in 2005.

Having been posted to Germany in 1993 whilst with the British Army, he trained with a WTF club for a year which enabled him to practice and learn the way the WTF like to kick, again improving his overall knowledge of Taekwon-Do. In 1998 he visited Canada whilst with the army, training at local ITF style clubs to increase his skills further.

When the British Army formed the AMAA (Army Martial Arts Association), he was selected for the British Army team and remained a team member until he left the forces, being awarded Army Colours every year for this achievement. Whilst in the British Army team he was both patterns and sparring champion several times and helped the Army Team to become Inter-Service Champions over several different years. Elliott left the army in 2002 to further his Taekwon-Do instruction and now teaches 5 times a week at his schools in Kent, UK.

I first met Elliott at the 'Kick It' tournaments in 2000. I recall at the time, someone told me my next competitor in the black belt sparring was on the Army Taekwon-Do squad, so I was thinking it was going to be a heavy contact, rough and tough type of bout. Much to my surprise, Elliott was more a classy fighter and didn't go the snot and blood route as he didn't need to and it made the bout a great game of 'cat and mouse'. Over the years we have competed on numerous occasions and our friendship truly underlines one of my sayings (regarding competitions) of: *'2 minutes of war, friends for life'*. A tough fighter and a great technician - these are the reasons I asked Elliott to be part of these books.

Elliott demonstrates pattern Ko-Dang. More information on Elliott can be found at *www.kent-taekwondo.co.uk*

Vikram Gautam, 3rd Degree

Vikram started Taekwon-Do when he was just aged 10 years old (in 1991). As a child he trained with my instructors Mr. David Bryan, 6th Degree and Mr. John Pepper, 2nd Degree at Wembley Taekwon-Do School, which was part of the BUTF (British United Taekwon-do Federation). He continued to train at this Wembley Taekwon-Do School under the exceptional guidance of Mr. David Bryan and Mr. John Pepper for the next 9 years achieving his 1st degree in 2000. Following his 1st degree he began assisting me at Rayners Lane Taekwon-Do Academy and eventually started training there full time due to university making it impossible to train at his former club due to conflicts in times. Vikram graded to 2nd degree in March 2006 and for 3rd degree in 2010 under legendary Taekwon-Do pioneer, Master Willie Lim, 8th degree.

I remember Vikram as a child student who was always inquisitive and eager to learn new stuff, so much so it seems he used to ask me to teach him a new kick every class. When he first competed as a blue belt, he stole the golds in both patterns and sparring and has continued in a similar vein ever since. Following his 1st degree, he competed and fought a Karate black belt who had turned his hand to Taekwon-Do and the fight ended within about 3 seconds as Vikram landed a superb flying back piercing kick as his first technique, which although controlled, hit his opponent straight in the face ending it as a TKO! Vikram's superb natural ability and technique is why I asked him to be part of these books.

Vikram demonstrates the patterns Do-San, Toi-Gye, Choong-Moo, Jee-Goo and Eui-Am.

Colin Avis, 2nd Degree

Colin began practicing Taekwon-Do in 2001 at Rayners Lane Academy and has trained there ever since. After around five years of training he attained the grade of 1st Degree in 2006. Having reached the coveted black belt ranks, Colin maintained the same work ethic he displayed during his formative coloured belt years up to 1st degree, swiftly achieving the rank of 2nd Degree in 2008. Colin was the first student of Rayners Lane Taekwon-Do Academy to be promoted all the way from 10th Kup to 2nd Degree.

Although a student of the Academy, Colin also assists in teaching and has done so for a number of years. He can always be seen supporting the Academy's endeavours in hosting and attending numerous seminars, tournaments etc. Colin is also a seasoned competitor himself and has won his fair share of silverware, with one of the highlights being a silver medal won for sparring at the world championships hosted by Grandmaster Hee Il Cho. He was also part of the Rayners Lane Men Sparring Team that took the silver at the same World Championships.

Colin has won more 'Student of the Month' awards than any other student, as well a being the only Academy student to ever have been named 'Student of the Year' on more than one occasion, winning it in both 2004 and 2007. Colin's passion for the art, commitment and consistency to both training and the Academy as well as his technical skills are why I asked him to be part of these books.

Colin demonstrates Saju Jirugi and Saju Tulgi, as well as patterns Won-Hyo, Hwa-rang, Ge-Baek, Choong-Jang and Jook-Am.

Lyndsey Reynolds, 2nd Degree

Lyndsey started training in Taekwon-do at Rayners Lane Academy in 2000, gaining her 1st Degree in March 2008 and in doing so, became the first female student to attain a dan grade at the Academy. She became the Academy's 'Student of the Year' in 2002 and still trains as diligently as she always has. Lyndsey graded for 2nd degree in 2011.

As a white belt, her first ever competition was a World Championships in 2000 and since then she has had a good competition career and is a fearsome fighter. Her most notable tournament success was at the 2004 World Championships where she achieved a gold in sparring, a silver in patterns and a further gold as part of the Rayners Lane female team in the team sparring division.

At Rayners Lane all students are equal and thus the girls mix it up with the boys which has transcended further for Lyndsey over the years with a memorable moment being when she was a yellow belt and there were no other ladies entered in her sparring division. The event organiser gave her the choice of a straight gold or fighting in the mens division. She chose the latter and despite some tough opponents took the bronze! This happened again recently as a black belt as well! Lyndsey's skills, guts and steadfast determination is why I asked her to be part of these books.

Lyndsey demonstrates the Silla Knife Form.

Parvez Sultan, 1st Degree

Parvez started Taekwon-Do in January 2000 at Rayners Lane Academy. Always training hard, he achieved his 1st degree in 2006 along side 'Slumdog Millionaire' start Dev Patel amongst others, making them the first students of the Academy to go from white to black belt. He also won the Academy's 'Student of the Year' award in 2001.

Parvez has had a good competition career winning many medals along the way, with his highlights being the World Championships in 2004 where, after a terrible first day at the event, he pulled it together for day 2 and won the combined middle and heavyweight brown/red belt sparring division, fighting some tremendous fighters along the way. One of his proudest moments was testing himself at the authors previous organisations tournament (the BUTF British Championships) and winning the gold in the mens senior kup division after many good fights, actually ending up facing a club mate in the finals who had come up on the other side of the table.

Through the years Parvez has been a dedicated student throughout the years, training hard and showing good skills and technique, which is why I asked him to be part of these books.

Parvez demonstrates the patterns Jee-Sang and Po-Eun.

Sushil Punj, 1st Degree

Sushil started Taekwon-Do at the Academy in 1999 at just 8 years old. After achieving his 2nd Kup he took a hiatus from training, returning to take his 1st Kup, before taking his 1st degree in April, 2009 at just 17 years old. He has competed in both national and international tournaments including a World Championships in 2004.

As a child student, Sushil unfortunately failed his 2nd kup grading and stopped training, as many young students do after such disappointments, however, unlike others he showed true indomitable spirit by resuming training a few years later being older and wiser, with a brand new and intense focus taking him passed the grading he previously failed and to 1st degree, making him one of the few black belts to have come from the Academy which are the reasons I asked Sushil to be part of these books.

Sushil demonstrates the patterns Chon-Ji, Dhan-Goon, Joong-Gun and Kwang-Gae.

Kate Barry, 1st Kup

Kate started training at Rayners Lane Taekwon-do Academy just after it was founded in April 1999 and has trained there ever since. At the time of writing these books, Kate was a 2nd kup. Now a 1st kup and due to take her black belt grading 2011, despite a nagging knee problem that has slowed her progress down.

Kate has competed in many tournaments over the years including two World Championships where she won a silver in points sparring, a bronze in continuous sparring and a gold as part of the women's team in the open grade team sparring divisions, but her most memorable moment comes from a competition when she was an 8th kup where, following a previous training session that involved practising front leg side kicks to score quickly, she employed what she had practised in extra time and as soon as the ref said 'sijak' she hit her opponent with the technique, not only scoring the winning point but also lifting them off the floor and back with the kick.

Kate is the longest 'still in training' student from the Academy, having been there from the early days. Always supportive of the Academy, a hard worker and a long term student are the reasons I asked Kate to be part of these books.

Kate features in the *'Differences Between Organisations'* section of the book, as well as being one of the main photographers.

Marek Handzel, 1st Kup

Marek started Taekwon-Do in September 2004 before joining Rayners Lane Taekwon-Do Academy in February 2005. At the time of writing these books he was a 2nd Kup. He is now a 1st kup and due to take his black belt grading in 2011.

His favourite achievement to date is achieving the *'Student of the year'* award in 2006. Marek has been an exceptional student throughout the years and truly epitomises the tenet of 'perseverance', which is why I asked him to be part of these books.

Marek demonstrates pattern Dan-Gun.

Jonathan Choi, 1st Kup

Jonathan started training at Rayners Lane Taekwon-Do Academy in 2007 and at the time of writing these books he was a 2nd Kup. He is now a 1st kup and due to take his black belt grading in 2011.

A highlight of his training so far was taking home two golds at his first ever tournament. As well as Taekwon-Do Jonathan has a passion for Wushu and was also part of the WTF for a short period whilst in China. Jonathan has also won the Academy's *'Student of the Year'* award in 2008. Jonathan trains hard and is a consummate student which is why I asked him to be part of these books.

Jonathan demonstrates Saju Makgi.

Richard Baker, 1st Kup

Richard started training at Rayners Lane Taekwon-Do Academy in December, 2006 and at the time of writing these books he was a 2nd Kup. He is now a 1st kup and due to take his black belt grading in 2011.

Richard has a good competition record so far, bringing home golds in both patterns and sparring divisions. Richard always gives 110% in training and is a good student which is why I asked him to be part of these books. Richard is due to take his black belt in 2011.

Richard features in the *'Differences Between Organisations'* section of the book.